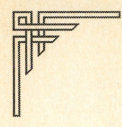

COMMUNICATE

STRATEGIES FOR
INTERNATIONAL TEACHING
ASSISTANTS

JAN SMITH
COLLEEN M. MEYERS
AMY J. BURKHALTER

Minnesota English Center
University of Minnesota

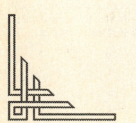

REGENTS / PRENTICE HALL
Englewood Cliffs, New Jersey 07632

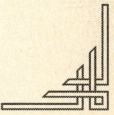

Library of Congress Cataloging-in-Publication Data

Smith, Jan, 1950–
    Communicate : strategies for international teaching assistants /
  Jan Smith, Colleen M. Meyers, Amy J. Burkhalter.
      p. cm.
    Includes bibliographical references and index.
    ISBN 0-13-137720-5 (pbk.)
      1. Graduate teaching assistants—Training of—United States.
  2. College teaching—United States. 3. Students, Foreign—United
States.   4. English language—United States—Study and teaching
(Higher)—Foreign speakers. I. Meyers, Colleen M., 1951–   .
II. Burkhalter, Amy J., 1956–   . III. Title.
LB2335.4.S65   1992
378.1'25—dc20   91-18916
                                          CIP

Publisher: *Tina B. Carver*
Acquisitions editor: *Anne Riddick*
Managing editor, production: *Sylvia Moore*
Editorial/production superviser and interior designer: *Janet S. Johnston*
Prepress buyer: *Ray Keating*
Manufacturing buyer: *Lori Bulwin*
Scheduler: *Leslie Coward*
In-house artist: *Warren Fischbach*
Cover coordinator: *Marianne Frasco*
Cover designer: *Carol Ceraldi*
Photographer: *Jan Smith*

 © 1992 by REGENTS/PRENTICE HALL
a Division of Simon & Schuster
Englewood Cliffs, New Jersey 07632

Printed in the United States of America

10   9   8   7   6   5

ISBN 0-13-137720-5

Sections in Appendix II are adapted from SPEAK® materials with
permission of Educational Testing Service, the copyright owner.

Test results using an adaptation of an ETS testing instrument should in no
way be construed as confirming or denying the validity of the original test
on which it is based, or as possessing any validity of the original test.
Furthermore, the test scores obtained from an ETS scoring scale used with
an adaptation of an ETS scoring rubric cannot be assumed to be equivalent
to scores obtained from the original, ETS-developed test and scoring
rubric.

Prentice-Hall International (UK) Limited, *London*
Prentice-Hall of Australia Pty. Limited, *Sydney*
Prentice-Hall Canada Inc., *Toronto*
Prentice-Hall Hispanoamericana, S.A., *Mexico*
Prentice-Hall of India Private Limited, *New Delhi*
Prentice-Hall of Japan, Inc., *Tokyo*
Simon & Schuster Asia Pte. Ltd., *Singapore*
Editoria Prentice-Hall do Brasil, Ltda., *Rio de Janeiro*

Contents

Preface

International teaching assistants (ITAs) teach at almost every U. S. university that offers graduate level education. International graduate students are sought after not only because of their skills as students and researchers but because of the knowledge, skills, and international perspectives they bring to the teaching of undergraduate students. There is every indication that the number of ITAs at U. S. universities will remain constant or even grow in the near future.

Most ITAs enroll in ITA training courses in order to improve their spoken English skills, but this textbook makes the assumption that ITAs need to develop more than their English proficiency in order to become effective teachers in the U. S. university classroom. The main task of all TAs in their new role as teachers is to communicate with undergraduate students. Although language skills are important to giving and receiving messages clearly, teaching skills are equally important to ensure that the messages are communicated in a way that is easily understood. In addition to language and teaching skills, ITAs need a third set of skills not demanded of native English-speaking TAs. To ensure clear communication with their students, they need to develop cross-cultural communication skills based on an awareness of differences between their culture and U. S. culture. Strong teaching skills and an awareness of cultural differences can often compensate for more slowly developing language skills. In fact, ITAs may never develop nativelike English, but they can learn to communicate clearly and to become excellent teachers who are greatly appreciated by their U. S. students.

ITAs who participate in ITA training courses will benefit most by taking responsibility for their own learning. This involves deciding what they want to learn and using all possible resources to that end: information from books, students, and teachers; observations of positive and negative role models among peers and instructors; and feedback on personal performance. The role of an ITA training course instructor thus becomes that of a facilitator who helps ITAs find resources for what they want to learn and opportunities to practice what they are learning. Another part of the instructor's facilitative role is to help ITAs use peer feedback and an expanding awareness of U. S. university classroom culture to develop an effective individual teaching style. Although training courses and textbooks such as this one can facilitate ITAs' acquisition of skills in language, teaching, and cultural awareness, it is important that ITAs make their own decisions about what kind of teaching style they want to develop and to what degree they want to adapt to U. S. cultural patterns of teaching. It is they who know best what resources they have to draw on, what weaknesses they need to compensate for, and what specific contexts they will need to function in.

Each of the **ten units** in this textbook includes work on teaching skills, language skills, and cultural awareness. Each unit centers around a common rhetorical teaching task in U. S. university classrooms: introducing oneself, introducing a syllabus, explaining a visual, defining a term, teaching a process, fielding questions, explaining something at a basic level, presenting information over several class periods, and leading a discussion. An introduction in each unit explains why the given rhetorical teaching task is important in U. S. university classrooms and introduces the important features of the assignment for the unit. The **appendix** includes feedback forms to guide feedback given to ITAs on their teaching; materials for the ITA Test, an exit test evaluating the skills taught in this text; and field-specific materials for language and teaching practice. The **bibliography** includes resources for further work with field-specific materials, cross-cultural communication skills, language skills, and teaching skills. It also lists resources for information on TA training in general, "the ITA problem," and ITA training.

Teaching Skills

The sections addressing teaching skills are the focuses, the functional language, the assignment preparation, and the assignment presentation. The **focus** sections introduce and provide practice with specific teaching skills. The **functional language** sections introduce and provide practice with vocabulary and expressions needed to perform the teaching task of each unit. The **assignment preparation** sections prepare ITAs for successful completion of the teaching assignments. The **assignment presentation** sections guide ITAs in preparing ten-minute microlessons for a small group of their peers.

Language Skills

Language skills are developed in the pronunciation and the grammar sections. The **grammar** sections work on grammatical problems common among ITAs and are usually related to the rhetorical teaching task of the unit. The **pronunciation** sections focus on the suprasegmental problems of stress, rhythm, and intonation that are common to ITAs of most language backgrounds. Problems with specific segmentals can vary widely in a group of ITAs with different native languages and are best treated in individual tutorials. For work on problematic segmentals, ITAs may use the many pronunciation textbooks listed in the bibliography.

Cultural Awareness

Culture, for the purposes of this textbook, refers to the immediate subculture in which ITAs find themselves—the U. S. university and their specific department at the university. This text does not try to develop cultural awareness by presenting information. Instead, the **needs assessment** in each unit asks ITAs to examine their own values and beliefs about teaching and sends them out to gather information directly from fellow teaching assistants, professors, and undergraduate students. By analyzing the information they collect, ITAs can assess for themselves what they need to learn about the U. S. university subculture in which they will be working. In this way, ITAs not only gain specific, individually relevant information but develop tools to do further investigative work as they interact with the individuals who can best help them perform their role as a TA effectively.

Field-specific Language Practice

Undergraduate textbook materials for fifteen academic fields are included in the **appendix** to provide relevant content for practicing teaching and language skills. Visuals, lists of terms, passages from textbooks, questions, topics of general interest, and problems are provided for the fifteen fields: biology, business administration, chemistry, civil engineering, computer science, economics, electrical engineering, industrial engineering, mathematics, mechanical engineering, physics, psychology, second languages, sociology, and statistics. ITAs in fields not included can either use materials from the field closest to their own or gather similar materials from undergraduate textbooks in their own fields.

Acknowledgments

This book is the fruit of numerous people's efforts. It is based on materials developed for a course in the TA English Program, a part of the Minnesota English Center at the University of Minnesota. We are indebted to all the teachers who participated in planning the original course, the teachers who have taught in and developed the course over the years, the teachers who field-tested these materials, and the international teaching assistants whose needs and contributions have shaped the course.

We thank NAFSA, who funded the development of the original course; Mark Landa, Susan Gillette, and Bill Perry, the designers of the original syllabus; and Mark Landa, again, for nurturing the course into a full-fledged program from his position as director of the Minnesota English Center.

For contributions to the materials in this book, we thank our colleagues Karin Smith, Eric Nelson, Susan Gillette, Linda Mealey, and Elaine Tarone from the University of Minnesota; Roberta Abraham and Barbara Plakans from Iowa State University; the Educational Testing Service; and the authors of the field-specific textbook materials included in the appendix.

We thank Eric Nelson for the editorial and teaching expertise with which he edited our manuscript, and Prentice Hall Regents' reviewers for their valuable critiques and suggestions.

Finally, we thank our partners, families, and friends, especially Chris Bauer, Jenise Rowekamp, Pat Eliason, and Kathy Hoffarth, for their support.

To the Instructor

Using This Textbook

ITA training programs vary in structure and number of training hours offered to ITAs. At the end of this section are **sample syllabi for three types of courses**: four-week intensive courses, ten-week quarter courses, and sixteen-week semester courses. Sections on teaching, language, and cross-cultural communication skills are combined in each unit to facilitate integration within a single course, but the skills are contained in clearly marked sections so that programs offering separate courses for each type of skill can use just those sections relevant to each class. The book then functions as a tool for coordination among instructors working with a single group of students.

No instructor should feel constrained to cover everything in this book. It is designed as a resource for addressing a wide variety of individual ITA problems, from which ITA instructors can choose the information, exercises, and activities most appropriate for their students. Instructors in ITA programs with insufficient instructional time to cover the entire textbook may choose to cover the **core sections of each unit**. The core sections in each unit are:

- **for teaching**—the focuses, the assignment presentation, and the feedback form;
- **for language**—the pronunciation section; and
- **for culture**—the needs assessment.

Using the core sections of the textbook, with some supplementary work on individual pronunciation problems, requires three to four hours per unit: one hour of group instruction, one microteaching class (one to two hours depending upon the number of ITAs in each group), and one tutorial per ITA per unit for ten units.

Instructors with more than sixteen weeks allotted to their training program would profit from building in more discussion time. This textbook does not always provide a formal method for processing the amount of information ITAs will gather in their needs assessments. Additional discussion time to compare their findings would give ITAs a valuable opportunity to integrate and synthesize this information.

Developing an ITA Training Course or Program

This book can be used most effectively if a program employs four important tools: videotape, microteaching sessions, constructive feedback from instructors and peers, and one-on-one tutorials between instructors and ITAs.

Videotape is an objective record of how teachers look and sound to their students. If programs do not have access to videotaping facilities, **audiotape** can provide a similar objective record of performance. Many ITAs are unaware of the strengths and weaknesses of their language and classroom communication skills. On videotape they can readily observe themselves as they appear to others and the effect of their behavior on others. Videotaping on a weekly basis allows ITAs and their instructors to note improvements and identify persistent problems. Videotape frees both instructors and ITAs from relying solely upon the subjective viewpoints of instructors for information about ITAs' progress in developing their classroom communication skills, and empowers ITAs to make their own choices about how to develop an effective teaching style.

Microteaching sessions allow ITAs to learn from and support each other as they develop their classroom communication skills. The ideal size of a microteaching group is no more than six ITAs, and preferably four or five. ITAs take turns teaching and playing the role of students. In the most successful microteaching sessions, ITAs take active roles as students by asking undergraduate-level questions. After each session they support each other by providing detailed comments about the strengths and weaknesses of each other's skills.

Constructive feedback from peers and instructors is essential to an individual seeking to become a confident and effective teacher. Positive feedback allows individuals to capitalize on strengths as they work on their weaknesses. The most helpful feedback immediately follows performance so that specific examples can be remembered. If feedback is limited to the one or two areas of language or teaching that most interfere with effective teaching, ITAs can gain confidence from their successes and focus on changing one or two problems at a time. It is helpful to use a unit's focuses as group goals and individual problematic areas as individual goals for improvement in each microteaching session.

Feedback sessions after microteaching can be limited to **peer feedback** if the instructor has tutorial sessions in which to give ITAs individual help. At the beginning of the course it may not be easy for some ITAs to give each other useful feedback, so instructors may need to model the types of feedback they feel are most appropriate for ITAs in their class. Using one of the **peer feedback forms** after each assignment can provide focus for feedback discussions because the forms are keyed to the focuses of the unit as well as to the assigned teaching task. Each listening ITA in the class should complete a form for each presenting ITA during the microteaching sessions. The forms may simply provide an outline for oral feedback, or they may be collected and given to the presenting ITA as a written record.

Regular **tutorials** between the instructor and each ITA offer the ideal opportunity for one-on-one feedback, review of the ITA's videotaped presentations, and individualized language instruction. The **instructor feedback form** (in the appendix) is a useful tool for organizing the issues dealt with in each tutorial session. This form is keyed to the focuses. By filling out this form during each microteaching session and discussing it with the ITA in a tutorial, an instructor can provide consistent feedback about the progress the individual is making. Copies of these filled-out forms will also document each ITA's development and help the instructor evaluate the ITA at the end of the term. Tutorials allow instructors to attend to the varied needs of different ITAs, and to serve as guides through the difficult linguistic, cultural, and personal transitions to becoming effective teachers in the U. S. university undergraduate classroom.

Final Evaluation

This textbook recommends evaluating each ITA at the close of the term, through the use of the **ITA Test** in the appendix. Individual ITAs present information for five minutes and answer questions for five minutes for a panel of ITA instructors or other designated members of the university community. ITAs are rated on presentation language skills, teaching skills, interactive language skills, and the overall impression they convey. ITAs receive final recommendations from the course or program based on this test and on their performance throughout the term.

Further Resources Available in the Teacher's Manual

A teacher's manual is available upon request from the publisher. It includes an **answer key,** suggestions **for further practice** of skills presented in each unit, and unit-by-unit **teacher's notes.**

SAMPLE SYLLABI FOR THREE TYPES OF COURSES

Sample 10-Week Quarter Syllabus

Week	Microteaching [1–2 hours]	Group Instruction [2–3 hours]	(Optional) or Homework	Individual Tutorial* [1 hour]
1	*Unit 1* Introduction to unit Functional Language Needs Assessment Assignment Presentation Feedback Form	*Unit 2* Introduction to unit Focuses 1 and 2 Functional Language Pronunciation	*Unit 2* Needs Assessment (Assignment Preparation) (Grammar)	*Unit 1* Videotape review [work with individual problems] Focus Pronunciation [Diagnostic] Grammar [Diagnostic]
2	*Unit 2* Assignment Presentation Feedback Form	*Unit 2* Discuss Needs Assessment *Unit 3* Introduction to unit Focuses 1 and 2 Functional Language Pronunciation	*Unit 3* Needs Assessment (Assignment Preparation) (Grammar)	*Unit 2* Videotape review [work with individual problems] *Unit 3* Follow-up on pronunciation
3–9	*Previous Unit (3–8)* Assignment Presentation Feedback Form	*Previous Unit (3–8)* Discuss Needs Assessment *Current Unit (4–9)* Introduction to unit Focuses 1 and 2 Functional Language Pronunciation	*Current Unit (4–9)* Needs Assessment (Assignment Preparation) (Grammar)	*Previous Unit (3–8)* Videotape review [work with individual problems] *Current Unit (4–9)* Follow-up on pronunciation
10	*Unit 9* Assignment Presentation Feedback Form	*Unit 9* Discuss Needs Assessment *Unit 10* Introduction to unit Focuses 1 and 2 Assignment Presentation Feedback Form	*Unit 10* Needs Assessment	*Unit 9* Videotape review [work with individual problems] Follow-up on pronunciation *Unit 10* (Preparation for ITA Test)

*For programs without tutorials, individual oral or written feedback should be included in microteaching sessions.

Sample 16-Week Semester Syllabus

Week	Teaching Preparation [1 hour]	Language Preparation [1 hour]	Micro Teaching [1 hour]	(Optional) or Homework	Individual Tutorial* [1 hour]
1	*Unit 1* Introduction to unit Needs Assessment	Functional Language	Assignment Presentation Feedback Form		Videotape review Focus Pronunciation [Diagnostic] Grammar [Diagnostic]
2	*Unit 2—first half* Introduction to unit Focuses 1 and 2	Func. Language	Assignment Preparation	Needs Assessment	Follow-up on pronunciation
3	*Unit 2—second half* Discuss Needs Assessment	Grammar	Assignment Presentation Feedback Form		Videotape review [work with individual problems]

For weeks 4–13, do units 3 through 7. Follow the suggested lesson plans for weeks 2 and 3, doing the first half of the unit on even weeks and the second half on odd weeks.

Week	Teaching Preparation [1 hour]	Language Preparation [1 hour]	Micro Teaching [1 hour]	(Optional) or Homework	Individual Tutorial* [1 hour]
14	*Unit 8* Introduction to unit Focus	Func. Language Pronunciation	Assignment Presentation Feedback Form	Needs Assessment (Assignment Preparation) (Grammar)	Videotape review [work with individual problems]
15	*Unit 8* Discuss Needs Assessment *Unit 9* Introduction to unit Focus	Func. Language Pronunciation	Assignment Presentation Feedback Form	Needs Assessment (Assignment Preparation) (Grammar)	Videotape review [work with individual problems]
16	*Unit 9* Discuss Needs Assessment *Unit 10* Introduction to unit	Focuses 1 and 2	Assignment Presentation Feedback Form	Needs Assessment	(Preparation for ITA Test)

*For programs without tutorials, individual oral or written feedback should be included in microteaching sessions.

Sample 4-Week Intensive Syllabus

Week	Monday	Tuesday	Wednesday	Thursday	Friday
1	Unit 1				
AM	*Teaching Prep* [2 hours] Introduction to program Introduction to unit	*Optional or Homework* [2 hours] Functional Language Needs Assessment	*Tutorial** [1 hour] Videotape review Focus	*Language Prep* [2 hours] Pronunciation Grammar	*Microteaching* [2 hours] Assignment Presentation Feedback Form
			Unit 2		
PM	*Language Prep* [2 hours] Pronunciation Grammar	*Microteaching* [2 hours] Assignment Presentation Feedback Form	*Teaching Prep* [2 hours] Introduction to unit Focuses Assignment Prep.	*Optional or Homework* [2 hours] Func. Language Needs Assessment	*Tutorial** [1 hour] Videotape review [Work with individual problems]
2	Unit 3				
AM	*Teaching Prep* [2 hours] Introduction to unit Focuses	*Optional or Homework* [2 hours] Func. Language Needs Assessment	*Tutorial** [1 hour] Videotape review [Work with individual problems]	*Language Prep* [2 hours] Pronunciation Grammar	*Microteaching* [2 hours] Assignment Presentation Feedback Form
			Unit 4		
PM	*Language Prep* [2 hours] Pronunciation Grammar	*Microteaching* [2 hours] Assignment Presentation Feedback Form	*Teaching Prep* [2 hours] Introduction to unit Focuses Assignment Prep.	*Optional or Homework* [2 hours] Func. Language Needs Assessment	*Tutorial** [1 hour] Videotape review [Work with individual problems]
3	Unit 5				
AM	*Teaching Prep* [2 hours] Introduction to unit Focuses	*Optional or Homework* [2 hours] Func. Language Needs Assessment	*Tutorial** [1 hour] Videotape review [Work with individual problems]	*Language Prep* [2 hours] Pronunciation Grammar	*Microteaching* [2 hours] Assignment Presentation Feedback Form
			Unit 6		
PM	*Language Prep* [2 hours] Pronunciation Grammar	*Microteaching* [2 hours] Assignment Feedback Form	*Teaching Prep* [2 hours] Introduction to unit Focuses Assignment Prep.	*Optional or Homework* [2 hours] Func. Language Needs Assessment	*Tutorial** [1 hour] Videotape review [Work with individual problems]

*For programs without tutorials, individual oral or written feedback should be included in microteaching sessions.

Week	Monday	Tuesday	Wednesday	Thursday	Friday
4	Unit 8**				
AM	*Teaching Prep* [2 hours] Introduction to unit Focus	*Optional or Homework* [2 hours] Func. Language Needs Assessment	*Tutorial** [1 hour] Videotape review [Work with individual problems]	*Language Prep* [2 hours] Pronunciation Grammar	*Microteaching* [2 hours] Assignment Presentation Feedback Form
			Unit 9		
PM	*Language Prep* [2 hours] Pronunciation Grammar	*Microteaching* [2 hours] Assignment Feedback Form	*Teaching Prep* [2 hours] Introduction to unit Focus Assignment Prep.	*Optional or Homework* [2 hours] Func. Language Needs Assessment	*Tutorial** [1 hour] Videotape review [Work with individual problems]

*For programs without tutorials, individual oral or written feedback should be included in microteaching sessions.

**Units 7 and 10 have been omitted due to time constraints.

UNIT 1
Introducing Yourself

Introducing oneself is an important part of establishing rapport with one's students.

In this unit your assignment will be to introduce yourself to the class. You will speak for five minutes and then answer questions for five minutes. You will be practicing for your first day of teaching, when you will introduce both yourself and the course to your students. Introductions are important; they provide the context for everything that follows, and your students' first impression may be a lasting one.

In the first session of this course, observe how your instructor introduces himself or herself and how he or she sets up the context for subsequent classes. As you watch your instructor's self-introduction, notice how he or she tries to make you comfortable. Watch for the different types of information your instructor chooses to give you about goals for the class and his or her professional background. Pay attention to the language your teacher uses. Listen for expressions to use in your own self-introduction.

Focus:
Objectives of the Course

The categories below correspond to the skills covered in this course. You will be evaluated in these skills at the end of this course. For you to learn efficiently with this textbook, it is a good idea to make an initial self-assessment similar to the final assessment that your instructor will make of your skills. First you will rate yourself on language and classroom communication skills. Then, after your first presentation, you and your instructor can compare your self-rating with your instructor's rating of your skills. Use the following scale for your self-rating. Be sure to fill in every blank.

1. My lack of skill in this area **would cause serious problems in teaching**.

2. My skill in this area **is not yet sufficient for good teaching,** but will not cause major problems.

3. My skill in this area **is sufficient for good teaching.**

LANGUAGE SKILLS

___ *Pronunciation*
Individual sounds
Stress
Intonation
Enunciation
Intelligibility

___ *Grammar*
Accurate form
Appropriate usage

___ *Fluency*
Phrasing
Pauses
Smooth rhythmic patterns

___ *Comprehensibility*
Pronunciation
Grammar
Fluency
Vocabulary

TEACHING SKILLS

___ *Organization of presentation*
Overall structure
Logical development
Transitional devices
Emphasis of important points

___ *Clarity of presentation*
Focus on topic
Sufficient information
Conciseness
Use of supporting detail

____ *Relevance of content*
Use of practical examples
Use of contexts familiar to students
Use of personal or real world
  experiences
Connection to previous knowledge
Focus on use of information

____ *Manner of speaking*
Appropriate volume
Appropriate speed
Appropriate tone of voice
Variation for intended effect

____ *Audience awareness*
Appropriate content
Appropriate vocabulary
Appropriate manner of presentation
Monitoring of audience responses
Adjustment to audience responses
Eye contact

____ *Teacher presence*
Confidence
Rapport with audience
Appropriate authority
Ease of performance

____ *Method of handling questions*
Quick response
Appropriate repetition or rephrasing
Appropriate check for comprehension

____ *Use of blackboard and visuals*
Appropriate choice of visuals
Organization of visuals
Integration of written and spoken
  material
Legibility
Correctness of spelling

____ *Nonverbal communication*
Posture
Gestures
Facial expressions
Head movements
Use of space
Body movements
Nonlanguage sounds
Eye contact and posture with visuals

____ *Interaction*
Interaction invited
Expectation of audience participation
  communicated
Friendly, non-judgmental responses
Encouragement of questions
Appropriate feedback to audience
  responses

____ *Aural comprehension*
Understanding of utterances spoken
  at a natural rate
Use of listening strategies
Negotiation of meaning through
  use of questions

____ *Clarity of response to questions*
Focus on topic of question
Direct answer
Sufficient information
Concise answer

OVERALL IMPRESSION

____ Can teach with ideal non-native TA performance

Functional Language:
Ending a Presentation

When you present information to a group, your job is not finished after you have finished giving the information. You have one more task—concluding your speech and letting your audience know you are finished. If you stop speaking without concluding, your audience may not know you are finished. While you are waiting for them to ask questions, they may be waiting for you to continue speaking.

A conclusion is similar to the brake lights on a car. Brake lights warn other people that a car is slowing down and give others time to adjust to the changing situation. Ending your speech with the expression "That's all" is like suddenly slamming on the brakes. Just as with other transitions from one topic to another, it is helpful to use organizational cues to let your audience know what to expect next.

Conclusions are used not only to warn the audience that the speech is about to end. They are also used to highlight whatever the speaker thinks is most important for the audience to remember. Folk wisdom in the United States says that audiences only remember the first and the last things a speaker says. If that is true, the introduction and conclusion are the most important parts of a teacher's presentation.

EXERCISE 1: Using conclusions for a purpose

Many expressions can be used to conclude a presentation. Which you use depends on what you wish to accomplish in your conclusion. Below are five purposes and five groups of expressions used to conclude presentations. Write the number of each purpose in front of the appropriate matching pair of expressions.

Purposes for conclusions	Concluding expressions
1. Summarizing information	a. ____ "Any questions?" "Is this clear?"
2. Inspiring the audience to use information	b. ____ "What I want you to remember is..." "So don't forget that..."
3. Emphasizing important points	c. ____ "As I said earlier, ..." "So what we've covered during this week is..."
4. Referring to previous information	d. ____ "To sum up, ..." "To conclude, ..."
5. Checking for comprehension	e. ____ "So I hope you understand how to..." "Now that you have learned this, I want you to..."

EXERCISE 2: Checking for comprehension of information

Checking for comprehension at the conclusion of a lesson is especially important for two reasons: (a) in the culture of the U. S. university classroom, one of the teacher's primary responsibilities is to make sure that students have understood; and (b) as a second-language speaker, you need to compensate for potential miscomprehension due to language problems. In small groups or pairs, brainstorm five sentences or questions you can use in the classroom to check whether your students have clearly understood the information you have presented. Draw on your memory of the language you have heard U. S. teachers use. Write the sentences on a separate piece of paper.

Review your answers, check for grammar mistakes, and have your teacher check them for idiomatic usage.

Assignment Presentation:
Introducing Yourself

In this unit your assignment is to introduce yourself to the class. Plan to speak for five minutes and answer questions for five minutes. Use the outline below and the suggested time as you plan your presentation. Do not write out your presentation, but make notes and speak from your notes.

Content	Concerns	Time
1. What is your name? What would you like to be called?	(Be sure others can pronounce the name.)	½ minute
2. Where are you from? Explain why you are in the United States.	(Use correct verb tenses here.)	1 minute
3. What field are you in? Talk about your area of specialization.	(You may want to define your area of specialization or give an example.)	1 minute
4. What experience have you had in teaching? Talk about any of the following: level and type of students, subject matter, range of responsibilities, or reactions to the experience.	(If you have no teaching experience, talk about another experience that is relevant to teaching.)	1 minute
5. What do you hope to learn in this class? Be specific.	(Think about this question. Try to give one or more specific goals.)	1 minute
6. What do you want to emphasize in your conclusion?	(Try not to stop suddenly.)	½ minute

Pronunciation:
Diagnosis of Problems

Read the following paragraph to yourself to become familiar with the ideas, and then read it aloud to your teacher. (You may need to read it more than once.) He or she will underline or circle words in which there is some problem that interferes with comprehensibility.

International teaching assistants face many challenges as they begin studying and teaching in the United States. Undergraduate students demand fluent and accurate language skills. They also expect international TAs to teach in the same way that native English-speaking TAs do. At the same time, ITAs must spend long hours trying to meet the demands of studying in a second language and culture. Is it better to think of these challenges as obstacles or opportunities? Should international TAs be required to have the same language and teaching skills as TAs from the United States? Some ITAs have found that their attitude makes a tremendous difference in dealing with these problems. The difficulties of living, studying, and teaching in a new environment can be a source of pain and anger or an opportunity to grow and develop as a human being. Which will they be for you?

The most common pronunciation problems of nonnative English speakers are listed below. Put a check beside what your instructor thinks are your three most serious problems.

SOUNDS

___ substituting incorrect sounds for correct ones. Example: _____

___ leaving out sounds that should not be left out. Example: _____

___ adding sounds that should not be pronounced. Example: _____

WORD STRESS

___ stressing the wrong syllable. Example: _____

___ not reducing vowels in unstressed syllables. Example: _____

THOUGHT GROUPS

___ not breaking the sentence into short phrases with one major stress in each group.

___ not pronouncing each thought group in one smooth breath.

RHYTHM AND LINKING

___ giving equal stress to all the syllables in a thought group.

___ stressing unimportant words in a sentence.

___ not blending the words of a thought group together so that they sound like a single word.

INTONATION

___ using rising instead of rising-falling intonation at the end of phrases, statements, and Wh- questions.

___ mixing up the intonation patterns of different kinds of questions: yes/no questions, Wh- questions, choice questions.

___ not using rising intonation for each item except the last in a series or not using rising-falling or sentence-final intonation for the last item in a series.

EMPHASIS

___ not emphasizing contrasting words or ideas in the sentence.

___ not emphasizing the words you want to focus on in the sentence.

___ starting sentences or phrases more than once before finishing them.

___ pausing in the middle of thought groups.

___ using too many fillers or hesitation sounds.

___ pausing between words rather than between thought groups.

Grammar: Diagnosis of Problems

To determine your grammar proficiency, complete the following partial sentences aloud.

1. By the time you get to the end of the book...
2. Because of the holiday next week...
3. When I have the time...
4. It will always be important...
5. If you use the method we discussed last week...
6. While I was preparing the exam...
7. Of the two books, I prefer the one...
8. In order to pass this course...
9. Before I talk about this chapter...
10. I suggest that you...
11. Even if you get an A on the final exam...
12. As soon as you finish the test...
13. By working hard in this class...
14. Unless you've done last week's homework correctly...
15. Between these two solutions, I recommend you choose...
16. If you failed the last test...
17. After you find the results...
18. Even though this problem looks easy...
19. A microscope is an object...
20. Since we can't finish all of this today...

   With your instructor, determine which of the following grammatical categories you need to learn about or monitor more carefully in your speech.

___ Verb form   ___ Articles

___ Verb use   ___ Relative clauses

___ Subject/verb agreement   ___ Pronouns

___ Subordination   ___ Infinitives and gerunds

___ Other _____

Needs Assessment:
Characteristics of a Good Teacher in Your Culture

Each culture has its own definition of what makes a good teacher. To compare ideas of teaching across cultures, first complete the following questionnaire by circling the answer or answers that you think best describe the characteristics of a good teacher in your culture. Then divide into small groups and compare your answers.

There are no universally right answers to this questionnaire. It is designed to try to help you realize that values vary from culture to culture. In the next unit you will interview one or two people from the United States and compare their description of a good teacher with your own.

1. A good teacher in my culture
   a. encourages students to ask questions in class.
   b. usually answers questions outside of class instead of in class.
   c. encourages students to answer questions by thinking for themselves.

2. A good teacher in my culture
   a. always knows the answer to student questions.
   b. is not afraid to admit that he or she does not know the answer to a question.
   c. must always appear to know the answer to student questions even if he or she does not.

3. A good teacher in my culture answers student questions by
   a. giving as much information as he or she can.
   b. going straight to the point and answering as simply as possible.
   c. asking the student, "What do you think?"

4. A good teacher in my culture
   a. asks questions periodically to see if students have understood the lesson.
   b. leaves it up to the students to ask questions if they do not understand.
   c. relies on test results, homework, and quizzes to determine if students have understood the lesson.

5. A good teacher in my culture
   a. lectures most of the time, believing that students learn best from the voice of authority and experience.
   b. encourages student participation in class to facilitate learning from student questions and comments.
   c. organizes experiences for students to learn by doing.

6. A good teacher in my culture
   a. is informal during class but keeps relationships with students more distant outside of class.
   b. treats students formally during class and after class.
   c. treats students formally during class but treats them like friends after class by socializing with them.

7. A good teacher in my culture
   a. makes the class fun by telling jokes and having the students do interesting things.
   b. is hardworking and serious. Students often get a lot of work done in his or her class.
   c. makes the class relevant by having the students discuss how the class material applies to their lives.

8. A good teacher in my culture
   a. is well-organized, has a plan for the day's lesson, and follows the plan exactly.
   b. has a general plan for the day but deviates depending on how things are going that day.
   c. is often unpredictable. Students almost never know what to expect. The teacher generally comes without a plan and does whatever comes to mind at that moment.

9. A good teacher in my culture
   a. tries to make the material as simple and easy as possible so that most students can understand and get high grades.
   b. tries to make the material difficult so that it is challenging to even the best students. Students must work very hard to get good grades.
   c. tries to make the material just challenging enough so that most students' grades are average.

10. A good teacher in my culture
    a. presents material quickly in order to cover as much as possible in the quarter.
    b. presents material at a pace that is adequate for most students to take notes, and periodically pauses for students to comprehend the material.
    c. presents material rather slowly so that even the slowest students can grasp information.

UNIT 2
Introducing a Syllabus

A dynamic presentation of the syllabus helps students
feel enthusiastic about the course.

In this unit your assignment will be to practice presenting a syllabus at the first meeting of a class. Plan a clear and well-ordered presentation of no more than five minutes in length. Your instructor and fellow ITAs will then ask you questions about the syllabus or the class for an additional five minutes.

As a TA, you will probably be required to present a syllabus or other course information on the first day that you meet your students. First impressions are often lasting ones, so it is important that you make a good first impression. If the students react negatively to the first class, they may decide to drop the course. In the United States students can choose their courses freely and may often be able to choose their instructors.

In this unit, you will learn techniques to ensure that you make the type of impression that you want and to present your course syllabus in a clear and interesting way. These techniques will help ensure that your students will return, on the second day of class, eager and willing to learn.

Focus 1:
Nonverbal Communication

Nonverbal communication refers to the information, attitudes, or feelings that we communicate to others without using words. We most commonly communicate without words by using hands and arms for gestures or touching, and by using facial expressions, body posture, and nonverbal sounds. Many other kinds of behavior also communicate information nonverbally: use of space, use of time, types of dress, and variations in the way we speak, such as volume, speed, and intonation.

A teacher's nonverbal communication often shows how the teacher is feeling and what his or her attitude is toward students. Teachers use nonverbal behavior both intentionally and unintentionally. Nonverbal communication can be used **intentionally** to make a presentation more interesting or easier to follow. Think of some nonverbal behaviors you have observed that your professors use to reinforce what they are saying. A teacher's nonverbal behavior may also **unintentionally** communicate his or her self-confidence, enthusiasm for the subject, or attitude toward the students. For example, a teacher who is constantly moving around the room with no purpose might be interpreted as being nervous and not very confident.

Students also communicate nonverbally, often displaying much more than they would ever say to a teacher directly. A student's nonverbal communication can indicate interest, boredom, confusion, or understanding. In what ways do you show your instructors how you are feeling about the class?

Cultures vary widely in their use of nonverbal communication. Newcomers to a culture often do not anticipate the differences. One example of this is the shock felt by many international students when they see U. S. students sitting with their feet on the chairs in front of them, drinking soft drinks in class, or reading newspapers while the teacher is lecturing. U. S. teachers may tolerate these behaviors from their students even if they do not like them.

Because we are often not aware of our own nonverbal communication and its effect upon others, it is important to learn about expectations regarding nonverbal behavior in a culture that is new to us. The best way to improve your awareness of nonverbal communication patterns in the United States is to sharpen your powers of observation and to ask questions about what you observe.

EXERCISE 1: Comparing cross-cultural differences in classroom
                nonverbal communication

Nonverbal classroom behavior in your country may differ from behavior in the United States. To begin focusing on these differences, observe your own teachers and fellow students this week and note any striking differences. Some points to compare:

Behavior	My Country	United States
1. Space		
How much do teachers move around?		
Do they stand? Sit? Where?		
2. Gestures		
How much do teachers move their hands?		
What do these movements mean?		
Do any gestures differ in meaning in the two cultures?		
3. Eye Contact		
Where do teachers look when teaching?		
If they make eye contact with students, do their eyes sweep across the group or focus on individuals?		
If they focus on individuals, how often and how long do they make eye contact?		
4. Facial Expressions and Head Movements		
How often do teachers smile?		
How do they show anger?		
What do they do when students ask questions?		
How do *students* indicate: boredom? interest? confusion? understanding?		
How do *teachers* indicate: agreement? disagreement? confusion? understanding?		
5. Touching		
Do teachers ever touch students?		

What does it mean if a teacher
touches a student?

In what situations, if any, would a
student touch a teacher?

In what situations, if any, would
students touch each other?

6. Time

How late to class can teachers be
without offending the students?

How late to class can students be
without offending the teacher?

What do people do or say when
they are late?

7. Classroom Behavior

Do students or teachers smoke,
drink, or eat in class?

How do students sit?

How do students get the teacher's
attention?

Under what circumstances do
students leave the class while it is
still in session? What do they do or
say if they want to leave?

8. Dress and Cleanliness

How do teachers dress for class?

How do students dress for class?

How important is cleanliness or
the lack of body odor?

9. Manner of Speaking

How loud a voice is appropriate
for lecturing?

Does appropriate loudness of
voice differ for men and women?

What speed of speaking is
appropriate for lecturing?

How much variation in pitch is
appropriate for a teacher?

What does it mean if a teacher's
voice varies too much or too little
in pitch?

Be prepared to talk about the differences which you find most striking and the
implications these differences have for your teaching in the United States.

Focus 2:
Teacher Presence

To have teacher presence means behaving in a way that allows other people to trust you and feel comfortable with you as a teacher. One of your roles as a teacher in the United States is to be an authority who shows confidence in his or her knowledge and ability to lead a group of students. Another role is to support student learning by showing interest in your students and concern about their needs. Both of these roles are important in establishing rapport (a comfortable relationship) with your students. It is important for you to be confident and comfortable with your position of authority and at the same time to be open, approachable, interested in the students, and concerned about their learning.

EXERCISE 2: Demonstrating confidence and approachability in the U. S. classroom

This exercise will help you think about the ways to demonstrate confidence and approachability in the U. S. university classroom. Check all the items that you feel are correct for each section. When you are finished, compare answers with a partner before discussing the exercise with the whole class. Some of the items below may be obvious, and others may be less obvious. The purpose of the exercise is to start you thinking about these issues.

A. TAs in U. S. universities can show **openness** to students by

 ___ 1. looking occasionally into the eyes of students when speaking.

 ___ 2. frequently encouraging students to ask questions in class.

 ___ 3. always remaining at the front of the class.

 ___ 4. asking students to hold their questions for office hours.

 ___ 5. using humor occasionally or laughing with the students.

 ___ 6. looking at the desk or floor or over the students' heads when speaking.

 ___ 7. maintaining a serious attitude.

 ___ 8. keeping their facial expressions neutral.

 ___ 9. occasionally walking close to the students.

 ___ 10. smiling occasionally.

B. TAs in U. S. universities can show **confidence** by

 ___ 1. using a loud voice.

 ___ 2. coming to each class well prepared.

 ___ 3. standing straight.

 ___ 4. speaking just loud enough for students to hear.

 ___ 5. using expressive gestures and facial expressions.

 ___ 6. speaking quickly to make sure that all the material is covered.

 ___ 7. admitting they do not know the answer to a question but will find out.

_____ 8. keeping their hands at their sides and avoiding changing facial expressions.

_____ 9. standing in a relaxed position.

_____ 10. providing students with a model of excellent scholarly ability.

_____ 11. speaking slowly so that students can understand easily.

_____ 12. demonstrating concern for student learning with a willingness to explain information simply and frequently.

_____ 13. inventing an answer based on their background in the field when they don't know the answer to a question.

_____ 14. depending on their expertise to conduct the class without preparation.

C. TAs in U. S. universities can show **concern** for students by

_____ 1. making each class as interesting as possible.

_____ 2. giving complex explanations to demonstrate their expertise in the field.

_____ 3. requiring students to pay attention regardless of the interest level of the material.

_____ 4. reacting to student questions as challenges to their authority.

_____ 5. checking with students frequently to see if they have understood the material.

_____ 6. urging students to ask questions even if the questions show ignorance or lack of attention to the class material.

_____ 7. answering every question with complete and detailed answers.

_____ 8. providing brief and direct answers before checking to see if students want more information.

_____ 9. giving students the responsibility to keep up with the material in the course.

_____ 10. making their explanations as simple and clear as possible.

D. TAs in U. S. universities can show **interest** in the students by

_____ 1. showing respect for their students through an awareness of cultural differences in the university-level classroom.

_____ 2. demonstrating that they know exactly what the student's question is even before the student has finished speaking.

_____ 3. speaking calmly and neutrally.

_____ 4. maintaining a proper distance from the students.

_____ 5. speaking energetically and enthusiastically.

_____ 6. considering student needs before making decisions about the course.

_____ 7. interacting and talking with the students frequently.

_____ 8. thinking that teachers generally know what is best for their students.

_____ 9. requiring students to show respect for their teachers by conforming to teacher expectations for the course.

_____ 10. listening carefully to student questions and trying to answer exactly what it is they want to know.

Functional Language:
Classroom Expressions and Terms

EXERCISE 3: Classroom terms

Students may ask about your testing or grading methods for the course. Test yourself by matching the term with its definition.

Terms:

1. Partial credit
2. Make-up policy
3. Grading on a curve
4. Essay test
5. Pass/fail
6. Multiple-choice question
7. Used textbook
8. Drop the course
9. Full credit
10. Open book test
11. Set grading scale
12. Cumulative exam
13. Study guide
14. Midterm exam
15. Supplementary textbook
16. Course credits
17. Make-up test
18. Closed-book test
19. Objective test
20. Incomplete
21. Review session
22. Take-home exam
23. Prerequisite
24. Extra credit

Definitions:

A. ____ A test that uses multiple-choice, true or false, matching, and fill-in-the-blank questions.

B. ____ A test answer that is not completely correct and receives less than the total number of possible points.

C. ____ An extra class held for those students who want to go over material to be covered on a test.

D. ____ An in-class test for which students can use their textbooks and notes.

E. ____ A test that poses open-ended questions to be answered by writing paragraphs or compositions.

F. ____ Additional points earned by a student who does work in addition to what is normally required.

G. ____ A test question that forces a student to select the best of several given answers.

H. ____ A textbook that is not required for the course but is recommended for additional study.

I. ____ A test answer that receives the total number of possible points.

J. ____ A set of materials designed to help a student perform better in the course.

K. ____ A policy in which grades are based on score cut-offs that were previously decided upon by the instructor.

L. ____ A test given again after the scheduled time for students who miss the original test due to illness or another unavoidable conflict.

M. ____ A test given halfway through a course that covers the course material up to that time.

N. ____ A course that must be taken before another course.

O. ____ A test on everything covered in the course up to the time of the test, including material covered on previous tests.

P. ____ A policy in which grades are based on a normal distribution curve.

Q. ____ A set of rules that determine when students may make up tests or hand in homework late.

R. ___ A student's cancelation of registration in a course.

S. ___ A test that students complete outside of class using their textbooks and notes.

T. ___ A non-letter grade, given by the instructor, that relieves the student of the pressure to achieve the highest grade possible.

U. ___ The units of value for a university course.

V. ___ A textbook owned by a previous student in the course that is sold to a new student in the course.

W. ___ A grade that allows the student to make up missed work during a subsequent quarter or semester.

X. ___ A test that students take in class without the use of their textbooks or notes.

EXERCISE 4: Using classroom expressions

Many expressions are specific to the U. S. university classroom. Test your knowledge of these expressions by completing the student and teacher dialogs below with the appropriate expressions. (Remember to use the grammatically correct forms.) Some of the expressions you have already learned in this unit; others are new. Use the context to decide which expression goes where.

Part 1
Expressions

speak up
go around
credit
share
pass . . . back
lose points
skip
move on
turn in
grade down
collect
hand in

Dialog

TA: Here's the syllabus for this course. (1) _____ these _____, please.

STUDENT: I didn't get one.

TA: I'm afraid there are not enough copies to (2) _____. You'll have to (3) _____ for now. I'll bring more next time.

STUDENT: I'm sorry I can't hear you back here. Would you say that again?

TA: I'll try to (4) _____. I said that I would bring more syllabuses next time.

TA: Would you look at the top of the page, please? I want to explain the attendance policy.

STUDENT: Will we be (5) _____ if we (6) _____ class?

TA: No, but I (7) _____ homework at the beginning of each class, and if yours isn't in, you'll (8) _____.

STUDENT: What happens if we're sick and can't (9) _____ the homework?

TA: You'll just have to see me during my office hours to (10) _____ your homework, but you won't get (11) _____ if you don't have a good excuse. OK, let's (12) _____ to the section in the middle of the handout, the one on the tests for this course. There will be two quizzes, a midterm and a final.

**Part 2
Expressions**

get back

open book

fill in

review session

go over

turn to

make up

count

be on the right
    track

partial credit

be out of

Dialog

STUDENT: Will the quizzes be (1) _____?

TA: Yes, you can use any notes or materials that you want for the quizzes but not for the midterms or final. Are there other questions about the tests?

STUDENT: Will you have a (2) _____ to (3) _____ what will be on the midterms and final? And how much will each test (4) _____?

TA: I'm not sure. If you need a review session to (5) _____ you _____ before one of the tests, just ask me and I'll see if I can organize one. The final will be one third of your grade, the midterms will each be one sixth, and the homework will be the other third. Now find the section toward the bottom where it talks about your calculations on the tests.

STUDENT: I don't understand. Will we be allowed to use a calculator?

TA: Yes, you can use a calculator, but I won't require you to actually finish the calculations. What I'm mainly interested in is how well you can analyze the problem. I'll even give you (6) _____ if you (7) _____.

STUDENT: (8) _____ to the homework, if we do badly on it, can we (9) _____ it _____?

TA: No, I'm sorry. I don't have time to grade extra homework. Try to get it right the first time. The last thing I want to talk about is the textbook. Do you all have a copy of it?

STUDENT: The bookstore (10) _____ them. What should we do?

TA: I'll see if I can get some more ordered right away. Are there any more questions about the syllabus? If not, those of you who have the books, would you (11) _____ page six? Please share with a neighbor if you don't have the book yet.

Assignment Preparation:
Introducing a Syllabus

To prepare for your presentation in this unit, work with a partner to present part of the sample syllabus given below. After each of you finishes presenting your part of the syllabus, give each other feedback on the presentation. Use the outline following the sample syllabus to help plan your part of the presentation.

SAMPLE SYLLABUS

Course Information

Course: American Studies 3300: An Introduction to American Culture
Class hours: M, W: 14:15–16:00
Place: 315 Johnson Hall

TA: (Your name)
             Smith Hall
             635-4832

Office hours: TH: 12:00-14:00
Text: *An Introduction to American Culture* by Stone (required)
             American Society by Jenkins (optional)

Topics

Weeks	Topics	Text pages	Tests/Papers
1–2	The American Family	1–150	
3–4	Social Customs	151–303	Midterm I
5–6	Treatment of the Elderly	304–459	
7–8	Attitudes toward Work	460–600	Midterm II
9–10	Religion in America	601–759	Final paper

Course Requirements

Homework: Weekly homework assignments are due every Friday.
                LATE HOMEWORK NOT ACCEPTED.
Exams: Two midterm exams on Wednesday of weeks 4 and 8, based on material from the textbook and the lectures. A make-up exam in week 10, available only to those who miss an exam for a good reason, such as a serious illness or death in the family.
Final paper: A required research paper of 5 to 7 pages on the topic of your choice. More details about this assignment later.

Grading Policy

Grading: On a curve, based on the highest score any student has received.

Homework assignments:	10 points each	=	100 points
Midquarter exams:	100 points each	=	200 points
Final paper	200 points each	=	<u>200 points</u>
			500 points

ITA 1 presents the following information, using the first half of the sample syllabus, Course Information and Topics.

1. Overview—Welcome the students to your class and tell them what you will cover during this period.
2. Self-Introduction—Tell the students your name, what you would like to be called in class, something about your background, and how you are specially prepared to teach this class.
3. Course Information—Hand out the syllabus and go over the key points of the top section. What do you need to include? What can be left out?
4. Topics—What can you say about the content of the course to stimulate interest in the students? What will you tell them about the amount of work that will be required and what they should do if problems arise?

ITA 2 presents the following information using the second half of the syllabus, Course Requirements and Grading Policy.

5. Course Requirements—What parts might you want to emphasize here? Do you need to read everything?
6. Grading Policy—What do students need to know about the attendance policy? What part(s) of this section need to be emphasized?
7. Closing—What could you say in closing to make the students feel like the class will be interesting and/or enjoyable? What impression will you give them concerning the difficulty of the course? What can you say about your role as the instructor? (For example, should they be independent, or depend on you for assistance?)

Assignment Presentation: Introducing a Syllabus

In this unit your assignment is to practice meeting your students on the first day of class. You will introduce yourself and present a syllabus for a course. Plan a clear and well-ordered presentation of no more than five minutes that covers the information below. Your instructor and fellow students will then ask you questions about the class for an additional five minutes.

Ask your TA supervisor, advisor, or fellow TAs for a copy of the syllabus of an undergraduate course in your department for which you may be asked to be a TA. This syllabus should include some or all of the following information:

1. Course name and number.
2. TA's name (That's you!).
3. Days and times the course will meet.
4. Textbooks: Required and supplemental.
5. TA's office, office phone number, and office hours.
6. Other course information including: materials to be covered each week, homework assignments, tests, grading and attendance policies.

CHECKLIST FOR ASSIGNMENT PRESENTATION

1. How will you give your students the syllabus? Will you bring photocopies, make an overhead transparency, or write the information on the board?

2. Research shows that information transfer increases with shared background: the more the students know about you, the easier it will be for them to learn from you. How will you introduce yourself? What information might you include about your background? What can you do to encourage students to accept you as their teacher? How can you show them that you are approachable, friendly, and concerned about their learning?

3. Students may be concerned about their ability to understand you and whether you will be able to understand them. It may be wise to approach this subject right from the beginning. You should keep in mind the advantage of **acknowledging** your English problems rather than **apologizing** for them. What might you say on the first day to put them at ease and to set the tone for the rest of the quarter? Think of strategies you and your students can use to prevent misunderstandings.

4. How will you introduce the basic information about the course? Will you just read it aloud or will your presentation differ from the visual information you supply?

5. How much of the syllabus will you talk about? (What aspects of the course are complicated or difficult to understand? What aspects are obvious and need no explanation?)

6. How will you know if students have understood you? Will you monitor their faces, ask frequently if they understand, encourage them to ask specific questions?

7. Consider what questions students might have on their first day in class. What information may not be clear? What additional information may be needed? You must be ready to answer questions such as when homework is due, how many tests there will be, and whether you will be available at any time other than office hours.

Pronunciation: Compensation Strategies

Pronunciation generally takes a long time to change, and you will probably not make all the changes you would like while taking this course. There are, however, specific techniques that can make your speech more comprehensible even if you still have pronunciation problems. We call these techniques **compensation strategies.** As your pronunciation improves, you may choose to stop using some of these strategies, but until then it is important to be sure that your listeners can understand you.

General Communication Compensation Strategies

1. Speak slowly and in short phrases.
2. Pronounce every sound as precisely as you can—perhaps even by exaggerating the movements of your mouth.
3. Use the written word to back up the spoken word—on the blackboard, on overhead projector transparencies, on handouts.

4. Be redundant: say each important idea several times in different ways.

5. Avoid the words or types of sentences that you know cause problems and find other ways to say the same thing.

6. Check the pronunciation of key vocabulary (common vocabulary from your field) before presentations.

EXERCISE 5: Using your dictionary

The two easiest ways to check the pronunciation of a word are to ask a native speaker of English how to pronounce the word, and to look the word up in an English-English dictionary. The second technique is complicated by the fact that not all dictionaries use the same symbols for a given sound. You have to become familiar with the system of symbols used in your dictionary. Most dictionaries have a pronunciation key for their system of symbols at the beginning of the dictionary; others have a pronunciation key at the bottom of each page.

1. Where is the pronunciation key in your dictionary?

2. What symbols does your dictionary use for the sounds underlined in the following words?

VOWELS:		CONSONANTS:			
____ seat		____ pit		____ zoo
____ sit		____ bit		____ she
____ say		____ tin		____ pleasure
____ set		____ din		____ hit
____ sat		____ cat		____ swim
____ sock		____ go		____ win
____ saw		____ chat		____ sing
____ stone		____ fudge		____ yes
____ stood		____ fat		____ we
____ soon		____ vat		____ where
____ sum		____ think		____ lock
____ salute		____ that		____ rock
____ side		____ sat		
____ sound				
____ soy				
____ stern				
____ steer				
____ stare				
____ sure				

3. Remember that in English, stressing the correct part of the word—saying it louder and at a higher pitch—is an important part of correct pronunciation. What mark does your dictionary use to show which part of the word should be stressed? Look up the following word in your dictionary and copy the stress mark it uses exactly as it appears.

cor rect

4. In the appendix, find the field-specific vocabulary list for the field that is closest to your major.

   a. First use any pronunciation rules you know to try to pronounce each word in the list.

   b. Then choose ten words from the list for which you are not sure of the pronunciation. Look up the words in an English-English dictionary and check the pronunciation shown between slash marks or in parentheses after the word.

   c. Remember to check for the correct word stress.

   d. If your pronunciation was different from that of the dictionary, underline the word in pencil and practice the correct pronunciation by saying it aloud first just once, then twice in a row, then three times in a row, then four times in a row, and finally five times in a row.

      EXAMPLE: correct
               correct, correct
               correct, correct, correct
               correct, correct, correct, correct
               correct, correct, correct, correct, correct,

   e. Each week before your presentation, come back to the vocabulary list. Go through the steps above with each underlined word, and if your pronunciation of the word matches the dictionary's pronunciation, erase the line under the word.

   f. As you master more words each week, look up others about which you are unsure. Continue working on the list each week until you feel confident of the pronunciation of all of the words on the list. If you finish the list, add your own field-specific words and continue the process of mastering the pronunciation of vocabulary from your field.

Specific Pronunciation Compensation Strategies

1. **Paraphrase**
   EXAMPLE: You: What do you sink?
           Native speaker: Sing?
                    You: I mean how do you feel about it?

2. **Give the more general category in which the term belongs**
   EXAMPLE: You: I always have lice with my meal.
           Native speaker: How disgusting!
                    You: No, I mean food—grain—lice.
           Native speaker: Oh, rice!

3. **Give more specific examples of a general term**
   EXAMPLE: You: Do you have hobeece?
           Native speaker: Say what?
                    You: Hobeece! Skiing, painting, playing a musical instrument.
           Native speaker: Oh, you mean hobbies!

4. **Say it together with commonly associated words (collocation)**
   EXAMPLE: You: Do you like bebber?
           Native speaker: Bobber? What's a bobber?
                    You: No, bebber! You know, like salt and bebber!

5. **Use synonyms**
   EXAMPLE: You: Is it rodge?
           Native speaker: Rog? Rog who? I don't know any Roger!
                    You: Rodge! Rodge! Big! Is it big?

6. Add information

EXAMPLE: You: He was jung.
         Native speaker: John? You have to go to the bathroom? The men's john is...
                    You: No, he was jung, very jung, just a teenager.

7. Build in redundancy

EXAMPLE: You: Heez book is beeger zan mine.
         Native speaker: Zanmine? What's a zanmine?
                    You: Heez book is beeger zan my book.

8. Establish the topic

EXAMPLE: You: Does it rain much in your country?
         Native speaker: Trains? In my country?
                    You: No, I'm asking about the weather. Does it rain much?
         Native speaker: Ohhh! Only during the summer.

Add examples from your own experience for the following additional strategies.

9. Contrast with an opposite

EXAMPLE: You:
         Native speaker:
                    You:

10. Demonstrate it

EXAMPLE: You:
         Native speaker:
                    You:

11. Write it

EXAMPLE: You:
         Native speaker:
                    You:

12. Spell it out

EXAMPLE: You:
         Native speaker:
                    You:

EXERCISE 6:   Practicing pronunciation compensation strategies

The first sentence of each of these exchanges is spoken by a nonnative English speaker. The word in parentheses is the word he or she meant to say. Respond to the English speaker's request for clarification with a sentence that will make the message clear. Then write the name of the strategy you used. The first item is done for you.

1. Nonnative speaker: It's on the light (right).
   Native speaker: On the light?
   Nonnative speaker: No, I mean the opposite of left. (CONTRASTING WITH AN
                             OPPOSITE)

2. Nonnative speaker: I don't have a co (coat).
   Native speaker: A co? What's a co?

3. Nonnative speaker: What spot (sport) do you like best?
   Native speaker: Spot? You mean where do I like to go?

4. Nonnative speaker:	Can I have a pier (pear) please?
Native speaker:	Excuse me? What do you want?
5. Nonnative speaker:	Do you have a peel (pill)?
Native speaker:	What do you want a peel for?
6. Nonnative speaker:	Please collect (correct) my mistakes.
Native speaker:	Collect them? Did you write them down?
7. Nonnative speaker:	What is this sing (thing)?
Native speaker:	You mean song?
8. Nonnative speaker:	Could you give me the book (books) please?
Native speaker:	Which one do you want?
9. Nonnative speaker:	Is it code (cold)?
Native speaker:	You mean like the Morse Code?
10. Nonnative speaker:	I sent most of my things by sheep (ship).
Native speaker:	By what?

Grammar:
Compensation Strategies

Using correct grammar is sometimes a problem for ITAs, especially when they are trying to concentrate on content or when they need to use complex structures. Of course, practice and careful observation when reading and listening to English are probably the best solutions for improving one's grammar, but in the meantime, compensation strategies may help you overcome grammar weaknesses.

If you have problems with any of the areas of English grammar listed below, try the suggested compensation strategies.

Problem: Difficulty with articles
Strategy: When you can, make it plural.

It is often quite difficult for learners of English to know what article to use. An easy way to avoid using articles when describing things that are generally true is to follow the rule **When you can, make it plural**. In other words, instead of saying "A whale is a mammal," you can simply say, "Whales are mammals." That way, you only have to add an *s* and you can forget about articles altogether. Remember that this rule does **not** hold true when describing things that are concrete and specific. For instance, when referring to specific chemicals students are using in a chemistry experiment, you must say, "Mix the chemicals slowly." You cannot say, "Mix chemicals slowly."

Problem: Difficulty with long, complicated sentences
Strategy: Use short, simple sentences instead of long, complex ones.

Using simple sentence construction is important for you as an ITA for at least two reasons: (a) It will be easier for your students to understand you, and (b) it will be easier for you to speak correctly and fluently because you will not need to pause to think about difficult English sentence construction.

The following example was chosen to demonstrate that shorter, simpler sentences are easier to produce and to understand.

EXAMPLE: one long, complicated sentence
"Even though this function is decreasing, the other one is increasing, so both of them will cancel each other out, and the net effect will be zero."

EXAMPLE: two short, simple sentences
"This function is decreasing and the other is increasing."
"As a result, they will cancel each other out, and their net effect will be zero."

Problem: Difficulty with complex grammatical constructions
Strategy: Be flexible and say it another way.

Of course you cannot always avoid using complex structures, but if it is difficult for you to say something one way, perhaps you can use a different construction. Look at the following example:

EXAMPLE: complex grammatical construction
"Even if you haven't finished this lab, you have to go on to the next one."

EXAMPLE: simpler grammatical construction
"I know that you haven't finished the lab, but you have to go on to the next one."

Problem: Leaving out the verb *be*
Strategy: Use a more descriptive verb instead of the verb *be*.

Many students whose native language has no equivalent of the verb *be* (indicating the existence of something) omit it in complex sentences. For example, a speaker of Chinese might say, "Why prices higher when inflation?" rather than, "Why are prices higher when there is inflation?"

A good strategy for dealing with this type of problem is to use more descriptive verbs, such as *exists* or *occurs*, to replace the verb *be*. For example, in our original question above, we could say, "Why do higher prices occur when inflation exists?"

Problem: Use of double connectors such as *because,... so*
Strategy: Avoid using the first of the two connectors.

Many students whose native language requires them to use two connectors when showing logical relationships (*because... so; although... but*) carry this over into an incorrect use of double connectors in English. One way to prevent this is to avoid using the first connector and automatically use the second one.

EXERCISE 7:   Practicing grammar compensation strategies

In preparation for your presentation in this unit, audiotape yourself. Listen to the tape to determine which of the following problems you need to work on. After choosing the most serious problem, use one of the compensation strategies listed above to improve your grammar for your class presentation. After you have given your presentation in class, ask your teacher or your classmates to give you feedback on how well you did.

articles	long, complicated sentences
complex constructions	*be* verb deletion
double connectors	other(s)

Needs Assessment:
Problem-Solving Strategies in the U. S. Classroom

Teachers have strategies to help them through difficult classroom situations. New teachers often consult experienced teachers to learn these strategies and thereby avoid difficult situations in the classroom.

Here are some common classroom situations. First think about how you would solve each problem. Then ask an experienced TA from your department how he or she would handle each problem.

1. You made a mistake in your calculations when writing on the board and notice it several minutes later.

   Your solution: _____

   Experienced TA solution: _____

2. During class a student asks you a question about your field and you do not know the answer.

   Your solution: _____

   Experienced TA solution: _____

3. Students are not paying attention in your class. They are talking or joking with each other, reading the newspaper, or sleeping.

   Your solution: _____

   Experienced TA solution: _____

4. A student tells you why you should give him more points for a particular answer on a quiz. He is very persistent and will not accept *no* for an answer.

   Your solution: _____

   Experienced TA solution: _____

5. Students complain that your quizzes are harder than those of other TAs and that you grade more harshly than other TAs.

   Your solution: _____

   Experienced TA solution: _____

6. Your students seem very passive and distant in class. They do not ask questions, and they are very reluctant to participate when you call on them.

   Your solution: _____

   Experienced TA solution: _____

7. Your students complain to the chair of the department about your teaching skills, but they have never told you directly that they have difficulty.

Your solution: _____

Experienced TA solution: _____

8. A number of your students consistently hand in homework late and often skip class. Then they come to your office hours and ask you to explain what they have missed.

Your solution: _____

Experienced TA solution: _____

UNIT 3
Explaining a Visual

Visuals add interest and clarity to your presentation.

Your assignment in this unit will be to explain a visual such as a graph, table, model, diagram, or flow chart. Many instructors use visual aids in every class session. If using visual aids is not a familiar experience, this is an opportunity for you to experiment with ways that visuals can contribute to your teaching. If you are familiar with using visual aids, this is a chance to experiment with ways to use them more effectively. Although this assignment may seem simple or unnecessary, being able to help students understand the organization and meaning of the information in a visual requires considerable skill and practice.

For visuals to be effective, they must be used for a purpose. When you use a visual, be sure you can answer the questions "How will this visual help me to communicate?" and "Why is this visual more effective than any other visual?" Classroom instructors may chose to use visuals for any of the following purposes:

- To get the attention of students.
- To keep students interested.
- To give students another way to understand a given concept.
- To give students something to refer to after listening to the instructor's explanation.
- As a compensation strategy for problems communicating with spoken language.

You may have heard the common saying "A picture is worth a thousand words." Think about whether this has been true in your experience as a student. Were the class sessions using visual aids such as graphs, diagrams, physical models, objects, movies, or pictures easier to understand than those in which you learned from speech or writing alone? A visual may not necessarily communicate better than words, but it usually communicates information more concisely. For example, look how much more difficult it is to grasp the most commonly assigned graduate TA duties from the statistics in the following paragraph than from the graph, Figure 3-1.

Teaching Assistant Responsibilities

Results from a survey of departmental TA duties at a major U. S. university indicate that the most common duty assigned to teaching assistants is grading exams, homework, and papers. Eighty-seven percent of the departments surveyed require their TAs to do some type of grading. In the large majority of departments employing teaching assistants, TA responsibilities include office hours (79%) and proctoring exams (70%). A smaller number of departments report assigning TAs to lead recitations (40%) or labs (34%). In some departments TAs may also be assigned to assist other instructors in labs (31%) or to set up equipment (25%). In contrast to this, 25 percent of the

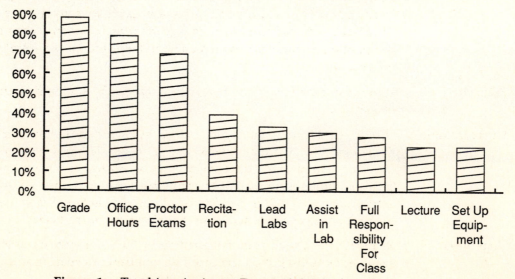

Figure 1. Teaching Assistant Reponsibilities

departments surveyed report that they require TAs to lecture, and 30 percent of the departments surveyed indicate that teaching assistants assume full responsibility for their classes.

In addition to graphs, many other visual aids can clarify or add interest to spoken or written information. Some options are the blackboard, handouts, posters, models, a volunteer from the audience, live demonstrations, physical objects, movies, videotapes, slides, photographs, transparencies on overhead projectors, or pictures on opaque projectors.

Focus 1: Blackboard and Visuals

For visuals to be fully effective, they must be carefully chosen to convey a specific point, be well-organized to reveal information clearly, be easy for all students to see, be legible, and be spelled correctly. The written or pictorial information should be smoothly integrated with information given orally. This means that all visuals must be presented with an oral explanation or they must directly support the oral information being given at the time.

When you choose a visual, it is important to consider the availability of the visual you want, the expense or difficulty of creating your own visual, and the availability of audio-visual equipment needed to present your visual. It is helpful to experiment with different types of visuals. You may find that you really like to use a certain type of visual or that students respond better to one type of visual than another.

The most common type of visual in U. S. universities is the blackboard. Using the blackboard seems very simple, but teachers must learn to use it effectively. Experienced teachers in the United States often give the following advice to new teachers.

Techniques for Presenting Information on the Blackboard

Legibility: Be sure that your handwriting or printing is neat and large enough to be easily read by anyone in the room. Write horizontally, not diagonally. Write only on parts of the board that are visible to everyone in the room. Spell words correctly and include important punctuation. When drawing complicated graphs, use colored chalk to help students interpret the information.

Efficiency: Write in outline form and abbreviate. To keep the students' attention, write quickly.

Organization: Use the blackboard to illustrate and clarify important points, starting on the left side and working toward the right side. Number your examples, steps, or main points. Leave space or draw vertical or horizontal lines between different topics. When defining a term, underline the word or words being defined. If possible, after your presentation move to the back of the room to evaluate what you have written on the board.

Repetition: Reinforce the title of your presentation or the main topic of each class segment by writing it on the board as you begin to speak about it. Be sure to write key words and definitions on the board.

Completeness: Include all steps, important details, signs, and symbols. Write the full definitions of terms. Label axes of graphs or rows and columns of tables. Remember that students need to be able to reconstruct your presentation from their notes.

Posture: When writing, don't turn your back to the students. Stand with your body facing the students at a 135 degree angle to the board.

Eye contact: Whenever possible, look at the students while using the blackboard. Whenever you pause to explain or stop to think about something, resume eye contact with your class.

Erasing: Before erasing the board, ask if anybody still needs to see the material you have written. If the answer is *yes*, write on another part of the board or stop and wait for them to finish copying it.

Spoken information: Be sure that your speech and the information on the board are well connected. Introduce information you are about to write on the board. Refer back to concepts previously covered by pointing to them on the board. Use the board to summarize information before making transitions to new information and also at the end of your class.

Courtesy: To avoid making the chalk squeak, break the chalk stick into smaller pieces and hold it loosely at a 45 degree angle to the board.

EXERCISE 1: Practicing techniques for presenting a specific visual

Work with a partner. Each person will choose one visual from the sample visuals in the appendix and think about how to present this visual on the board. Then, using the suggestions above, each person will practice presenting his or her visual by using the board. The other person will play the role of the student and give feedback regarding how well the suggestions above were applied.

Focus 2: Organization

In an organized presentation, the ideas to be presented are grouped and ordered in a way that makes the information easy to understand and remember. The organization is made clear by using organizational cues to signal the relationships between groups of ideas and by using transitions to signal a shift from one group of ideas to another. Important points are clearly emphasized so that students have no problem distinguishing between ideas they need to remember and those which are presented simply to help them understand the main ideas better.

In this unit you will learn how to organize presentations for your class. Some benefits of careful organization are listed below.

• By organizing your presentation in advance you will demonstrate to your students that you are taking your TA responsibilities seriously.

• Organizing your presentation beforehand will help you use your limited time more efficiently.

• Organizing your presentation ahead of time will help you feel more comfortable speaking English.

Two aspects of organization are particularly important: (1) using an outline to plan and give your presentation and (2) using a method of logical development which is appropriate for what you are trying to say.

A. Outlines

Cultures differ in the way they organize material. For example, in some cultures the main point does not come until the end, while in the culture of the United States, it is stated at the very beginning. A common rule that teachers in the United States like to follow when making a presentation is "First, tell what you will say, then say it, and then tell what you have said." Although this type of organization is not the only way to give a lecture, and it may not be the most interesting, it is the method that U. S. students expect their instructors will use.

When giving a presentation, it is important to use a method that allows you to plan what you will say and then to present your information exactly as you have planned to do it. The easiest way to do this is to prepare an outline of what you will say and then follow your outline as you present. Some information about outlining is presented below in outline form.

USING AN OUTLINE TO ORGANIZE INFORMATION FOR A PRESENTATION

I. Introduction: Function of an outline
   A. An outline helps you clarify your most important points.
   B. It also helps you decide what information you need to make those important points clear.

II. Form of an outline
   A. Notice the pattern of indentation in this outline.
      1. Where do you find the most important and most general points?
      2. Where do you find the most detailed points?
   B. Notice the Roman numerals, letters, and numbers that organize this outline.
      1. This is the most traditional way of labeling an outline.
      2. A less formal way to organize outlines is to use different degrees of indentation without letters and numbers.

III. Sample outline of a class
   A. Beginning
      1. Greeting
         a. Get everyone's attention.
         b. Get started.
      2. Introduction—tell the overall format of the presentation.
   B. Middle
      1. Background
         a. Give important contextual information.
         b. Define important terms.
      2. Body
         a. Present main ideas.
         b. Illustrate main ideas with supporting details.
      3. Summary—focus on important points.
   C. End
      1. Question period
         a. Give feedback to students.
         b. Get feedback from students.

2. Closing
    a. Signal the end of class.
IV. Conclusion: Reasons for using an outline
    A. An outline helps you to clarify the most important points and to remember to include information to make those important points clear.
    B. Outlines can help you prepare to introduce information, explain it in detail, and then summarize what you have said.

EXERCISE 2: Recognizing the logical order for content in an outline

Below is a scrambled outline of a short presentation on preparing for an academic career. Develop your skills in using an outline to organize information by putting the numbers of the phrases on the right in logical order in the outline on the left.

Preparing for an Academic Career

I. _n_
    A. ___
        1. ___
        2. ___
        3. ___
    B. ___
        1. ___
        2. ___
        3. ___
II. ___
    A. ___
        1. ___
        2. ___
        3. ___
    B. ___
        1. ___
        2. ___
        3. ___

a. Maintain a high grade-point average in order to get into graduate school.

b. Improve skills in spoken English in order to teach effectively.

c. Undergraduate work

d. Focus on publishing research articles to obtain tenure.

e. Learn about the needs and expectations of students.

f. Select courses in preparation for graduate work.

g. Learn how to write journal articles and present papers at conferences.

h. Work as a teaching assistant.

i. Assume full responsibility for lectures, assignments, tests, and grading in assigned courses.

j. Graduate work

k. Develop skills in thinking and writing in preparation for graduate work.

l. Obtain a position as an instructor or assistant professor.

m. Develop skills in lecturing, lab supervision, and holding office hours.

n. Education

o. Become comfortable in discussions with scholars in the field.

p. Learn how to supervise graduate assistants

q. Focus on one area of research for a dissertation.

r. Experience

B. Types of Organizational Structure (Logical Development)

In organizing the information you want to present, you will also need to choose a method of logically organizing the points that you want your students to learn. One way of organizing may do this better for some types of information, and another way of organizing may do this better for other types of information. For example, a series of historical events may be easiest to understand when organized chronologically (in the order in which it happened), whereas a single historical problem may be understood more clearly if information is organized by cause and effect.

Organizational cues or expressions help make the way you have organized your information clear to U. S. students. These cues or expressions are like road markers or maps—they allow the students to prepare for what is coming in the lecture and to avoid getting lost. They also indicate what is important for students to pay attention to and remember.

Some of the most common methods of organizing information are by:

A. *ANALYSIS:* Breaking a large subject into smaller parts to help clarify the nature of the parts or to clarify the relationship of the parts.

B. *CHRONOLOGY OR SEQUENCE:* Ordering events or steps in a process as they occur in time.

C. *PROBLEM/SOLUTION:* Posing a problem and then (1) explaining how to solve it, or (2) examining different possible solutions.

D. *COMPARISON AND CONTRAST:* Showing the similarities and differences between two similar concepts, or showing the advantages and the disadvantages of each.

E. *CAUSE AND EFFECT:* Focusing on the various contributing causes leading up to a particular effect or event, or on the various effects stemming from a particular cause or event.

F. *HYPOTHESIS AND SUPPORT:* Presenting an assertion and justifying it by bringing in evidence, supporting arguments, and refutations of counterarguments.

G. *CASE STUDY:* Using a particular example to help establish, prove, or disprove a generalization.

EXERCISE 3: Identifying types of organizational methods

Use the preceding list of organizational methods to identify which method is being used in each of the following presentation outlines. Write the letter of the method used next to the number of each outline. Note that the following examples also demonstrate possible ways to use letters, numbers, and other symbols to label each item in an outline.

____ 1. **Profile of Jane Frost**
   1. Graduate student applying for a TA position
   2. Expertise in major field
      • Undergraduate degree in field
      • Graduated with honors
      • Strong research interests
   3. Work experience
      • Peer tutor, junior year in college
      • Lab research assistant, one semester

____ 2. **Reasons for the Increase in the Number of ITAs at U. S. Universities**
   1. Demographic
      a. Decrease in number of U. S. students attending graduate school
         —High paying jobs in business and industry are currently available to holders of undergraduate degrees.
      b. Increase in international students attending graduate school
         —Developing countries lack sufficient graduate level institutions.
         —Fall of the dollar allows more international students to consider attending U. S. universities.

2. Legal
  a. International students who lack sufficient funds for tuition and living expenses have severe restrictions on off-campus work.
  b. International student visas permit graduate assistant work.
3. Academic
  a. U. S. institutions lack sufficient numbers of U. S. graduate students for teaching and research.
  b. U. S. institutions can attract international graduate students by offering graduate assistantships.
    —Few graduate fellowships are available to support international students.
    —Research assistantships are often reserved for more advanced students.
    —Teaching assistantships are often the only form of financial support available to newly arrived international graduate students.

____ 3. **Effective Communication Strategies**

Problem: Not understanding what someone has said
  • Ask them to repeat what they have just said.
  • Try to figure out from the context what they must have said.
  • Ask a third person what the speaker said.
Problem: Not being able to think of the English word for what you want to say
  • Explain the meaning of the word.
  • Give an example instead of using the word.
  • Use a gesture or a demonstration to illustrate the word.

____ 4. **Spoken Skills**
  A. **Pronunciation**
    1. Individual sounds
    2. Word stress
    3. Phrasal Stress
    4. Intonation
    5. Enunciation
  B. **Grammar**
    1. Accuracy
    2. Usage
  C. **Fluency**
    1. Pauses
    2. Smoothness

____ 5. **Some Differences Between Professors and Teaching Assistants**
  I. **Professors**
    A. Research
    B. Publish
    C. Teach
      1. Large undergraduate classes
        a. Plan course
        b. Lecture
      2. Small upper-level and graduate classes
    D. Advise graduate students
    E. Supervise graduate assistants
  II. **Teaching Assistants**
    A. Take classes and study
    B. Pass graduate exams
    C. Research and write thesis
    D. Teach
      1. Labs, recitations, lectures
        a. Present information
        b. Interact with students
      2. Office hours
      3. Grading

____ 6. **Steps in Learning a New Vocabulary Item**
  1. Recognize that the word is unknown.
  2. Decide that knowledge of the word would be of benefit.
  3. Look up the unfamiliar word.
  4. When the word appears again, recognize the word as one you have looked up, but cannot remember, and look it up again.
  5. Remember the general nature of the word, even if you cannot remember its exact meaning.
  6. Wait until you see or hear the word again and look it up one more time.

7. Remember its exact meaning.
8. Consciously choose to use the word in a particular context.
9. Use the word without thinking.

_____ 7. **ITAs and Their U. S. Students**

ITAs who get to know their students and try to meet their students' needs will be more successful than ITAs who speak English well but do not make a special effort to get to know their students. There are several generalizations which support this hypothesis:

—U. S. students will usually try harder to understand their TA when they feel that the TA is concerned with their welfare.

—U. S. students expect their teachers to make the class material interesting and relevant to student needs.

—U. S. students look to their teachers for help and advice.

Functional Language: Describing Visuals

When using a visual to present information, it is important to know what to call the visual, how to choose the best type of visual for your information, and how to refer your students to specific locations and different types of graphics on a visual.

EXERCISE 4: Identifying types of visuals

Check your knowledge of the various types of classroom visuals by identifying the visuals on the next three pages. Each visual is labeled with a figure number. Put the number of the visual next to its definition in the following list:

_____ a. Coordinate graph: The plot of a series of points representing X and Y values.

_____ b. Bar graph: A drawing that represents quantities with proportional lengths of bars.

_____ c. Pie graph: A circular drawing that represents percentages as pieces of a pie.

_____ d. Diagram: A drawing or plan of the parts or components of an object.

_____ e. Table: Words, numbers, or pictures arranged in columns and rows.

_____ f. Flow chart: A drawing that represents the order of the steps of a process.

_____ g. Model: A three-dimensional representation of an object or concept.

	n is even	n is odd
a is a positive real number	$\sqrt[n]{a}$ is a positive real number	$\sqrt[n]{a}$ is a positive real number
a is a negative real number	$\sqrt[n]{a}$ is not a real number (it is imaginary)	$\sqrt[n]{a}$ is a negative real number
a is 0	$\sqrt[n]{0} = 0$	$\sqrt[n]{0} = 0$

Figure 2. Odd/Even Roots of Real Numbers (Angel 1988, p. 307)

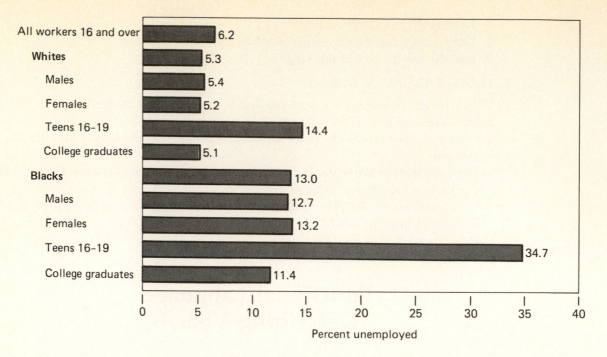

Figure 3.   Official Unemployment Rate Among Various Categories of Americans, 1987
(Macionis 1989, p. 507)

Figure 4.   Demonstrating a Chemical Compound

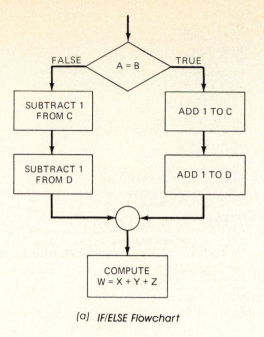

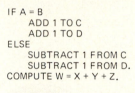

(a) *IF/ELSE Flowchart*

```
IF A = B
        ADD 1 TO C
        ADD 1 TO D
ELSE
        SUBTRACT 1 FROM C
        SUBTRACT 1 FROM D.
COMPUTE W = X + Y + Z.
```

(b) *COBOL Code*

Figure 5. The *If* Statement in COBOL (Grauer 1985, p. 71)

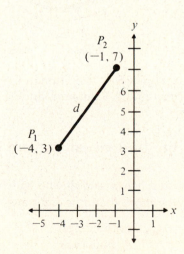

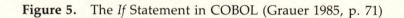

Figure 6. Determining the Distance Between Points (Angel 1988, p. 92)

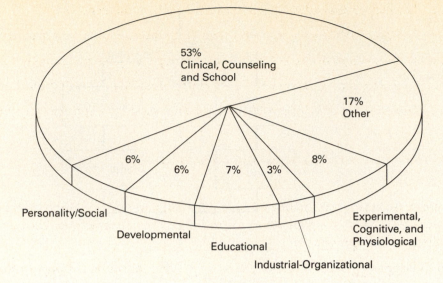

Figure 7. Percent of Psychologists Engaged in Work in Major Subfields of Psychology (Worchel and Shebilske 1989, p. 17)

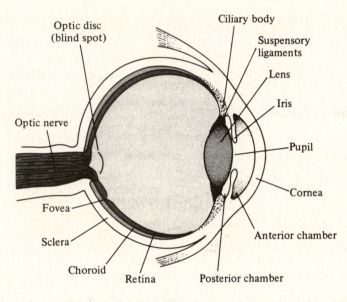

Figure 8. The Human Eye in Section
(Barrett, Abramoff, Kumaran, and Millington 1986, p. 460)

EXERCISE 5: Choosing the best visual for your data

Look at the types of data listed below and decide which type of visual is most appropriate for each data type. There may be more than one right answer.

    a. coordinate graph   b. pie graph   c. bar graph
    d. table   e. flow chart   f. model
    g. diagram

1. ____ The course of a disease from start to finish.

2. ____ The percentage of a person's budget that goes for food and housing.

3. ____ The comparison of the properties of five chemical elements.

4. ____ The position of the sun, moon, and earth during a solar and a lunar eclipse.

5. ____ A comparison of the percentage of GNP spent by various nations on defense.

6. ____ A comparison of the relative strength of earthquake shocks over time.

7. ____ The names and locations of various components of a gasoline engine.

EXERCISE 6: Describing location on a handout

These expressions can be used to describe the location of information on the following handout. Place the letter for each of the following expressions in the spot on the handout that the expression describes.

a. in the upper right-hand corner

b. in the left-hand margin

c. at the bottom of the page

d. in the upper left-hand corner

e. one fourth of the way up from the bottom

f. halfway down the page

g. in the lower right corner

h. one third of the way down from the top

TA Development Workshop   **AV Equipment Procedures**

HOW TO USE AN OVERHEAD PROJECTOR

*Plan Ahead

*1. Ask your departmental secretary whether your department has an overhead projector available for your use.

2. Use the classroom projection screen or an unobstructed white wall to project the image.

*3. Find a supply of overhead transparencies.

4. Select the visual you wish to transfer to an overhead projector transparency.

*5. Use a photocopier to transfer the image to the transparency.

6. Place the transparency on the overhead projector so that the top of the page points toward the students.

7. Do not obstruct the students' view of the screen.

8. Face the students and, as you talk, use your pen to point to parts of the handout on the projector or a pointer to point to the projected image on the screen.

9. Try to use the overhead projector in creative and interesting ways to keep students awake and interested in what you are saying.

Reminders

1. After turning the overhead projector off, allow it to cool down before moving it.

2. Find out where to locate a spare bulb in case one burns out.

Page 5

The list below identifies the components of Figure 9. Write the letter of the correct term on the graph next to the item it describes.

a. X-axis
b. curved line
c. dotted line
d. dashed line

e. Y-axis
f. shaded area
g. cross-hatched area
h. blackened area

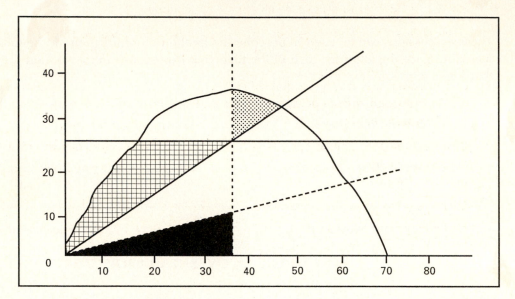

Figure 9. Common Visual Graphics

Assignment Preparation: Explaining a Visual

In this unit you will practice a very structured method for explaining a visual. This method is one way to be sure that students understand a complex visual. Less complex visuals may not require all these steps, and some of the steps may not be appropriate for all visuals. In addition, you may want to reorder the steps for a particular visual in order to encourage students to take a more active role in interpreting the information in the visual.

Work with a partner and take turns explaining a visual from the appendix or from the sample visuals in this unit. Follow the steps below and use the expressions provided to describe your visual. After both partners have finished, work together to write down one additional expression that could be used for each step in the process.

1. Introduce the visual by giving its title, name, or purpose:
   a. "The title of this (graph) is..."
   b. "This (model) is called a..."
   c. "This (chart) shows the relationship between..."
   d. "I think this (diagram) will help you understand..."

2. Discuss the overall organization, layout, or structure of the visual:
   a. "In this (graph), the (x-axis) represents... and the (y-axis) represents..."
   b. "This (mechanism) has (four) main parts:..."

3. Explain any symbols, terms, or other information that may be new for your audience:
   a. "Let's look at the (key). As you can see,..."
   b. "Notice that (A) denotes... and (B) denotes..."

4. Give at least one specific example which demonstrates the type of information the visual contains:
   a. "Let's look at one point on the (graph)..."
   b. "If you look at the (first) item in the (left) column..."

5. Discuss overall trends or patterns or make predictions based on the information conveyed by the visual:
   a. "Note the (peaks) at..."
   b. "In general, you can see that..."
   c. "If this trend continues, we will find that..."
   d. "This information suggests that..."

6. Close by summarizing the points you wish to emphasize regarding the visual:
   a. "In summary,..."
   b. "To conclude,..."

7. Elicit questions from the audience:
   a. "Is this clear?"
   b. "Any questions?"

Assignment Presentation: Explaining a Visual

Your assignment in this unit is to give a presentation explaining a graph, table, model, diagram, or flow chart from your academic field. Decide whether to present your visual on a handout, on the blackboard, or on an overhead projector transparency. Use the following steps to present the visual, but remember that some visuals may require you to omit a particular step or to follow the steps in a different order. You will have five minutes to present your visual to the class and another five minutes to answer questions about your visual.

1. What is the title, name, or purpose of the visual?

2. How can you help students understand the way in which information is organized in the visual?

3. What symbols or terms do you need to explain or clarify for the students?

4. What specific examples can you pick out to show the students how to interpret the visual?

5. What overall trends or patterns does the visual show? Can you make any predictions based on information from the visual?

6. What major points would you like to summarize or mention again for emphasis?

Pronunciation: Word Stress

Word stress means pronouncing one syllable of a multisyllable word more loudly, with a longer vowel, and with a higher pitch than the other syllables in the word. Several generalizations are helpful in figuring out which syllable to stress in English words.

1. Most **two-syllable words** are stressed on the first syllable, especially if the word is a noun.

   cy′ cle   **e′** qual   **stand′** ard

2. Many **two-syllable noun and verb pairs** differ according to stress. Nouns are stressed on the first syllable, and verbs on the second syllable.

Noun	Verb	Noun	Verb
pro′ ject	pro **ject′**	**con′** trast	con **trast′**
pro′ duct	pro **duce′**	**re′** call	re **call′**
ob′ ject	ob **ject′**	**sur′** vey	sur **vey′**

3. **Words with three syllables or more** may follow one of several patterns that are difficult to predict. In some of the patterns there is a primary stress [′ after letters in boldface type] and a secondary stress [` after letters in regular type]. The word stress patterns for individual multisyllable words must be memorized because there are no generalizations to help predict where the stress will fall.

at′ mos phere	**cat′** e go` ry	dy **na′** mics	mag **ne′** si um
cir′ cu lar	**com′** pro mis` ing	ad **van′** tage	com **par′** i son
cer′ tain ty	**la′** bo ra to` ry*	con **tain′** ment	pa **ra′** bo la
tem′ pera ture*	**au′** di to` ry	di **ver′** gent	phe **no′** me na
so′ di um	**an′** a lyz` ing	in **er′** tia	o **rig′** i nate

*The syllable division in these words is as pronounced, not as written. The second *e* in *temperature* is usually not pronounced. The first *o* in *laboratory* is usually not pronounced in American English.

ap` pa **ra′** tus	per` pen **dic′** u lar
fun` da **men′** tal	rec` og **ni′** za ble
cir` cum **stan′** tial	u′ ni **ver′** si ty
cor` re **spond′** ing	pa` ral **lel′** o gram
in` stru **men′** tal	sup` ple **men′**ta ry

4. Words with the following suffixes have primary stress on the syllable just before the suffix: **-ic(s), -i cal, -i ty, -tion, -sion, -cian, -u lar, -gra phy,** and **-gra pher.** The addition of the suffix may also cause a secondary stress to occur earlier in the word.

ac **cel′** er ate`	e′ du cate`
ac cel` er **a′** tion	e` du **ca′** tion
mol′ e cule`	math` e **mat′** ics
mo **lec′** u lar	math` e **mat′** i cal
mo lec` u **lar′** i ty	math` e ma **ti′** cian
e **co′** no my	**pho′** to graph`
e **con′** o mist	pho **tog′** ra phy
e` co **nom′** ics	pho **tog′** ra pher
e` co **nom′** i cal	pho` to **gra′** phic

5. Most **other prefixes and suffixes** do not change the stress of the original word unless they are given extra stress to ensure that the listener can hear them.

Original Word	With Prefix	With Suffix
a **gree′**	<u>dis</u> a **gree′**	dis a **gree′** ment
di **rect′**	in` di **rect′**	in` di **rect′** ness
pass′	sur **pass′**	sur **pas′** sa <u>ble</u>
press′	com **press′**	com **pres′** sor
re **spond′**	<u>cor′</u> re **spond′**	cor′ re **spon′** dence
syn′ the sis	<u>pho`</u> to **syn′** the sis	pho` to **syn′** the <u>size</u>

6. Similar sounding **two-syllable numbers** can best be distinguished if they are pronounced as follows:

thir` **teen′***	**thir′** ty**
four` **teen′**	**for′** ty
fif′ teen′	**fif′** ty
six` **teen′**	**six′** ty
seven` **teen′**	**se′** ven ty

*When a number like *thirteen* precedes a noun, the two syllables are stressed equally.
**The second *t* in a word like *thirty* is pronounced with a <u>d</u>-like sound.

7. **Compound nouns** have primary stress on the first noun of the compound. **Compound verbs** have primary stress on the second verb of the compound. The primary stress in **two-word verbs** falls on the particle following the verb. The other noun or verb of the compound or two-word verb receives secondary stress.

Compound Nouns		Compound Verbs		Two-Word Verbs*			
First Noun	Second Noun	First Verb	Second Verb				
black′	board`	out`	**run′**	hand` **in′**		bring` **up′**	
class′	room`	o` ver	**look′**	pass` **out′**		fill` **in′**	
news′	paper`	o` ver	**see′**	hand` **out′**		move` **on′**	
green′	house`	un` der	**stand′**	go` **o′ver**		look` **o′ver**	

*When two-word verbs are separated by a pronoun, both parts of the verb receive primary stress, as in *hand′it in′* and *bring′it up′*.

8. The stress on **three-noun compounds** is more difficult to predict. A good strategy is to try to determine which two of the nouns are linked together in meaning to form a two-noun compound that then joins with the third noun. The first noun of the two-noun compound receives primary stress while the third element receives secondary stress as in the following examples.

Third Noun before	Two-Noun Compound	Two-Compound Noun before	Third Noun
con sum` er	**price′** in dex	**weight′** loss	pro` gram
mag net` ic	**force′** field	**street′** car	line`
o per a` tions	con **trol′** cen ter	**chi′** square	test`

9. The primary stress on **adjective and noun combinations** is always on the noun.

Adjective	Noun
af firm` a tive	**ac′** tion
pas` sive	**trans′** port
or gan` ic	**com′** pound
cri` ti cal	**tem′** pera ture
rec tan` gu lar	ar **ray′**

EXERCISE 8: Identifying correct word stress

Mark the stress on these words according to the preceding nine rules.

Two-Syllable Nouns	Noun/Verb Pairs	
po wer	con tract	con tract
sym bol	in cline	in cline
cir cle	prog ress	prog ress
but ton	re cord	re cord

Stress Change with Suffixes

							Numbers		
e lec tric		mul ti ple					eigh teen	eigh ty	
e lec tri ci ty		mul ti ply					nine teen	nine ty	
e lec tri cal		mul ti pli ci ty							
e lec tron ics		mul ti pli ca tion							
e lec tri fi ca tion		mul ti pli ca tion al							

Compound Nouns	Compound Verbs	Two-Word Verbs	
lab man u al	un der take	run out	make up
ware house	with draw	turn in	fill out

Three-Noun Compounds		Adjective-Noun Combinations	
mas ter's de gree pro gram		e lec tric cur rent	
hu man re source man age ment		re stric tive clause	
gra d u ate le vel clas ses		an gu lar pro spec tive	
strength re duc tion fac tor		ra di ant en er gy	

EXERCISE 9: Identifying correct word stress in related forms of words

The stress in one of each group of three words is marked for you. Mark the primary stress in the other two related words. Make a guess about where secondary stress might fall and mark it as well.

Noun	Verb	Adjective
char' ac ter	to char ac ter ize	char ac ter is tic
cir cu la tion	to **cir'** cu late`	cir cu la to ry
dif ference*	to dif fer	**dif'** ferent*
di rec tion	to di rect	di **rec'** tive
ex pla na tion	to ex plain	ex **pla'** na to` ry
gra' vi ty	to gra vi tate	gra vi ta tion al
mag net	to **mag'** net ize`	mag net ic
pre sen ta tion	to pre **sent'**	pre sent a ble
spec i fi ci ty	to spec i fy	spe **cif'** ic
syn' the sis	to syn the size	syn thet ic

*The first *e* in *difference* and *different* is usually not pronounced.

EXERCISE 10: Practicing word stress

Gilbert (1978) suggests using a rubber band to practice correct word stress. Hold a strong rubber band between the fingers of both of your hands while practicing the pronunciation of the words in Exercises 8 and 9 above. Stretch the rubber band a lot when you pronounce syllables with primary stress and somewhat less when you pronounce syllables with secondary stress. Stretch the rubber band only a little when you pronounce syllables without stress. Use this practice with rubber bands to help control your production of stress and remember the correct placement of stress in the words you have practiced.

EXERCISE 11: Word stress for field-specific terms

Find the list of **field-specific terms** in the section of the appendix that is closest to your academic field. Use the rules you have just learned to mark the stress pattern for each word of more than one syllable or for each expression of more than one word. Look in your English-English dictionary for any words you do not know how to stress. Practice the pronunciation of the words on your field-specific list ten times.

EXERCISE 12: Word stress for subtechnical vocabulary

Find the list of **subtechnical vocabulary** in the appendix. Identify the words that are used in your field and use the rules you have just learned to mark the stress pattern for each of them. Look in your English-English dictionary for any words you do not know how to stress. Practice the pronunciation of each of the words that are used in your field five times.

Grammar:
Levels of Directness

U. S. teachers often use modal verbs such as *would, could, may*, and *might* to demonstrate politeness when making requests or suggestions. These indirect expressions show respect without lessening the effect of the request or suggestion. A teacher who omits these indirect expressions of politeness sounds overly authoritarian and unnecessarily brusque.

A. Indirect Expressions

Requesting That Students Do Something

"Would you (please) (VERB)...?"
"Could you (please) (VERB)...?"
"Would you mind (GERUND)...?"

"I would like you (INFINITIVE)...?"
"I wonder if you could/would (VERB)...?"
"I would appreciate it if you would (VERB)...?"

Asking Students for Permission to Do Something

"May I (VERB)...?"
"Could we (VERB)...?"

"Do you mind if I (VERB)...?"
"Would you mind if I (PAST TENSE VERB)...?"

Suggesting That Students Do Something

"How about (GERUND)...?"
"What about (GERUND)...?"
"Why not (VERB)...?"
"Why don't you/we (VERB)...?"
"Couldn't you/we (VERB)...?"

"I think that you/we should (VERB)..."
"Perhaps you/we should (VERB)..."
"You/we can (VERB)..."
"It might/would (not) be a good idea (INFINITIVE)..."

EXERCISE 13: Suggesting or requesting politely

Use one of the expressions above to politely make each of the following suggestions or requests. Not all expressions are appropriate for each situation. Write out your suggestions and requests. Ask your instructor or a native speaker if you have questions.

1. Request that the students do the next problem on their own.
2. Suggest that a student make an appointment with the professor to discuss that particular question.
3. Ask permission to erase what you have already written on the blackboard.
4. Request that a student read problem number 3 for the class.
5. Request that the students tell you when your pronunciation is not clear.
6. Suggest that a student try a different solution to the problem.
7. Suggest that the students use a chart in the appendix of the lab manual to find the answer to the problem.
8. Ask students for permission to skip over that particular question until the end of the class.
9. Suggest that the students heat the solution in order to speed up the reaction.
10. Request that the students hand in their homework at the beginning of the next class session.

B. Direct Expressions

Sometimes you may want or need to be more direct with your students. For example, if they do something that interferes with the smooth running of the class, or if their actions could be dangerous to other students, you may need to use a more authoritative tone. The following phrases may be useful for such situations. Note that your **tone of voice** (the emotional or attitudinal impact of your voice) can make a difference in how direct you sound. Have your instructor pronounce sample sentences using the following structures with different levels of directness in the tone of his or her voice.

Insisting that Students Do Something

"I want you (INFINITIVE)..."   "It's important (for you) (INFINITIVE)..."
"I expect you (INFINITIVE)..."   "You have to (VERB)..."
"It's important that you (VERB)..."   "I insist that you (VERB)..."

The following phrases are used when students are doing something that the instructor disapproves of. They are usually spoken in an angry tone. Be careful when using them because they are very strong.

Commanding or Warning Students About Their Actions

"You must (not) (VERB)...!"   "If you (don't) (VERB), I will (VERB)...!"
"Stop (GERUND)...!"   "You cannot (VERB)..., or... will happen!"
"(Please) (VERB)...!"   "You are (not) (INFINITIVE)...!"
"Don't (VERB)...!"

EXERCISE 14:   Being more directive with your students

Select one of the previous expressions to be more directive in the following situations. After writing out the exercise, pronounce the phrases for your instructor to get feedback on correct stress and tone of voice.

1. Some of your students have been arriving late to class. Insist that they be on time so that they will not miss important information.

2. During the last lab, some of the students were not wearing their safety goggles. Emphasize how important it is for students to wear safety goggles to protect their eyes from possible explosions.

3. You call a student into your office because she is failing the class. You want to emphasize how important it is that she do her homework and prepare for tests.

4. A student is talking and joking with the other students while you are lecturing. You feel that it is disruptive to other students in the class. Make him stop.

5. You have just handed out a midterm exam. Warn the students about cheating on this or any exam, and remind them of the serious consequences of cheating.

6. For the third time, a student has handed in an incomplete and hard-to-read assignment. Insist that she do it over legibly and hand in a completed version by Monday.

7. You suddenly notice a student in your lab is going to connect two dangerous high-voltage wires. Warn him!

8. Similar homework papers for the last assignment suggest that several students have copied from each other. Remind the students that they should do their work independently, and that working together on a homework assignment is the same as cheating.

9. Several students in your recitation have been handing in their homework late. Remind them that in order to get full credit, they must hand in the homework on time.

10. It is the first day of preparation for the lab, and students do not know the lab requirements. Remind them that they cannot work in the lab unless they have a special card that allows them to check out equipment.

Needs Assessment: Characteristics of a Good Teacher in the United States

In the previous unit, you compared ideas about good teaching across cultures and found that not all cultures agree on what makes a good teacher. In this unit, you will interview people from the United States to find out what they consider the characteristics of a good teacher to be, and you will compare their answers with the answers you gave in the last unit.

A. A Good Teacher in the United States

Find someone in your academic department to interview. People in the United States are often busy, so it is polite to first ask them if they have time to help you and then to make your request. Some typical expressions you can use to approach people are:

1. "Do you have a few minutes to answer some questions? I'm doing an interview for my TA training course."
2. "Can you spare a few minutes? I wonder if I could interview you as part of an assignment for a course I'm taking."
3. "I'd like to ask you some questions for an assignment I have. Do you mind? It will only take a few minutes of your time."

EXERCISE 15: Interviewing people from the United States about the qualities of a good teacher

To get a better idea of the U. S. perspective on teaching, interview at least two people from the United States. Try to choose different kinds of people, for example, a man and a woman, or a first year student and an experienced professor. Ask the following question and write down each person's answers.

"In your opinion, what **three** things make a good teacher?"

Share your results with the other students in your class. Did you get similar answers? How do these qualities compare with the qualities of a good teacher in your culture? Are the characteristics the same or different?

In the cases in which your expectations of a good teacher differ from those of your students, you have several options for using the information:

- Ignore the differences and teach as if you were in your own culture.
- Change your teaching style to meet the expectations of your students.
- Learn a second teaching style so you can choose whichever one is more appropriate in a given situation.

Discuss the implications of each option and decide which one is best for you.

B. The Ideal Teacher

Teachers from different cultures may not realize that their roles differ across cultures, and each may assume that his or her experience with teaching is typical of all teachers. When differences in teaching styles are not acknowledged in classrooms where the teacher and students come from different cultural backgrounds, problems can result. By anticipating the expectations students and teachers have of each other in U. S. classrooms, ITAs can avoid potential problems.

EXERCISE 16: Comparing the ideal teacher in your culture with the ideal teacher in the United States

Use an X to indicate on the following chart what you think are the characteristics of an ideal teacher according to your own culture. Then, ask a native English-speaking TA from your department to use an * to indicate what he or she thinks are the characteristics of an ideal TA in a U. S. university. Bring your results to class and compare them with those of ITAs from other countries and other departments.

The Ideal University Level Teacher in My Culture and in the United States

	Somewhat	Equally	Somewhat	
Open-minded				Closed-minded
Active				Passive
Judgmental				Accepting
Friendly				Distant
Formal				Informal
Hesitant				Self-confident
Unconcerned				Sympathetic
a Facilitator				an Expert
a Talker				a Listener

UNIT 4

Defining a Term

Defining new terms in ways that are relevant to the students' experience is crucial.

In this unit your assignment will be to define a term from your academic field. You will speak for five minutes, presenting a definition of the term and then explaining and clarifying it.

You can realize the importance of being able to define terms clearly by observing how often your teachers define terms for their students. Teachers are also expected to clarify definitions of terms in reading materials. Some typical situations in which teachers define terms are listed below:

- The students have not been introduced to the term.
- The students were introduced to the term previously but may have forgotten it or did not totally understand it.
- The students know the term but are not familiar with how it is used in a particular field.
- The term is confusing and is often mixed up with another term.

A formal definition often has three parts:

1	2	3
The item you are defining	**A category to which it belongs**	**The differentiation of the item from all other members of its class**
Kinetic energy	is a type of energy	that is related to the motion of a body.

A formal definition may be very precise, but students do not always grasp the meaning immediately. To help students, teachers try to present definitions in ways students can readily understand. The following section discusses some of those ways.

Focus 1:
Relevance of Content

Students in a U. S. classroom expect teachers to make new information relevant (applicable) to their lives. They want to know why they should study the information and how it will be useful to them. They expect teachers to show how new information is related to familiar contexts, and they need new ideas illustrated by good examples. They expect teachers to refer to practical examples or personal experiences when demonstrating the importance of, or illustrating, the information.

This section will focus on making the definitions of terms relevant to students so that the meanings of the terms are clear and presented in ways that students can easily understand. Definitions can be made relevant in several ways by:

1. **Practical example: Give an example from the students' experience.** Use information they already know to help them learn what they do not know. Try to choose examples that are creative and interesting.

   "To understand what a *fulcrum* is, think of two children on a seesaw. As you know, children sit on the two ends of the long seesaw board. The point where the board touches the seesaw's base is called the fulcrum."

2. **Personal example: Give an example from your own experience.** Use a story or event from your own life to help students learn new material. Research (Nelson 1989, 1992) has shown this to be a very effective method.

"To help you understand what *deja vu* is, let me share a personal experience. One evening I was at a party talking to my supervisor's wife, whom I had never met before. As I was listening to her speak, I knew exactly what she was going to say because I had dreamed it earlier. As I answered her, I felt compelled to repeat what I had said in the dream, just like an actor following a script. This is *deja vu*, which means 'seen before,' a sense of being in a situation that is happening for the second time."

3. **Analogy: Make an analogy to some other concept that students know.** Think about a pattern, relationship, or function that is similar to the concept you are defining.

"The structure of an *atom* is like that of the solar system. Electrons orbit around a nucleus the same way that planets orbit around the sun."

4. **Comparison or contrast: Compare the term with a similar term or contrast it with an opposing term.** Many terms have an opposite term or a similar term that differs in a specific way.

Similar: "*Nuclear fusion* is similar to *nuclear fission* because mass is converted to energy, but different because fusion involves the union of atomic nuclei and fission involves the splitting of atomic nuclei."

Opposite: "*Parallel* lines can never intersect and *perpendicular* lines intersect at right angles."

5. **Word origin: Tell about the origin of the term.** Did it come from another language? Does it have a prefix or suffix that can help students understand its meaning? Is it an acronym (an abbreviation consisting of the first letters of several words)? Has the meaning of the term changed over time?

"*Prefix* comes from Latin. It has two parts: *pre*, which means 'before,' and *fix*, from *fixus*, the past participle of *figere*, 'to attach.' A prefix is a particle that we attach to the beginning of a word to modify the word's meaning."

"*Radar* is an acronym that stands for radio detecting and ranging. Radar is a device that uses echoes of radio waves to detect the presence or location of an object."

6. **Visual means: Provide a visual illustration or model of the term: a picture, drawing, diagram, or chart.** Be sure to consider if illustrations or models from books need altering in some way to make them more understandable. Several of the examples of strategies listed above could include simple visual illustrations.

EXERCISE 1: Thinking of ways to make explanations relevant

Choose six words from your field's list of terms in the appendix. For each word, use the strategy indicated to make the word's meaning relevant to your students.

Word used in your field	Type of strategy	Your idea for the strategy
1. _____	Practical example	_____
		_____
2. _____	Personal example	_____
		_____
3. _____	Analogy	_____
		_____

Word used in your field	Type of strategy	Your idea for the strategy
4. _____	Comparison/contrast with another term	_____ _____
5. _____	Word origin	_____ _____ _____
6. _____	Visual	_____ _____

Focus 2:
Manner of Speaking

Our voices have many qualities that can either help or hinder our teaching. The most noticeable qualities are volume, speed, and tone of voice.

Of these, the most important is **volume**. A voice that is loud enough helps the teacher appear confident and trustworthy. Speaking loudly enough for students to hear easily also helps them concentrate on what is being said.

Another important voice quality is **speed**. Is it easier for you to understand native speakers of English when they speak quickly or slowly? Most of you will answer, "Slowly," just as your students will answer if you ask them how you should speak. This is especially true when you are using many words with three or more syllables.

A final important voice quality is **tone**, the voice quality that reflects our emotions or attitudes, such as impatience, happiness, or anger. The same words may be spoken with several different attitudes and thus with several tones of voice. A common saying in English is "It's not **what** you say; it's **how** you say it." Ask your teacher or a native speaker of English to say the following sentences for you with the indicated tone of voice. Pay special attention to the pitch and tension of the voice, and observe the speaker's nonverbal communication, such as facial expressions and body tension.

anger:	"I'd like you to hand in your papers on time!"
politeness:	"I'd like you to hand in your papers on time."
impatience:	"You have to finish the test in five minutes!"
patience:	"You have to finish the test in five minutes."

You may have noticed that positive attitudes differed from negative attitudes through different uses of pitch, voice tension, body tension, and facial expressions.

Each good voice quality can become a bad quality if it is carried to an extreme. What impression do you get when people speak **too** loudly, **too** slowly, or in an **inappropriate** tone of voice? Remember that different cultures may have different ideas of what volume, speed, or tone of voice is appropriate. Also remember that the volume, speed, or tone of voice that is appropriate when you talk with friends may be different from what is appropriate when you are speaking to a classroom full of students.

EXERCISE 2: Reading aloud to practice appropriate volume, speed, or tone of voice

Ask your teacher for his or her impression of your use of your voice in these three areas. If you have trouble with volume, speed, or tone, you may need special practice to change your habits. With the help of your teacher, choose one problem below that you need to work on.

Turn to the passage from your field in the appendix, and read it out loud to practice at least one of the suggestions listed below for solving your problem. An effective way to practice is to (a) read one phrase at a time, and then (b) look up and say the phrase from memory.

Speaking too softly

1. Become aware of the abdominal muscles you use when you make sudden loud noises, such as when you try to scare someone by shouting. If you breathe using the muscles below your navel, your voice has much more strength. This style of breathing is called **diaphragmatic breathing**. You can develop awareness of your abdominal muscles by doing the following exercises:

   a. Make both hands into fists, put your knuckles together, and place your fists on your stomach below your belt, with your fingers and the insides of your arms facing up. Lean against a wall with your fists between you and the wall. As you breathe in, let your stomach expand naturally, pushing your body away from the wall. As you breathe out, feel your body move back toward the wall.

   b. Stand in the same position, but instead of breathing gently in and out, tighten your stomach muscles suddenly as you say "HO!" and again, "HO!" and again, "HO!"

   c. Stand up straight, take a deep breath (letting your stomach expand), and begin reading your field-specific paragraph, speaking as long as possible without taking a breath, and tightening your stomach muscles as you get to the end of a breath so that you can squeeze out the last bit of air that is left in your lungs.

2. Tape yourself speaking in the largest room available to you. Stand at one end and place the tape recorder at the opposite end. Speak loudly enough to make your voice clearly understandable on the tape.

3. Practice taping yourself speaking against some kind of background noise, such as a fan or music, and make sure that what you say can still be understood.

Speaking too quickly

1. Write "Slow down" at the top, middle, and bottom of each page of notes you use when you speak.

2. Underline or circle every word in your notes that has three or more syllables to remind you to say it slowly and to pronounce every syllable.

Speaking too slowly

1. Practice giving your presentation out loud several times to improve your familiarity with what you want to say.

2. Speak English as much as possible in your daily life to improve your fluency and comfort with the language.

Being unaware of tone of voice

1. A good way to control tone of voice is to say the same sentence using a different tone each time. Practice saying the following sentences using varied tones of voice that are appropriate for each emotion or attitude indicated in the parentheses. Ask your teacher or a native English speaker for feedback.

   a. "It's important to come to class on time." (anger; concern)
   b. "Hurry up! The lab time is almost over!" (impatience; patience)
   c. "Why did all of you get such a low score on the test? Didn't you study?" (disbelief; concern; anger)
   d. "Any schoolchild knows the answer to that question." (sarcasm; humor)
   e. "What's taking you so long to do the experiment?" (concern; anger)

Tone of voice interpreted as too angry

1. Get feedback on whether your volume, pitch, and range of intonation are interpreted as expressing anger and adjust them accordingly.
2. Relax your voice before speaking by breathing in deeply and breathing out while saying the word "aah" in a drawn-out fashion.
3. Pay attention to the tenseness of your body. Concentrate on relaxing each part of your body while speaking.
4. Pay attention to your facial expressions. Focus on maintaining relaxed facial muscles and on smiling while speaking.
5. Substitute modals or less direct expressions for direct speech, especially when giving students directions or advice. (See Unit 3, Grammar, for specific expressions.)

Tone of voice interpreted as not authoritative enough

1. Stand straight with your head held up straight.
2. Lower the general pitch of your voice.
3. At the end of phrases and sentences, be sure that the pitch of your voice falls. In English, if the pitch of your voice rises and then does not fall at the end of phrases or sentences, your listeners may feel that you are uncertain about what you are saying.
4. Reduce tension in your voice by relaxing (opening) your throat and supporting your speech with deep diaphragmatic breathing.
5. Speak more loudly, with clear enunciation (very precise pronunciation) of each sound.

Functional Language: Organizational Cues

Certain words or phrases can signal that an instructor is introducing a new idea. For example, to let you know that there are several important points, the instructor may say, "First,...", "second,..." and so on.

EXERCISE 3: Functions of organizational cues

To help you identify the types of phrases that are used to organize presentations, look at the following transcript taken from a lecture entitled "Cross-Cultural Differences in Nonverbal Communication." The organizational cues are underlined. Decide what purpose each cue plays and write the letter identifying the type of cue in the appropriate space. Choose from the following list:

    A. Giving an overview (telling what you are going to cover in the lecture)
    B. Emphasizing a main point
    C. Giving an example
    D. Making a transition (moving from one part of a lecture to another)
    E. Closing (ending a major section of a lecture)

1. ____ "Today, I'd like to define nonverbal communication. It's a very simple definition. It is all the communication that is going on which is not verbal—not words. So, as I speak to you today I'm communicating to you in various ways.

2. ⎯ "So, for example, eye contact—how I use my eyes, how I use my face, my gestures, even the way that I'm dressed, my posture—how I stand,—all of that is nonverbal communication.

3. ⎯ "Now, there are two things that are really important about nonverbal communication if you're moving into another culture.

4. ⎯ "First, you need to know that cultures differ in the way that they use nonverbal communication. The patterns which you learned in your culture are different from the patterns that I learned in my culture. So, in a way, nonverbal communication is like language.

5. ⎯ "For instance, when I was born in California, I didn't just learn English. I learned how to move, how to use my eyes, how to use my hands. When you were born in Hong Kong, or Taiwan, or Ethiopia, you did the same.

6. ⎯ "The thing that adds to this, however, is that when you learned that, it was unconscious. Nobody sat down and said, 'All right, Elaine, I'm going to teach you how to use your hands.' I learned all those things, but I learned them unconsciously. And because I did that, unconsciously, I believe that every one of us does the same thing. All right? So, when I move into a new culture, I'm in for a big shock, right? Something is different, but I'm not quite sure what it is. Suddenly people seem to be acting differently, but I can't quite tell you what it is.

7. ⎯ "Let me say again that much of that is nonverbal communication, which is below my level of consciousness.

8. ⎯ "To summarize, let me say that nonverbal communication not only differs from culture to culture, but that it is also below our level of consciousness."

EXERCISE 4:   Using phrases for organizational cues

Below is a list of common words and phrases that are used to signal ideas in presentations. Choose the letter from the following list which best describes the function of each word or phrase and write it in the blank. The first one has been done for you. When you finish, practice saying the expressions for fluency and intonation.

a. Giving an overview
b. Emphasizing a main point
c. Giving an example

d. Making a transition between ideas
e. Closing

_d_ 1. "All right. Let's go on to another aspect of..."

⎯ 2. "In conclusion,..."

⎯ 3. "Take, for example,..."

⎯ 4. "The main thing is..."

⎯ 5. "This morning we're going to look at..."

⎯ 6. "Let me say again that..."

⎯ 7. "To summarize, let me say that..."

⎯ 8. "Now, let's take a look at..."

⎯ 9. "Today's lecture will focus on..."

⎯ 10. "Let me give you an example to show..."

⎯ 11. "Let me end by saying..."

_____ 12. "In this lab I plan to cover..."

_____ 13. "OK. Just as a general conclusion, then,..."

_____ 14. "An example of this is..."

_____ 15. "Today, I'd like to talk about..."

_____ 16. "This is important because..."

_____ 17. "First,... Second,... Third,..."

_____ 18. "The key point is..."

_____ 19. "OK. Let's move on to the next part of..."

_____ 20. "For instance,..."

_____ 21. "Next,..."

_____ 22. "Finally,..."

EXERCISE 5: Practicing with organizational cues

Work with a partner and present the following presentation on the "Differences in the Use of
Eye Contact." Choose cues from the lists below to organize your part of the presentation,
and write the letter of each cue on the blanks provided.

TA 1:
a. "Now,..."   c. "For instance,..."   e. "First of all,..."
b. "Second,..."   d. "Today, I'd like to talk about..."   f. "For example,..."

Cues   Outline

_____ 1.   *DIFFERENCES IN THE USE OF EYE CONTACT*

_____ 2.   I. Eye contact communicates two things in the United States

_____ 3.   A. Listener is paying attention.

_____ 4.   E.g., Students must look at lecturers.

_____ 5.   B. Intensity of feeling.

_____ 6.   E.g., More than three seconds means intense feeling, such as love or
                         anger.

TA 2:
a. "Ok. Let's move on to..."   d. "One difference is..."   g. "Let me give you an
b. "An example of this is..."   e. "Finally, let's look at..."   example."
c. "To summarize,..."   f. "The third difference is..."   h. "Another difference is..."

Cues   Outline

_____ 7.   II. Cultural differences

_____ 8.   A. Eye contact shows respect in some cultures and disrespect in others.

_____ 9.   E.g., Asian and African children look down when scolded, but U. S.
                         kids look at their parents.

_____ 10.   B. Little or no eye contact conveys deference to authority in some cultures, but in the U. S. it conveys a desire to hide something.

_____ 11.   E.g., In the United States, little eye contact means a person is untrustworthy.

_____ 12.   C. Length of eye contact differs among cultures.

_____ 13.   III. Gender differences in people's use of eye contact in the United States.

           On the street men generally look at women much longer than women look at men.

_____ 14.   IV. Eye contact is a complex phenomenon that conveys more than one thing in the United States, is used differently in different countries, and is used differently by men and women.

Assignment Preparation: Defining a Term

1. Divide into small groups of two to four.

2. In your small group, choose a word from the list below for the group to define.

pineapple	thermometer	scissors
gymnasium	motorcycle	zebra
telephone	bilingual dictionary	glove

3. Taking turns, each person will assist in defining the term by answering one of the questions from the following list of steps. The first person will answer the first question, the second person will answer the second question, and so on, until the group has completed the definition.
   a. What is the term and why is it important?
   b. What is a formal definition for the term you have chosen?
      • The item you are defining.
      • A category to which it belongs.
      • The differentiation of the item from all other members of its class.
   c. After hearing a formal definition, a person may need further explanation to understand the term completely. How can you make the definition clearer? (Think about giving examples, making analogies, drawing diagrams, etc.). Also, how can you make the definition relevant to your listeners?
   d. What can you say to conclude your explanation and let your audience know you have finished your presentation?
   e. What can you say or ask to see if the audience has understood everything?

4. After the group has finished defining one of the words from the list, go on to a second term and follow the same procedure with each member of the group answering a different step of the presentation.

5. As you listen to the other members of your group, write down any transitions they use that you might find helpful in explaining your field-specific definition for the assignment in this unit.

Assignment Presentation:
Defining a Term

Your assignment is to define a term from your field of study. Your presentation should be five minutes in length, and you will be given five minutes to answer questions. Cover all of the following points:

1. What is the term, and why is it important?

2. What is a formal definition for the term you have chosen?

3. What examples, analogies, or diagrams can you use to make your definition clearer and more relevant to your listeners?

4. How can you conclude your explanation and let your audience know you have finished?

5. What can you say or ask to see if the audience has understood everything?

6. If students ask questions, what phrases can you use to restate the question in your own words? Restating questions will (a) ensure that **you** understand the question and do not waste time answering the wrong questions and (b) make it easier for other students to catch what was asked in case they did not understand, or didn't hear, the question.

Pronunciation:
Stress and Intonation in Thought Groups

One of the the most important aspects of your pronunciation in your work as a TA is the way you use thought groups, stress, and intonation. If you are unable to deliver spoken English patterns like a native-English speaker, your students may become tired, irritated, or unable to concentrate. If you can develop native speaker-like thought groups, stress, and intonation, your students will be able to respond positively to the **content** of what you are teaching instead of becoming distracted by the **way** in which you teach the content.

Definitions

- A **thought group** is a group of approximately **two to five words that form a unit of meaning**. A thought group could also be called a **phrase**. The following sentence has three thought groups:

    The English language / uses thought groups / for clear communication.

- **Phrasal stress** is the **stressing of one syllable in a thought group** and the lessening of stress in all other syllables in the group. In American English, the syllable that receives phrasal stress is usually the syllable with primary stress in the last stressed word in the thought group.

    the Eng'lish **lan**'guage

    Your maintaining of a regular pattern of phrasal stress will help your listeners concentrate on the message rather than on the form of what you are saying. Native speakers of English assume that any changes in phrasal stress are to emphasize the importance of particular words or phrases in the sentence. If you are not able to maintain the expected pattern of English phrases, your listeners will become confused or tired from trying to understand you.

- **Phrasal intonation** is the regular pattern of pitch change in thought groups. In American English, the syllables that come before the phrasal stress are pronounced with a **mid-level** pitch, and the syllable with phrasal stress is pronounced with a **high-level** pitch. Any syllables after the phrasal stress that are part of the thought group are pronounced with a **mid-level** pitch. If the syllable with the phrasal stress ends the thought group, it is pronounced with a pitch that falls from high to mid-level.

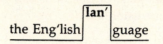

- **Sentence-final intonation** is the lowering of pitch on the syllables following the phrasal stress in the **last thought group** in a sentence. In most sentences the pitch at the end of the last thought group falls from mid-level to **low-level** to indicate that the sentence is complete.

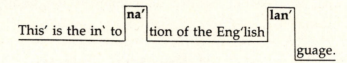

Sentence-final intonation adds meaning to what you are saying. In a later unit, you will practice the various forms of sentence-final intonation with questions.

Thought Groups

Thought groups are formed by dividing speech into meaningful units of approximately two to five words. Although thought groups can consist of only one word or of more than five words, nonnative speakers of English are most easily understood if they try to speak in thought groups that are usually from three to five words long. You can learn to divide speech into thought groups by thinking about grammatical structure. Thought groups may consist of many different combinations, such as the following:

Structure:	Example:
Article + adjective + noun	the large molecule
Subordinating conjunction + noun + verb	because the experiment failed
Preposition + article + noun	in the graph
Verb + object	use a dictionary
Relative pronoun + noun + verb	which she dissolved
Verb + adverb	rotated quickly
Article + noun + verb	the student agreed
Verb + direct object + preposition + indirect object	hand it to him

EXERCISE 6: Recognizing and reading aloud in thought groups

Divide the following passage into thought groups by using slash marks (/). Practice saying the paragraph several times. As you speak, pause briefly after pronouncing each thought group.

> For Americans, distance in social conversation is about an arm's length to four feet. Less space in the American culture may be associated with greater intimacy or aggressive behavior. The common practice of saying ''Excuse me'' or ''Pardon me'' for the slightest accidental touching of another person reveals an American attitude about personal space. Thus when a person's ''space'' is intruded upon by someone, he or she may feel threatened and react defensively. In cultures where close physical contact is acceptable and desirable, Americans may be perceived as cold and distant.
>
> Deena R. Levine and Mara B. Adelman, *Beyond Language*, p. 47

Phrasal Stress

Speakers of American English usually put phrasal stress on the last stressed syllable of each thought group. This syllable is stressed more than other stressed syllables within the thought group. The syllable with the phrasal stress is most often part of a noun, a verb, or a phrase-final adjective or adverb. It is usually not part of a pronoun, auxiliary verb, or conjunction. When speakers want to emphasize a particular meaning, they may shift the phrasal stress to another word in the phrase.

EXERCISE 7: Phrasal stress and vowel lengthening

Mark the phrasal stress for each thought group below with an accent mark ('). Then practice saying the thought groups by taking a rubber band and stretching it for each syllable of the thought group. For the syllables at the beginning and in the middle of each thought group, stretch the rubber band only a little. For the syllable with phrasal stress in each thought group, stretch the rubber band a lot. This will give you an idea of the difference in length between the shorter less-stressed syllables and the one long-stressed syllable in each thought group.

How can I get / my students / to understand me? / If I slow down* / by dividing my words / into thought groups* / and if I apply / a regular pattern / of stress and intonation, / I can speak / with expression / and accuracy. / Most speakers / of American English / speak like this. / Their stress is regular, / and their intonation / is controlled. / If you learn / to speak like this, / your students will hear / what's important / and ignore what isn't.

*Be careful where you place the phrasal stress in phrases with compound nouns and two-word verbs.

EXERCISE 8: Applying phrasal stress

Now apply phrasal stress to the paragraph you worked on in Exercise 6. Mark the phrasal stress with accent marks (as in the example below) before you practice saying the paragraph several times.

For Amer'icans, / distance in social conversa'tion / is about an arm's' length / to four feet'.

Phrasal Intonation and Sentence-Final Intonation

Phrasal stress is always accompanied by a rise and fall in pitch. The pitch rises on the syllable receiving phrasal stress and falls on the final syllable(s) of the thought group (as in phrases 1 and 2 below). At the end of the sentence, the pitch falls to an even lower level to indicate the end of the sentence (as in phrase 3 below).

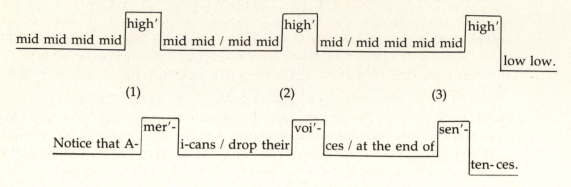

If there are no more syllables in the thought group after the phrasal stress, the pitch rises and falls on the same syllable (as in phrase 3 below).

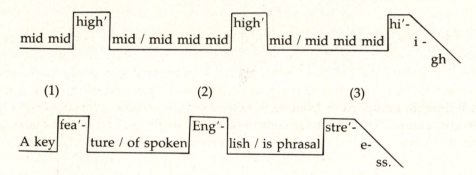

EXERCISE 9: Applying phrasal intonation and sentence-final intonation

Now apply phrasal intonation and sentence-final intonation to the paragraph in Exercise 6. Draw in the contours, as in the example below, before you practice reading the paragraph aloud several times.

For A⌐mer'⌐icans, / distance in social conver⌐sa'⌐tion / is about an⌐arm's'⌐length / to four⌐feet'.

EXERCISE 10: Practicing phrasal intonation and sentence-final intonation

Gilbert (1978) suggests using a kazoo (a special humming instrument) to practice thought groups. Use a kazoo to practice the thought groups in Exercise 6, making sure your pitch corresponds with the rules for phrasal intonation and sentence-final intonation. If you do not have a kazoo, hum the phrases. This will give you an idea of how the pitch changes within each thought group. After mastering the intonation patterns of the thought groups with the kazoo or by humming, speak the phrases with the same intonation you used to hum them.

Applying the Rules of Phrasal Stress and Intonation to Speech

By following the steps below you can begin to develop a more nativelike pattern of stress and intonation. If you practice this method daily by reading aloud or reciting, you will develop more control of your pronunciation with this new way of speaking.

- Slow down and focus on **how** you are speaking as well as on **what** you are saying.
- Divide your utterances into thought groups of about four or five words each. If you have trouble with this, start with two to three, or three to four, words per thought group and later increase the length to four or five words per thought group.
- Apply phrasal stress and intonation to each thought group.
- Be sure to use sentence-final intonation at the end of each sentence.
- At first, make your thought groups approximately the same length and apply the same amount of phrasal stress and intonation to the last stressed syllable of each thought group. Later, experiment with thought groups of different lengths and apply more (or less) phrasal stress to emphasize important words or phrases.

EXERCISE 11: Marking a field-specific passage for phrasal stress and intonation

Find the reading passage from your field in the appendix. Work on the **first** of the two paragraphs by dividing it into thought groups of about four or five words, as you did with Exercise 6. Mark the last stressed syllable of each thought group with an accent mark, as in Exercise 8. Draw a contour line for the phrasal intonation or sentence-final intonation for each thought group, as in Exercise 9. Read the passage aloud, pausing briefly between thought groups. Try for precise control of each thought group. Read the passage aloud at least ten times.

EXERCISE 12: Reading an unmarked passage in thought groups with phrasal stress and intonation

Work with the **second** of the two paragraphs from your field. This time do not mark the passage as you practice it. Read each phrase silently to yourself, remembering what you have read, then look up and say the phrase without looking down. Continue phrase by phrase until you have read the whole passage. As you do this, remember to apply the concepts of thought groups, phrasal stress, and phrasal intonation. After you have practiced the passage phrase by phrase, read the complete passage aloud at least ten times.

EXERCISE 13: Developing a native speaker-like pattern of stress and intonation

Practice reading aloud each of the two field-specific passages, or other paragraphs from your textbooks or other sources, with your instructor in order to develop a more nativelike pattern of stress and intonation. Clap or tap your finger as you pronounce the last stressed syllable of each thought group while (a) repeating after your instructor line by line, (b) reading aloud together with your instructor, and (c) reading aloud alone.

Tape record yourself in order to compare your speech to that of your instructor and to listen for the correct application of the rules in this section.

Grammar:
Relative Clauses in Definitions

Definitions are sometimes difficult to recognize. Can you tell which word is being defined in the examples below?

    a. A pediatrician treats children.

    b. We can see objects invisible to the naked eye through a microscope.

    c. People can stop to rest along the highway at a wayside rest.

It is not immediately obvious which words were defined in the previous examples. A way to make definitions obvious and clear is to use a relative clause.

EXERCISE 14: Making definitions clear by using relative clauses

Look at the first example below. Then define the other words by following the same pattern. Use the information above.

An X	is	a (noun)	+	(relative clause)
1. A pediatrician	is	a doctor		who treats children.
2. A microscope				
3. A wayside rest				

EXERCISE 15: Defining field-specific terms using relative clauses

Practice with definitions from your own field by choosing ten terms from the vocabulary lists in the appendix. Follow the pattern above and write a definition for each.

Needs Assessment:
The "International TA Problem" in U. S. Universities

The number of international TAs in U. S. classrooms has caused problems between U. S. undergraduate students and ITAs. Numerous articles have been written about the "international TA problem." You may have read some of these articles or you may have already heard something about this issue. In this section, you will have the opportunity to research this complex issue further.

EXERCISE 16: Researching articles on the international TA problem

Form groups of three or four students. Each student will be responsible for researching one article or for interviewing one person on the international TA problem. Use the list of resources below and answer the following questions. Later you will discuss your findings with other members of your group.

Resources:

1. Refer to the list in the appendix of articles on the international TA problem.

2. Ask your teacher for copies or references of articles from your own university newspaper that deal with this problem.

3. Interview your professors or international student advisors for information about ITAs at your university.

Questions:

1. Why are there so many ITAs in the United States at the present time? What implications does this have for undergraduate teaching at most major universities?

2. What exactly is the international TA problem, and what factors contribute to it?

3. Articles on the international TA problem often mention that U. S. students sometimes feel a sense of superiority over people from other countries. Have you observed anything that supports this claim? If so, what can you do about this perceived sense of superiority on the part of people in the United States?

4. Different groups of people in the United States may have different views on ITAs. Students and their parents may have one point of view; professors and university administrators may have another; state legislators and taxpayers may have a third. What differences do you think these groups may have regarding international TAs?

5. What possible solutions to the problem have been proposed? Do you think these solutions would be effective? Why?

UNIT 5
Teaching a Process

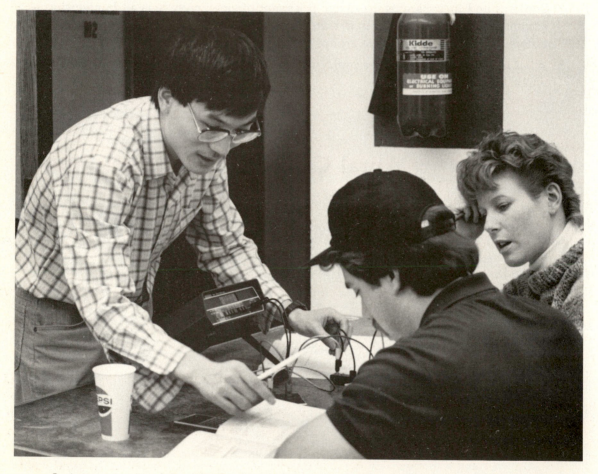

In interactive teaching, the teacher helps students discover ideas and information for themselves.

As a TA you will often have to teach such processes as the steps for an experiment, the stages of some natural phenomenon, or the instructions for solving a problem. In this unit, you will practice teaching a process. In addition, you will begin teaching in a more **interactive** way by asking questions throughout the lesson and responding to your students' answers.

In interactive teaching the teacher helps the students discover and internalize ideas and information in an active rather than a passive way. This means that the teacher does not **spoonfeed** information (give the information to students in the way that parents do when using a spoon to feed their children). Instead, the teacher encourages the students to think and to come up with the answers themselves.

One kind of interaction is asking and answering questions. There are several advantages to making classes more interactive through the question-and-answer process. Can you think of some of them? When asking and answering questions, it is important for you and the students to understand each others' language. It is also important to know how to encourage your students, whether their answers are correct or incorrect.

Another kind of interaction is to have your students do something with the information they are to learn. You may want them to work in small groups or pairs on a particular task. You may give them an in-class reading, an exercise, or questions for an all-group discussion. You might bring in models or equipment for them to work with individually or in groups. An essential aspect of teaching interactively is ensuring that students have direct access to the material to be learned. Another essential aspect of teaching interactively is providing feedback to students on their success or failure in learning.

Focus 1:
Aural Comprehension

The two important aspects to aural (listening) comprehension in English are understanding what you hear and getting the information you need when you do not understand what you hear.

The ability to understand native speakers speaking at a natural rate is partially dependent on your general knowledge of English and your exposure to spoken English. Your general listening proficiency will increase steadily, but it will take some time. You can compensate for weaknesses in your listening comprehension by using listening strategies to focus on the most important things to understand, such as the main idea or the direct answer to your specific question.

This section focuses on **getting the information you need when you do not understand what you hear the first time**. You need to ask questions of and get answers from the speaker until both of you are satisfied that you understand one another. It is a skill you can develop quickly in settings such as teaching, where you have a chance to interact with the person to whom you are listening.

The first key to getting the information you need when you do not understand what you hear is to follow an American English pattern of conversation called the **three-second rule**. Research (McLaughlin 1984) has shown that people in the United States are uncomfortable with silences longer than three seconds, unless the conversationalists are involved in some sort of nonverbal activity. For example, after one person asks a question, if the other does not respond within three seconds, the original speaker will usually begin talking again. To respond to the question does not necessarily mean to answer the question. You may want to use a hesitation device such as "Umm" or "Let me think." Or you may want to repeat or rephrase the question to verify exactly what the question was.

Learning to follow the three-second rule may take some practice, because longer silences are normal and acceptable for conversations in many other languages. If you wait more than three seconds to respond to a question, however, your U. S. students are likely to think that you either did not hear what was asked or that you do not know or want to answer.

Possible Responses to Questions

If you **understand** the question:

1. Answer the question if you know the answer.

2. If you do not know the answer, say so.

3. Gain time to think by using **thinking noises** or **hesitation devices**:
   "Uhh" or "Umm."
   "Let's see" or "Let me think."
   "That's a good (or difficult) question."

4. Rephrase the question to check your comprehension and give you more time to think.

If you **do not understand** the question:

1. If you are not sure why you did not understand, ask the student to repeat the question. If you still do not understand, another repetition probably will not help. Ask the student to say the question in a different way:
   "I'm sorry, I didn't catch your question."
   "Could you ask that another way?"

2. If possible, focus on the part of the question that you did not understand or on the reason you did not understand the question.
   a. If you did not understand **a particular word**, ask:
      "What does _____ mean?"
      (repeat the word)
   b. If you did not understand **the last part of their question**, ask:
      "_____ **what**?"
      (repeat the words you understood)
   c. If you did not understand one of the grammatical parts of the sentence, ask questions like these:
      "You want to go **where**?"
      "You want me to explain **what**?"
      "**Who** will be late?"
   d. If you did not understand **because the person spoke too quickly (or too softly)**, ask the person: "Would you please repeat that more slowly (loudly)?"

3. Use strategies to guess what was said and then check whether your guess is correct.
   a. Listen to the **intonation** to decide what kind of answer is appropriate:
      Rising intonation—usually needs a yes or no answer.
      Falling intonation—usually needs an informational answer to a Wh- question.
      Rising and then falling intonation—usually needs a choice of one of two options given.
   b. Remember the **first and last words** of the question. They may indicate what kind of help the student wants:
      Repetition: "Could you . . . again?"
      A fact: "When . . . happen?"
      An opinion: "Do you think . . . ?"
   c. Consider the **context**. It will probably give you the topic of the question as in these examples:

- If you just handed back a graded test, the question is probably about the grade or about the answer to one of the questions.
- If the topic you just covered is confusing, you may be able to assume **that** is the source of the student's confusion.

d. Listen for expressions that signal a **change of topic** so you know the question is **not** about the immediate context. Some examples are:

"By the way,..."

"Getting back to..."

"About [the quiz]..."

EXERCISE 1:   Using the three-second rule

Practice the three-second rule with the questions below, using responses from the examples above. Work in pairs. One person should read one of the following questions and then snap his or her fingers (or clap softly) three times, at one-second intervals. The second person should listen to (not read) the question and make some kind of response before the third snap (or clap). Take turns so that each person answers half of the questions. There are no incorrect answers for this exercise, because the answers themselves are not important.

Questions with Obvious Answers

1. What was your previous address?
2. What time did you wake up today?
3. How many months until your birthday?
4. How many credits are you taking now?
5. What's your favorite city in the world?

6. What's your campus address?
7. What did you eat for breakfast?
8. How many hours did you sleep last night?
9. How long have you been in the U. S.?
10. What's one of your favorite foods?

Questions Needing Time to Be Answered

1. What's the tallest mountain in the world?
2. What do you think is the most important problem in the world?
3. Do you know any common euphemisms for *death*?
4. In what year were you five years old?
5. How much tip would you leave for a $13.45 meal?

6. What country is the Tigris River in?
7. What do you think is the best solution for the population explosion?
8. What's the difference between *slang* and *idioms*?
9. How old was your mother when you were born?
10. What's the best way to go from this building to where you live?

Focus 2: Interaction

Educators in the United States generally value learning through active thinking more than learning through passive absorption of information. This implies that a teacher's role is not simply to present information, but to **interact** with the students to help them reflect on, interpret, analyze, and synthesize information. It is the teacher's responsibility to facilitate interaction by clearly communicating his or her expectations about student participation, inviting interaction and questions, and helping students feel comfortable speaking in class by giving them friendly, nonjudgmental responses and feedback.

Encouraging student interaction is one of the main techniques for promoting active learning within the context of lectures, recitations, or discussion groups. This section will focus on three aspects of using questions to stimulate active thinking: clarity of questions, level of thinking required by questions, and timing in waiting for answers.

Clarity of Questions

Questions used to encourage student interaction should be specific and clear. They should not be too difficult for students to answer.

Imagine that you are teaching a class on "Effective Study Skills" and you want to make it more interactive by asking questions. Which of the following two questions would be easier for students to answer and why? Which is clearer and why?

1. What study habits are best?
2. A certain student usually reviews for tests by rereading the textbook, but he often gets poor grades. Suppose he has an essay test in his psychology class next week. What could he do to improve his study habits for the test? Why?

EXERCISE 2: Making broad questions more specific

The following questions are too broad. Rewrite each to make it more specific.

1. What do you think about the United States?
2. What type of person are you?
3. Are people in your country happy?
4. How much do people earn in your country?
5. How do people learn languages?

Encouraging Higher-Level Thinking

Effective questions are those that will elicit the type of thinking we want. Questions that merely require students to respond with memorized information, such as facts or figures, require **lower-level** thinking. Questions that require students to form opinions, analyze choices, or draw conclusions usually require a **higher-level** of thinking. Which do you think are most useful for encouraging student interaction and why?

Look at the following questions about the Chinese and Russian revolutions. Which question would require students to use higher-level thinking skills? Which one would require lower-level thinking skills? How do you know?

1. In what year did the Chinese communist revolution begin?
2. Experts say that the types of communism that evolved in Russia and in China as a result of their revolutions are vastly different. Using your knowledge of both systems of communism, tell whether you agree or disagree with this viewpoint and why you think so.

Of course there are times when you may want to use both types of questions, or to sequence them from lower-level to higher-level.

EXERCISE 3: Identifying the level of thinking required by questions

With a partner, look at the following questions from a class on "Effective Study Skills" and decide whether each one would require lower-level (L) thinking or higher-level (H) thinking. Mark each accordingly. Be prepared to tell why you chose each answer.

____ 1. Yesterday we talked about how the usefulness of a particular study method depends on the learner's background. Which method (A or B) would be better for you to use in this class and why?

____ 2. In what year was Method A first introduced into the public schools?

____ 3. Based on your knowledge of these two methods, why do you think most students prefer Method A?

____ 4. According to recent statistics, do most high school students prefer Method A or Method B?

____ 5. If you use Method A, what can we conclude about your style of learning?

____ 6. According to your text, which study methods are most effective and why?

____ 7. Can you think of any advantages of using Study Method A instead of Method B?

____ 8. According to your text, Method A worked best for students who get high grades. Do you think it would also work best for students who generally get poor grades?

EXERCISE 4: Creating and analyzing questions for interaction

Suppose you want to help your students think through the basic steps they should take in writing a research paper. You have prepared the outline below and want to teach the material interactively.

Steps for Writing a Research Paper

1. Do background investigation and formulate a research question.
2. Gather information from various sources (library, interviews, experimentation).
3. Integrate and organize the information.
4. Plan the paper.
5. Write the paper.
6. Get feedback and revise the paper.

For each step, write one question that will help students think actively about that step. Analyze each question by considering the following points. Rewrite your questions if necessary.

• Which of the questions require lower-level thinking and which require higher-level thinking?
• Which question(s) would be most difficult for students?
• Which would be easiest?
• Are any questions unclear?
• Are any questions too broad?
• Is your grammar correct?

Timing in Waiting for Answers

Some hints about waiting for an answer:

1. In general, pause longer than you would in a conversation—more than the typical three seconds. The longer you wait, the more pressure there is on students to respond. Do not wait too long, however, or students will become embarrassed.

2. If you wait a few seconds and no one answers, repeat the question, then ask if they have understood it.

3. If you still do not get a response, reword the question. It is also a good idea to add a phrase such as, "Can anyone tell me...?"

Students take longer before responding if they are uncertain who you want to answer and how they are to answer. You want all students to think about the answer, but do you want only one person to answer or everyone to say it aloud? The following suggestions may help:

1. If your eyes are focused on the students rather than on the board, it is obvious that you are asking a question. To keep everyone thinking, move your eyes around the room without focusing on any one student.

2. If you want only one person to answer, focus your eyes on that person's face or call him or her by name. Here are some examples of what you could say:
   "(Joe), what do you think?"
   "Any ideas?"
   "Would you like to try it?"
   "How about you?"

3. If you want everyone to answer, you can say, "How many say (x)? Raise your hands." "How many say (no)?" This works best with yes/no and either/or questions.

4. If students are reluctant, you can encourage them with phrases such as:
   "Relax! Give it a try."
   "It's okay if your answer is wrong."
   "Don't be afraid to give a wrong answer. Nothing will happen."

EXERCISE 5:   Practicing asking and timing your questions

- For fluency, intonation, and correct phrasing, practice asking your questions in Exercise 4 out loud.

- To practice pausing, imagine that the student did not understand the question and repeat or reword it after waiting long enough to allow the students to think.

- After repeating or rewording the question, add one of the phrases introduced above to encourage students to respond.

Functional Language:
Responding to Student Answers

Making a class interactive by asking questions involves not only knowing how to ask **questions** effectively but also how to deal with **answers**. Students need encouragement whether their answers are correct or incorrect so that they want to volunteer answers again.

They need to be told when and why their answers are not correct, but in a way that does not embarrass them in front of their peers. What are some ways you can encourage students to keep on trying after they have given an incorrect answer?

Look at the following two examples of interaction between students and their TA. Which do you like better? Which would you like better as a student?

TA: Can anyone tell me what theorem we should use to solve this problem?
STUDENT: I think the Chain Rule would work here.
TA: Wrong. The Chain Rule will not work here. You have to use U-substitution.
STUDENT: (Silence.)

TA: Can anyone tell me what theorem we should use to solve this problem?
STUDENT: I think the Chain Rule would work here.
TA: Think about the Chain Rule carefully. Do we have the necessary conditions for using the Chain Rule here?
STUDENT: Oh, I see. Not really. How about U-substitution?
TA: What do the rest of you think? Should we use U-substitution here?
STUDENT: Yes.
TA: You're right. But can anyone tell me why we should use it?

Language for Student-Teacher Interaction

Listed below are some common phrases used to deal with student responses. Study them carefully.

Responses to incorrect answers:
  "Good guess, but that's not it."
  "Do the rest of you agree? Is that right?"
  "What do the rest of you think?"

Responses to partially correct answers:
  "Not quite."
  "Nice try, but not exactly."
  "So far so good."

Responses to correct answers:
  "Good job!"
  "You've got it!"
  "Right!"
  "Uh-huh."
  (Nod your head up and down.)

Paraphrasing student responses
  "His suggestion is..."
  "Did everyone hear what she said?"
  "She thinks that..."

Giving hints:
  "If we..., what will happen?"
  "Why did you... and not...?"
  "Wait a minute. If you do that, what will happen?"

Follow-up (checking to be sure everyone has understood the correct response):
  "Does everyone see how we got this?"
  "Do we need to go over this again?"
  "Any more problems?"
  "Anything else?"
  "Is it clear now?"
  "If it's still not clear, feel free to see me after class or during my office hours."

EXERCISE 6: Correcting student answers

Choose a field-specific visual from the appendix that is closely related to your field. Imagine that you will teach a concept represented by the visual to students from a different field.

1. To elicit interaction from your students, plan a question that will help them become interested in, interpret, or understand the visual.

2. Think of a possible incorrect answer to your question.

3. Think of a way to respond to the incorrect answer.

4. Think of any hints you could give students to encourage them to keep on trying.

Example:

Question:	"What is the *x* intercept of this function?"
Possible wrong answer:	"The cubed root of 2."
Possible TA response:	"Do the rest of you agree?"
Hint:	"Think about the value for the *y* intercept."

EXERCISE 7:   Affirming student answers

Using the same visual and question you chose for Exercise 6, think of:

1. a possible correct answer to the question;

2. what response you could give to let students know they are right; and

3. what phrase you could use to check to be sure the rest of the class understands the correct response.

Example:

Question:	"What is the *x* intercept of this function?"
Possible correct answer:	"Oh. It's the **square** root of 2."
Possible TA response:	"Right!"
Follow-up:	"Does everybody see how we got this?"

EXERCISE 8:   Practice responding to student answers

Prepare several interactive questions you could use to introduce a partner to a concept represented by your chosen visual. For each question, go through the following steps to prepare for some possible answers to your questions. When you are prepared, meet with a partner, introduce your concept using interactive questions, and respond appropriately to each correct or incorrect answer.

Steps:

1. Prepare your questions for interaction.

2. For each question, think of a possible wrong answer.

3. Write a possible response to the wrong answer.

4. Think of a hint to help the student come up with the correct answer.

5. Think of a possible correct student answer.

6. Write a possible response for the correct answer.

7. Write what you would say to make sure everyone has understood the correct answer and to encourage additional questions.

Example:

Question:	"What is the *x* intercept of this function?"
Possible wrong answer:	"The cubed root of 2."
Possible TA response:	"Do the rest of you agree?"

Hint:	"Think about the value for the y intercept."
Possible correct answer:	"Oh. It's the **square** root of 2."
Possible TA response:	"Right!"
Follow-up:	"Does everybody see how we got this?"

Assignment Preparation:
Teaching a Process

In pairs, practice teaching a process interactively by taking turns presenting the process outlined below. Assume that your students can read the outline on a handout or overhead transparency.

Steps in Analyzing Cultural Patterns

1. Choose a U. S. cultural pattern you have observed.
2. Decide on possible reasons for the pattern.
3. Write the possible reasons in the form of questions to test the accuracy of each one.
4. Choose a sample group of people from the U. S. to interview. Try to ensure that the sample is large enough and broad enough to give accurate results.
5. Conduct the interviews and record the findings.
6. Analyze the data for patterns.
7. Draw conclusions based on the findings.

As you present this information, use questions to encourage the students to interact with you and with each other. You may want to prepare questions that elicit the following:

- examples of the step.
- factors that could influence the step.
- problems that may occur in carrying out the step.
- any questions students have about the step.

Assignment Presentation:
Teaching a Process

Your assignment is to teach a process from your field using an interactive method. Plan to ask questions and work with the answers you receive to teach the process. Use the full ten minutes of your presentation for interacting with the other members of the class.

1. Choose a process from your field, such as the steps for an experiment, the stages of some natural phenomenon, or the instructions for solving a problem.

2. What kind of information can you make available to your students to help them contribute to teaching the process? Plan to bring in lab equipment, models, posters, overhead transparencies, handouts, in-class readings, or exercises. Think about how students can do something with the information as you talk with them.

3. Think about how much detail to include in teaching your process. How much can you expect your students to master in ten minutes? How can you limit the information they are to absorb so that they can have a successful learning experience?

4. Think about the steps in the process you will teach. What organizational cues will you use to ensure that students understand the order of the steps? What steps are crucial and deserve special attention? How can you help the students master the steps of the process?

5. What questions will you ask your students to get them involved in the topic you are teaching? What incorrect and correct answers could you expect, and how could you respond to each possibility? Follow this pattern:

Question: _____

Incorrect answer: _____

Possible response and hint: _____

Correct answer: _____

Possible response: _____

6. How will you know if the students have learned the process? Will you know by their answers to your questions? Should you ask one volunteer or all of the students to perform or demonstrate the process?

Pronunciation: Reduction, Linking, and Rhythm

Spoken language can be very different from written language. A major difference between spoken and written English is in the way that the processes of reduction and linking make spoken English smooth and easy to pronounce.

- **Reduction** is the modification or omission of individual sounds in the unstressed syllables of certain common function words to make the words easier to pronounce. Examples of reduction are contractions such as *I'll*, *she's*, and *we're*.

- **Linking** means the blending of sounds across the syllable boundaries of a thought group for ease of pronunciation. Word-final sounds are blended with the initial sounds of following words, as in: *Hand' it to me.* = *Han' di to me.*

- **Rhythm** refers to the regular pattern of phrasal stress and intonation. The techniques of reduction and linking make it easier to speak English with a natural rhythm.

To discuss reduction and linking, it is necessary to use phonetic symbols that represent the individual sounds within words. The symbols used in this textbook and their equivalent pronunciation are as follows:

Vowel	Example	Consonant	Example
iy	keep	p	plane
ɪ	did	b	bell
ey	take	t	table
ɛ	get	d	date
æ	have	k	card
ə	done	g	group

Vowel	Example	Consonant	Example
a	dr<u>o</u>p	f	<u>f</u>act
uw	d<u>o</u>	v	<u>v</u>alue
ʊ	p<u>u</u>t	s	<u>s</u>ign
ow	g<u>o</u>	z	<u>z</u>oo
ɔ	f<u>a</u>ll	š	<u>sh</u>ip
ay	p<u>ie</u>	ž	mea<u>s</u>ure
aw	f<u>ou</u>nd	č	<u>ch</u>ain
oy	b<u>oy</u>	ǰ	<u>j</u>udge
		θ	<u>th</u>ing
		ð	<u>th</u>is
		m	<u>m</u>ap
		n	<u>n</u>ose
		ŋ	wro<u>ng</u>
		r	<u>r</u>ate
		l	<u>l</u>eaf
		y	<u>y</u>ear
		w	<u>w</u>ire

Reduction

Native speakers of English do not pronounce every sound of every word exactly the way it is written. A number of predictable sounds are modified or omitted in speech. Native-speaking listeners know which sounds have been reduced or omitted and understand what they hear as if the sounds were still there. Because nonnative speakers of English often try to pronounce every sound, their speech may sound less smooth than that of native speakers.

Interactive teachers inspire their students to think independently.

The following predictable sounds in English are usually reduced or omitted:

1. **Unstressed vowels:** Vowels in syllables that are not stressed are often reduced to an [ə] or an [ɪ] sound. This vowel is produced in the middle of the mouth by relaxing the jaw in an open position. When vowels in unstressed syllables are reduced to this vowel sound, the mouth is able to rest. Native-speaking listeners tend to ignore the reduced vowels and listen only for the unreduced vowels in the stressed syllables of the sentence.

   C<u>o</u>m mun <u>i</u> ca t<u>io</u>n <u>is</u> <u>im</u> por t<u>a</u>nt. = [kə myu'nə key'šən ɪs ɪm powr' tənt]

2. **[t] between vowels:** When the sound [t] occurs between a stressed and an unstressed vowel or between a vowel and the sound [l], it is reduced to a sound that is symbolized with a [D] and pronounced something like a fast [d]. This happens even when the first vowel and the [t] are in one word and the second vowel is in another word.

$$he\underline{at}er = [hiy' Dər]$$
$$he\underline{at} \underline{it} = [hiy' Dɪt]$$
$$li\underline{ttl}e = [lɪD' əl]$$

3. **Consonant clusters:** When groups of three or more consonants are difficult to pronounce, native speakers of English often reduce consonant clusters by dropping out the middle consonant. This can also occur between words.

$$a\underline{sks} = [æsks] = [æss]$$
$$si\underline{xths} = [sɪkθs] = [sɪks]$$
$$la\underline{st} \underline{Th}ursday = [læs ðərz'dey]$$

EXERCISE 9: Practicing reducing vowels and consonants

Practice reducing the underlined vowels and consonants when you say the phrases below.

a wa<u>t</u>er bo<u>tt</u>le	a<u>sks</u> a quest<u>io</u>n	continu<u>ou</u>s partici<u>p</u>at<u>io</u>n
simpli<u>f</u>ying fact<u>o</u>r	tensi<u>l</u>e strength	mete<u>o</u>rology
gener<u>a</u>t<u>o</u>r	four ten<u>ths</u>	standa<u>r</u>d proced<u>u</u>re

4. **Function words:** Approximately one-fourth of the words in spoken English are function words. Function words can be articles, pronouns, prepositions, auxiliary verbs, modals, or conjunctions. Function words usually undergo reduction when they are not stressed in the thought group. Each of the function words below has a particular reduced form that is recognized by native speakers. Reducing the function word in any other way will cause confusion. The vowels in function words are almost always reduced to [ə] or [ɪ], but the reduction of the consonants is not quite as predictable.

articles:	a	Take <u>a</u> seat.	= [teykəsiyt']
	an	Get <u>an</u> A.	= [gɛDəney']
pronouns:	you	Did <u>you</u> do it?	= [dɪdyəduw'ɪt]
	he	Will <u>he</u> do it?	= [wɪliyduw'ɪt]
	him	Tell <u>him</u>.	= [tɛl'ɪm]
	her	Ask <u>her</u>.	= [æsk'ər]
	them	Talk to <u>them</u>.	= [tɔk'tuwəm]

prepositions:	to	I need to know.	= [ayniydtənow']
		It's two to three.	= [Itstuw'Dəθriy']
	of	Outside of class.	= [awtsaydəklæs']
	for	Work for a grade.	= [wərkfərəgreyd']
	as	Do as homework.	= [duw'əzhowm'wərk]
possessives:	his	Take his paper.	= [teyk'Ispey'pər]
	her	Grade her problem.	= [greyd'ərpra'bləm]
	your	What's your name?	= [wətsyərneym']
conjunctions:	and	Add and subtract.	= [æd'ənsəbtrækt']
	or	One or two.	= [wən'ərtuw']
modals:	can	Who can do it?	= [huwkınduw'It]
	will	I'll try it.	= [ayəltray'It]
	would	She'd like it.	= [šiydlayk'It]
	want to	Want to learn it?	= [wanələrn'It]
	has to	He has to go.	= [hiyhæstəgow']
	have to	We have to study.	= [wiyhæftəstəd'iy]
	have got to	You've got to ask.	= [yuwvgadəæsk']
auxiliaries:	is	He's busy.	= [hiyzbIz'iy]
	are	They're absent.	= [ðeyəræb'sənt]
	has	She's finished.	= [šiyzfınıšt']
	have	We've taken the test.	= [wiyvtey'kənðətɛst']
	had	If you'd passed.	= [Ifyuwdpæst']
	do	Do you see it?	= [dyəsiy'It]
	going to	I'm going to do it.	= [aymgənəduw'It]
	could have	I could have done it.	= [aykʊdədən'It]
	should have	We should have gone.	= [wiyšʊdəgɔn']
	would have	He would have asked.	= [hiywʊ'dəæskt']
verb endings:	-ing	He's teaching math.	= [hiyztiyč'ınmæθ']

EXERCISE 10: Comprehending reduced function words

The function words that would normally be reduced have been underlined in the following sentences. Listen while your instructor pronounces each sentence, and use the list above to identify the reduced form of each function word. Although it is important to learn to recognize these reduced function words, it is not necessary to be able to pronounce them accurately. You may, however, want to try to see how closely you can imitate native speakers of American English.

1. You can work together on your lab reports.

2. I want to ask you to hand them in on time.

3. You have to solve this problem with a computer.

4. We're going to work on this unit for a week and a half.

5. He has got to cancel his office hour because he has to go to an appointment.

6. Why are you sitting back there? You can sit closer if you want to.

7. Wasn't she coming to the review session? I should have reminded her about it.

8. Do you want to try these problems? I will help you with them.

9. Are you ready to hand in your papers or can you use another day to work on them?

10. The professor told me you could have used your calculators during the test.

11. They <u>should have</u> turned in their papers <u>as</u> soon <u>as</u> they <u>could have</u>.

12. I <u>would have</u> given <u>you</u> more time <u>to</u> do the homework if <u>you</u> <u>had</u> asked <u>for</u> it.

Linking

Native speakers of English often make their speech smoother by linking the last sound of a word with the first sound of the next word within the thought group, thus pronouncing the two words as one word. Many combinations of word-initial and word-final sounds are possible. When linking, continue the final sound of the first word until you begin to pronounce the initial sound of the second word.

Vowel plus vowel

| ey + ow | say over | | ow + ə | grow up |
| iy + ɛ | see anything | | ay + ə | buy up |

Consonant plus vowel

r	answer it		č	teach a lesson
l	spell it		ǰ	judge a case
n	learn anything		p	stop everything
m	claim everything		b	cube it
f	graph it		t	make it even
v	give out		d	read about
s	pass it		k	talk over
š	push out		g	log it in

Identical consonants

p	keep practicing		t	get twenty
d	had difficulty		k	take care
s	miss something			

EXERCISE 11: Practicing linking

Pronounce the following phrases using the linking patterns listed above.

Vowel plus vowel	Consonant plus vowel	Identical consonants
data analysis	x axis	parallel lines
amino acid	human intelligence	mass society
go over	scientific evidence	oblique cone
stay after class	physical ability	business cycle
do a problem	radiant energy	organic compound

Rhythm

By using reduction and linking within thought groups, native speakers of English can follow the regular beat of phrasal stress in their speech. This means that different thought groups are spoken in approximately the same amount of time, even if the number of words in the groups varies greatly.

EXERCISE 12: Practicing thought groups with a regular rhythm

Prator and Robinett (1985) suggest practicing the rhythm of American English by clapping your hands or tapping your finger as you pronounce the syllable with primary stress for each thought group in a sentence. By keeping a regular rhythm and applying the principles of reduction and linking, you will be able to add words to individual thought groups without increasing the length of time needed to pronounce the sentence. Work with your instructor to pronounce the following groups of sentences according to the same rhythmic beats.

(Clap)	(Clap)	(Clap)
Teachers	like	students.
The teachers	like	students.
The teachers	like	their students.
The teachers	should like	their students.
The teachers	should have liked	their students.
The teachers	should have liked	some of their students.
The TAs	passed	the course.
The TAs	could pass	the course.
The TAs	could pass	this course.
Some TAs	could pass	this course.
Some TAs	could have passed	this course.
Some of the TAs	could have passed	this course.

EXERCISE 13: Practicing reductions and linking

This transcript of a native English-speaking TA's lab presentation has been divided into thought groups. Practice reductions and linking by reading the passage aloud at the same time and with the same rhythm as your instructor. Make a tape recording of your reading of the passage to compare your rhythm with that of your instructor.

Hooke's Law (F = kx)

Today's lab / is the forces / in Hooke's Law lab. / Hooke's Law / is something everyone / should be familiar with. / Let me write it on the board. / Hooke's Law simply states / that the force on a spring / equals some constant / times the displacement. / Here x is the displacement / from its original equilibrium position. / Okay? / This is familiar. / We've all used Hooke's Law before. / And it makes sense. / If you stretch a spring / twice as much, / you expect the spring / to pull back twice as hard. / It's a natural type / of expectation.

Now let's see, / the places where this is used in real life, / for example, / would be the shock absorbers in your car./ When you go over a pothole, / your shock absorbers / will push the tires down / so that your car / doesn't shake too much./ Okay? / So that's one place / where we'd use springs, / and one place where the engineers / would have to deal with Hooke's Law / to develop a good shock absorber.

Now the main point of this lab / is twofold. / Hooke's Law is a simple concept / that you all know about, / so we're not going to learn / anything really about Hooke's Law. / But there's two main points to the lab. / First, / graphing / and interpreting a graph, / which is so important / in whatever field you go into. / Learning how to deal with graphs / is very valuable. / And the second one / is to point out that physics is empirical. / What that means is / it's the experiments that drive the physics. / For example, / the way this Hooke's Law came about / was not that Hooke sat around and said, / "Hm, / let me write down this equation / and then all the springs / will obey it." /That's not the way it works, / where you take a spring / and put masses on it / and then put forces on it / and measure them / and then sit back and say, "Hm, / what's the pattern here?"

Grammar: Indicative and Imperative Verbs

The type of language a teacher uses when giving instructions is important in helping a student find his or her own answer to a problem. The form of the verb can make a big difference in the teacher's message. When giving instructions, teachers may choose one of two types of verbs:

Indicative: First, *you put* this component into that slot.
               First, *we put* this component into that slot.
               First, *one puts* this component into that slot.
               First, *the experimenter puts* this component into that slot.
Imperative: First, *put* this component into that slot.

The difference between these two types of verbs is in the attitude of the speaker toward the listener. **Indicative** verbs are statements; **imperative** verbs are commands.

Each of the verb forms above conveys a different feeling. The pronouns *you* or *we* with the indicative form make your language friendlier. Using the third person (*one* or a name—e.g., the experimenter) adds distance and formality. Use of the imperative can imply some sort of power relationship between you and your students like that of expert and novice.

When giving instructions, many teachers in the United States avoid using the indicative form with *one* or the imperative form. If you want to sound less authoritarian, use the indicative with the pronouns *you* or *we*.

EXERCISE 14:   Giving instructions in a friendly manner

Here are some directions for fixing a flat tire on a car. Practice giving these instructions to a partner, using the indicative with the pronouns *you* or *we*, and try to sound friendly and concerned. (Be careful with two-word verbs and negatives, and remember that you do not have to use *you* more than once in each sentence.) After you have finished, ask your partner to evaluate you. Then switch roles and repeat the exercise.

Fixing a Flat Tire on a Car

First, (engage) _____ the parking brake and (block) _____ the wheels with a piece of wood. Second, (check) _____ the air pressure in the spare tire and (add) _____ air if necessary. Then, (use) _____ a tire iron to loosen the lug nuts. Next, (jack up) _____ the car. After that, (take off) _____ the lug nuts and and (remove) _____ the wheel. Then (put on) _____ the new wheel and (replace) _____ the lug nuts, but (not tighten) _____ them. Finally, (lower) _____ the car to the ground and (tighten) _____ the lug nuts with the tire iron. Then (unblock) _____ the wheels and (drive _____ away) the car.

EXERCISE 15:   Giving instructions for completing a task

Imagine that you need to give your students instructions for completing one of the following tasks. Practice giving oral instructions to a partner in a friendly manner.

How to plot a graph.

How to use a particular instrument for measurement.

How to calculate the results of an experiment.

How to do a particular homework assignment.

Needs Assessment:
Student Roles, Issues, Learning Styles

In the first unit, you looked at what characteristics make good teachers. In this unit, you will look at the other side of the equation: the students' roles and responsibilities and the students' expectations of their teachers. The information will help you teach your students more effectively.

EXERCISE 16: Characterizing U. S. undergraduate students

The following questionnaire contains a series of statements about U. S. undergraduate students. Follow these steps in filling out the questionnaire:

1. Read each statement and check the blank beside it to indicate whether you agree or disagree with it. You may agree (or disagree) with more than one statement in each category, so check all that apply.

2. Ask a native English-speaking TA from your department to indicate his or her opinion about each statement by marking the agree or disagree column.

3. Bring your results to class and compare them with those of TAs from other countries and other departments. What conclusions can you make about strategies you may want to use as a ITA in your field in the United States?

Characteristics of the Average U. S. Undergraduate Student

	Your opinion		Native English-speaker opinion	
	Agree	Disagree	Agree	Disagree
Goal orientation				
goal-oriented; know what they want to study and what type of job they want after graduation	___	___	___	___
none; in college to have fun.	___	___	___	___
Consider cheating to be...				
acceptable; will often copy other students' homework or exams.	___	___	___	___
acceptable only in extreme cases, such as when under extreme pressure.	___	___	___	___
dishonest and unacceptable.	___	___	___	___
Motivation				
low: in school for social reasons, parental pressure, or inability to find a job after high school.	___	___	___	___

	Your opinion		Native English-speaker opinion	
	Agree	Disagree	Agree	Disagree
high to do well in elective courses, but may not be equally interested in required courses.	____	____	____	____
high in all levels and classes.	____	____	____	____

Preparation for college

better prepared than students from most other countries, especially in the sciences.	____	____	____	____
varies widely for any given academic area.	____	____	____	____
more poorly prepared than students from most other countries.	____	____	____	____

Classroom behavior

informal: joking, talking, drinking or eating.	____	____	____	____
reading the newspaper or listening to the radio with headphones on during class.	____	____	____	____
formal; show respect for the teacher when in the classroom.	____	____	____	____

Priorities

social life equally as important as academic life.	____	____	____	____
part-time jobs more important than schoolwork.	____	____	____	____
studies more important than any other aspect of their life, including family, friends, job, etc.	____	____	____	____

Attitudes toward other nationalities

consider people from other countries to be superior to those from the U. S., and due a high degree of respect.	____	____	____	____
consider people from other countries to be equal to those from the U. S., and therefore treat them as they would any other human being.	____	____	____	____

Expectations of teachers

expect their teachers to be friendly toward them.	____	____	____	____
expect their teachers to show authority and demand respect.	____	____	____	____
want their teachers to entertain them and make the class fun and interesting.	____	____	____	____

Access to education

feel that education is a luxury given only to a few and therefore value their education highly.	____	____	____	____
feel that education is a right that should be available to everyone.	____	____	____	____
feel that education should be reserved only for those who can afford it.	____	____	____	____

Learning Styles

Kolb (1981) has hypothesized that there are four distinct types of learners whom he calls the **practitioner**, the **facilitator** (or **motivator**), the **applied scientist**, and the **theoretical** (or **basic**) **scientist**.

The Practitioner

This type of learner gets excited by new experiences, enjoys taking risks, and adapts well to change. This person tends to focus on learning by doing and by integrating application with experience.

The Facilitator or Motivator

This type of learner gets excited by working with people and enjoys generating and sharing ideas with others. This person also tends to become very involved in learning.

The Applied Scientist

This learner gets excited by working with things rather than with people and wants concrete answers to questions. This person enjoys hands-on experiences and wants quick answers.

The Theoretical or Basic Scientist

This learner gets excited by working with ideas, such as the theoretical aspects of problems, creating conceptual models, and combining diverse ideas. He or she tends to be analytical and to enjoy inductive approaches.

EXERCISE 17: Comparing your learning style with that of undergraduate students

1. Look over the above descriptions given for the four principal types of learners and decide which category best describes you. Write it here: _____.

2. Interview a native English-speaking TA from your department to find out what learning style or styles best describe the undergraduate students you will be teaching. Show the TA the list above and ask for the following information:

   a. What percentage of students in undergraduate courses in this department are majors? What percentage are non-majors?
   b. Which learning style listed above do you think best describes majors in the undergraduate courses?
   c. Which of the learning styles listed above best describes non-majors in undergraduate courses in this department?
   d. Do you take different learning styles into consideration when planning lessons for your undergraduate courses? If so, what specifically do you do?

EXERCISE 18: Planning your course to accommodate different learning styles

Kolb's 1981 study analyzed students from various academic disciplines in terms of their learning styles. He found that students in the social sciences tended to be Practitioners, those in the humanities were mainly Facilitators, those in the physical sciences were mostly Applied Scientists, and those in the natural sciences were principally Theoretical (Basic) Scientists. This implies that if you teach courses required for non-majors, those students not majoring in your field may have learning styles different from your own. Their learning styles will probably be more similar to the learning style of their particular major.

The following exercise will help you think about activities most appropriate for the various learning styles.

1. Look at the list of classroom activities listed below and check the ones you think would be most appropriate for students from each of the four major learning-style categories.

2. Think about the most common learning styles among undergraduate students in **your** field, and circle the activities you think would help them learn best.

	Practitioners	Facilitators	Applied Scientists	Basic Scientists
1. Lectures	_____	_____	_____	_____
2. Personal journal keeping	_____	_____	_____	_____
3. Practical problem solving	_____	_____	_____	_____
4. Independent study	_____	_____	_____	_____
5. Group activities	_____	_____	_____	_____
6. Abstract problem solving	_____	_____	_____	_____
7. Lab experiments	_____	_____	_____	_____
8. Interviewing	_____	_____	_____	_____
9. Self-discovery activities	_____	_____	_____	_____
10. Demonstrations	_____	_____	_____	_____

UNIT 6
Fielding Questions

Encouraging questions establishes an atmosphere of
active thinking in the classroom.

Your assignment in this unit will be to prepare for an exercise in **fielding questions** in which you will spontaneously respond to questions posed by your classmates. (The term *fielding* is borrowed from the game of baseball, in which players in the field catch and return the ball.) You will be asked to field several questions from your classmates and instructor, and you will prepare several questions to ask each of your classmates. These questions will be about your field of study or about some aspect of classroom management, such as tests, homework, or lab assignments.

Teachers in the United States welcome questions. They feel that, in general, students who ask questions in the class are alert and interested, and students who do not ask questions may be bored, intimidated, or unable to understand the content of the class. In most cases, students who ask questions in class do not intend to challenge the teacher but genuinely want to know the answer to the question.

One of the most challenging tasks you will face as a TA is answering spontaneous questions. This is a complex process because it involves:

a. letting the student know that you have heard the question,
b. making sure that you and the other students understand what is being asked,
c. answering the question appropriately, and
d. checking to make sure the student is satisfied with your response.

In addition to giving you practice in these four basic areas, this unit will help you become aware of important cultural differences between the ways teachers field questions in your culture and how they field questions in the United States.

To begin thinking about fielding questions in the U. S. classroom, consider possible solutions to this real-life situation an international TA encountered.

It was the end of a math recitation, and the international TA had just announced that she wanted her students to hand in their homework on the due date. (Many of them had been handing in their homework late.) At that point, a U. S. student asked if he could hand in the homework that was due for class that day during her office hour, which was at a later time on the same day. At first she laughed. When he repeated his question, she paused for a long time. At that point, the bell rang, so everyone started picking up their belongings and standing up to leave, which created a lot of noise in the room. The student who had not yet received an answer to his question asked the question again in a different way: "Do you want 'em now or can we hang onto 'em?" She answered, "Right," an inappropriate response for a question using *or*. He asked one more time, and she finally gave him an answer, but there was so much noise that hardly anyone heard her.

The student later reported that he thought the ITA had misunderstood his question because of her inappropriate responses. During an interview after the class, however, the ITA said that she had in fact understood his question but was unprepared to answer it because she had not expected it. Both the student and the ITA said that all the noise and movement made the situation even worse.

EXERCISE 1: Responding to student questions

Work alone or in groups to brainstorm possible solutions to the following problems faced by the ITA in the story. Try to think of common expressions that the ITA could have used to try to solve the problem.

1. You cannot understand the student's question.

2. You think you understand the student's question but are not completely sure.

3. You understand the student's question, but you have not thought about the issue or you do not know the policy of your professor or department.

4. You cannot hear the student's question because of noise or movement in the classroom.

5. The student's question is not relevant.

Focus 1:
Method of Handling Questions

A teacher's **method** of handling questions is as important as the **content** of the answers to the students asking the questions. An effective method of answering a question usually includes a verification of what the question is, a quick response (even if it is a request for clarification rather than an answer), a clear answer, and a check to be sure that the students understand and are satisfied with the answer. Experienced teachers in the United States will often follow certain steps in answering student questions in a large group. Although there are many methods for answering questions effectively, international TAs can compensate for imperfect language skills by following these steps very closely.

1. Make some kind of **verbal or nonverbal response** to the question **within three seconds** to acknowledge the question.

2. **Repeat or rephrase** the question in order to
   a. verify that you have understood the question correctly.
   b. make sure all of the students have heard the question.
   c. change the question, if necessary, into one that is more appropriate for the class.
   d. give yourself more time to think about the answer.

3. **Answer**
   a. clearly so that the students will understand.
   b. concisely in order not to waste time.

4. **Check** with the student who originally asked the question to see if you answered in a satisfactory way.

Previously you learned about the three-second rule for responding to questions. In this section you will learn to restate questions and to check to see if you have answered them satisfactorily. Later you will learn about concise answers to student questions.

Restating Questions

Restating questions means repeating the question, if it is short, or rephrasing it, if it is longer. It is important for nonnative speakers of English to restate questions to ensure correct comprehension and to allow thinking time before answering. Restating questions benefits the whole class: students who did not hear the original question do not miss any information, and the teacher is able to change irrelevant or confusing questions into questions that will be of use to the entire class.

One of the difficulties of restating questions is getting the grammar right. Look at the following examples. What differences do you notice between the original question and the restatement?

Yes/No Question:	Can we hand in our assignments tomorrow?
Possible Restatement:	You would like to know if (whether) you can hand in your assignments tomorrow.
Wh- Question:	How long do we have to do the assignment?
Possible Restatement:	You would like to know how long you have to do the assignment.

You have probably noticed that you must make **three** changes in the grammar:

1. The addition of *if* or *whether* for Yes/No questions
2. A change in the subject from *we* to *you*

    Can *we* hand in...?   ... if *you* can hand in...

3. A change in the word order of the question from **question word order** (verb-subject) to **statement word order** (subject-verb) for most questions

    Can *we* hand in...?   ... *you can* hand in...
    V S   S V

EXERCISE 2:   Restating simple questions

Imagine you are teaching a lab and you are asked the following questions. Restate each question to ensure everyone hears it. Use the phrases in parentheses. Pay attention to word order, use of pronouns, and use of *if* or *whether*.

1. "What is the lab assignment for this week?" (Her question is, ...)
   Answer: "Her question is what the lab assignment is for this week."

2. "When do we have to turn in the assignment?" (He wants to know...)

3. "Is there going to be a make-up lab?" (She's asking...)

4. "Can we hand in the assignment next week instead?" (Repeat the question but watch the pronouns.)

5. "Could you go over the last reason again?" (What you're asking is...)

6. "Why aren't we going to have a quiz this week?" (You want to know...)

7. "Do you want us to hand in our reports now or later?" (If I'm not mistaken, you'd like to know...)

8. "Are we going to have a review session before the test?" (He wants to know...)

EXERCISE 3:   Restating questions in context

Most questions asked by students relate to a particular context because they are based on material that you have covered in class. The following questions relate to the equation below. Imagine that you have just explained the solution to this equation and its application to your field. Your students ask you the following questions, which you restate. For this exercise, use any phrase for restating the question that you think would be appropriate.

$$a = 3 + \left\{ [2(b - \frac{C^2 \sqrt{k}}{4M}] + 2.5) \right\} 10^{-6}$$

1. "In this problem, is it absolutely necessary to carry out the calculations to five decimal places?"

2. "I was wondering if you could tell us again what M stands for."

3. "Can we apply this equation to any system or does it only hold true for closed systems?"

4. "Are there other ways of solving this equation?"

5. "What would happen if we substituted R for C^2? Would we obtain the same results or not?"

6. "I didn't follow what you said about the relationship between the square root of *k* and *M*. Could you explain it again?"

7. "Do you mind if we do the assignment with a friend?"

8. "How do we know that this equation accounts for the observed phenomenon? Couldn't other factors besides these be responsible for the results?"

EXERCISE 4:   Rephrasing questions in nonstandard form

After many years of studying English, most ITAs recognize the standard Wh-, Yes/No, and choice questions using *or*. Unfortunately, the questions that students ask are often not in one of these standard forms, and they are sometimes difficult to recognize as questions. The following questions illustrate the types of confusing questions that you may be asked. Rephrase each question in a clear way, as you would if you were trying to answer the question in the classroom. Look at this example:

> QUESTION: How come we have to use the Riemann sum to figure out an integral if we already have formulas for it?

> PARAPHRASE: Why is it necessary to use the Riemann sum to calculate an integral if we already have formulas for it?

1. "It says here in the book that after closing the accounts for a certain accounting period, we have to adjust them somehow. I don't understand. Did we cover that? What does it mean?"

2. "In your example where there are two people on a raft and one jumps off, and the weight pushes the raft in the opposite direction, I'm not sure if I understand how to calculate the effect of the jump on the raft. Could you do that one again for me?"

3. "But I thought that you said that it didn't matter if we left the minus sign in here because we're not worried about the direction of the vectors in this lab. How come you're worried about it now?"

4. "I didn't quite get how the core of the nuclear reactor is lowered into position and what role the water plays in terms of the actual nuclear reaction. Could you go into that a little bit more?"

5. "So, if we know the equilibrium price, we can determine the equilibrium quantity."

6. "Antibodies neutralize antigens, don't they? At least that's what I thought you said the other day."

7. "You lost me when you were talking about why there's so much political instability in Latin American countries. First, it sounded like the main reason was economic, but then you talked about the historical part about—uh—the Spaniards and all. What's the point?"

8. "How come the twin brother, Tom, didn't grow old, but his sister, Mary, did? I mean, I know you can't go over the whole Theory of Relativity, but what does it boil down to?"

9. "I thought you said last week that we have to use the Chain Rule to solve this kind of problem, and now you're telling us we have to use this other rule. I'm totally confused. What I'm trying to get at is, when do we use this new rule and when do we use the other one?"

10. "I didn't catch what you said about why work and power are different. You said something about holding a book in your hand not being work because there's no movement so there's no distance involved, which means it can't be work, right?"

Checking to See if You Have Answered the Question

Have you ever asked a teacher a question, listened to the answer, and then realized that the teacher has not answered your question? This is an uncomfortable situation for students. Teachers can help by checking with students to make sure they are satisfied with the teacher's answer. Here are some useful expressions to use when checking to see if you have answered your students' questions.

"Did I answer your question?"   "Is that clear?"

"Do you understand now?"   "Is that what you wanted to know?"

"Is that what you were asking for?"   "OK?"

"Does that help?"

EXERCISE 5: Monitoring student comprehension

1. Think about students you have observed in classes. When someone asks them if they have understood, what responses will they make if they have understood? These can be verbal or nonverbal responses. List at least four.

2. What responses do students make if they do not understand? Again try to think of four verbal or nonverbal responses.

3. List four reasons why students might not be willing to tell you that you did not answer their question or that they did not understand your answer.

Focus 2:
Clarity of Response to Questions

U. S. students usually want answers to be focused, direct, and brief yet substantial. They do not require that teachers prove their expertise or impress their students with their extensive knowledge. U. S. students do not want to hear everything that might possibly relate to their questions; they expect their teachers to respond concisely with one or two details or examples, then check whether the students are satisfied with the answer, and to move on to the next question.

After you have made sure that you understand the question, the best way to respond is by following these steps:

1. Give a one-sentence answer to the question.

2. Supply an example or several facts related to the question. Be careful to stay on the topic of the question and avoid other questions that were not asked.

3. Check with the student to be sure you have answered the question. Unless the student requests more information, go on to the next question.

4. If the student indicates a lack of understanding, repeat the information in a slightly different way.

5. If, after a second attempt, the student still does not understand, invite him or her to speak to you after class or during your office hours.

The following example illustrates these five steps.

STUDENT: "Can you go over the Doppler effect again? I'm not sure I got it the other day."

TA: "The Doppler effect is the change in the frequency with which waves from a given source reach an observer. The frequency varies with the speed at which the source and observer move away from or toward each other with a corresponding change in pitch. Is that clear?"

STUDENT: "I still don't get it."

TA: "Let me put it this way. You're probably familiar with the common example of the increase in pitch you experience as you hear a train approaching. This is the Doppler effect. Does that help?"

STUDENT: "That helps, but I still don't completely understand."

TA: "Why don't you see me after class and I can go into it in more detail, OK?"

STUDENT: "OK."

These useful expressions will help you make your answers as concise as possible.

"In general,..."

"That's a complicated issue, but in simple terms..."

"The simple answer is..., but let me explain in a little more detail."

"I don't want to go into..., so let's just say that the answer is..."

"For our purposes, we can assume..."

"What you need to know about this for this class is..."

EXERCISE 6: Giving concise answers

Work in pairs and take turns answering the following questions concisely. For the sake of practice, limit your answers to two sentences.

1. What makes a good graduate student?
2. Do you think a TA should try to make his or her class interesting? Why?
3. What makes a good teacher?
4. What do **you** think is the most rewarding aspect of being a teacher?
5. In your opinion, should students expect their TAs to solve problems for them?
6. Do you want students to ask questions while you are teaching the class? Why?
7. Which is more important—your work as a TA or as a graduate student?
8. Should TAs plan their class for the best or worst students? Why?

Functional Language: Purposes of Restating Questions

There are many reasons for restating questions. How you choose to restate, rephrase, or repeat a question depends on your reasons for doing it.

PURPOSE: TO VERIFY THAT YOU HAVE UNDERSTOOD THE QUESTION

Do this if you have any doubt about what the question is. Get into the habit of doing this as a check on your ability to understand what your students are saying.

Examples:

If you think you understand the question:
"Your question is..."
"What you're asking is..."
If you are unsure of what the question was:
"Do you mean . . ?"
"If I understand you correctly..."
"I think what you're asking is..."
If you did not understand the question at all:
"Would you repeat your question, please? I didn't understand you."
"I'm sorry, what did you say?"
"Excuse me, I didn't understand you. Would you repeat that please?"

PURPOSE: TO MAKE SURE THAT ALL THE STUDENTS HAVE HEARD THE QUESTION

Often classrooms are large and noisy or students have not been paying attention. Restate questions in this way to alert students to the importance of the answer and to avoid having to answer the same question more than once.

Examples:

"Did everyone hear that? Her question was..."
"That's a good question. He wants to know..."
"I want to make sure everyone heard you. Would you repeat your question?"

PURPOSE: TO CHANGE THE QUESTION INTO ONE THAT IS MORE APPROPRIATE FOR THE CLASS

Students may not know how best to ask the question or they may be asking a question that is not relevant to your particular class. In the United States, teachers feel that no question is stupid or useless because students who ask questions are generally interested in doing well in the class. Restating the question in a clearer or more relevant way will help everyone in the class. The following example illustrates how a teacher can change a broad question into a more relevant one:

STUDENT: "What's the difference between the midterm and the final?"
TA: "Do you mean relative weight, types of questions, content,...?"

Examples:

"Let me ask that question another way."
"I think what you want to know is... Am I right?"
"In this class we don't have to worry about that, but what we do want to know is..."

PURPOSE: TO GIVE YOURSELF TIME TO THINK ABOUT THE ANSWER

Sometimes you may not know the answer to a question right away. Restate the question in order to give yourself time to think without making students feel that you did not hear their questions. If you then decide you do not know the answer, the best procedure is to tell the students that you do not know and will try to find out before the next session.

Examples:

"Yes. I see what you are asking. You want to know... Let me think..."
"Your question is... That's a very interesting question. I need to think for a bit before I answer."

"So you want to know . . . I don't know the answer to that question, but I'll try to find out for you by the next class."

"Let me check on it and get back to you next time."

EXERCISE 7: Restating questions with a purpose

Restate each of the following questions for the purpose listed after it.

1. "When do we have to turn in our term project?" Restate to be sure everyone has heard the question.

2. "When Professor Collins talks about *fear of failure*, I think she means something different than what you mean." Restate to give yourself time to think.

3. "I know what an *arithmetic progression* is, but what's a *geometric progression*?" Restate to verify you have understood the question.

4. "I am not sure about what I want to ask, but I don't really know what you are talking about when you tell us to integrate a function. I'm really lost." Restate to find out **exactly** what the question is.

5. "Can we call you at home? I can't come to your office hour, and no one ever seems to answer your office phone." Restate to give yourself time to decide whether or not this request is appropriate for you.

6. "I just wanted to ask what a [mumble mumble] is." Ask for repetition to find out what the question is.

7. "When you talked about class one objects, I started wondering about class two and class three objects. How are they the same or different? Are we going to cover them this quarter?" Restate to clarify what the student will need to know for this class.

8. "What's the answer for number six on the quiz from yesterday?" Restate in order to be sure the class knows the student is asking about yesterday's quiz.

Assignment Preparation: Fielding Questions

In this unit you will be fielding questions from your classmates about your field of study. You will be focusing on the four steps for fielding questions that were covered in this and the previous units:

1. The three-second rule: answering within three seconds
2. Restatement: restating or paraphrasing the question
3. Clarity: answering directly, succinctly, and completely.
4. Comprehension check: checking to see if the student is satisfied with your response

Practice these steps by choosing a partner and finding the list of questions in the appendix that is most closely related to your partner's field of study. Play the role of a student and ask your partner the first question from the list. Your partner will answer the question, focusing on the four steps listed above. Then give feedback on how effectively your partner fielded the question. Alternate back and forth until you cover as many questions as time permits. The following diagram may help you understand the procedure more easily:

Student asks question one from the teacher's field.
Teacher answers question one.
Student gives the teacher feedback on his or her answer.
Then switch roles.

Assignment Presentation:
Fielding Questions

You will prepare questions to ask your classmates, and you will be asked to field several questions from your classmates and instructor. These questions will be about your field of study.

1. Write down the name of each ITA in your class or group and the field in which he or she will teach.

2. Prepare two questions to ask each ITA about his or her field. Try to imagine what a U. S. undergraduate student might want to know and make your language sound like his or hers. Practice saying each of the questions several times for fluency. If possible, ask your teacher to give you feedback on your grammar and intonation.

   You will field questions from the group for ten minutes. You may be asked up to two questions by each of the members of the group who are playing the role of students. For each question you field, follow these steps:

   1. Make some kind of response within 3 seconds.
   2. Restate the question.
   3. Answer clearly and concisely.
   4. Check to see if you have answered the question.

   Try to focus more on the method of handling questions than on the actual content of your answer. During your ten minutes, answer as many questions as you can in an efficient, courteous, and interactive manner. Your classmates will be evaluating you on whether you have followed the four steps for each question.

Pronunciation:
Intonation for Questions

In a previous unit you practiced the sentence-final intonation pattern that is used for the majority of English sentences. Most exceptions to this pattern occur in the intonation patterns for questions. It is important that you be able to recognize these patterns when people ask you questions, because different intonation patterns signal the need for different kinds of answers. For the same reason, it is important to use correct intonation in the questions that you ask because your listener will become confused if your intonation indicates the need for one kind of answer and your words a different answer.

Wh- Questions

Questions that begin with *Who, What, When, Where, Why,* and *How* are commonly called **Wh- questions**. The intonation pattern of these questions is the same as sentence-final intonation: the pitch rises on the the last stressed syllable of the final thought group and then falls below the pitch level of the rest of the sentence. This intonation pattern is called **falling intonation**.

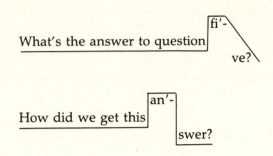

Yes/No Questions

Questions that begin with auxiliary verbs (such as *can't* and *will*) require a yes or no answer and are called **yes/no questions**. The intonation of these questions differs from that of Wh- questions in that when the pitch rises on the last stressed syllable of the final thought group, it does not fall but continues to rise until the end of the sentence. This intonation pattern is called **rising intonation**.

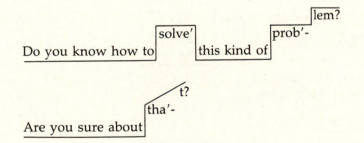

The information carried by rising intonation is so important that any statement can be changed into a yes/no-question without changing the order of the words, simply by using rising intonation instead of falling intonation.

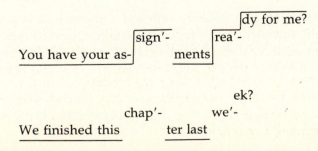

Echo Questions

Rising intonation can also be used to repeat someone else's Wh question, conveying without words the question *Did you ask...?* These questions are often called **echo-questions**.

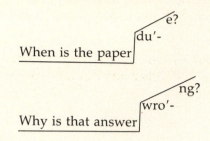

Choice Questions

A **choice question** (sometimes called an alternative question) lists two or more possible answers, uses the word *or* between the last two possible answers, and expects the listener to choose one of the possibilities to answer the question. Choice questions have a rising intonation pattern for each possible answer before the word *or*, and then falling intonation for the last possibility.

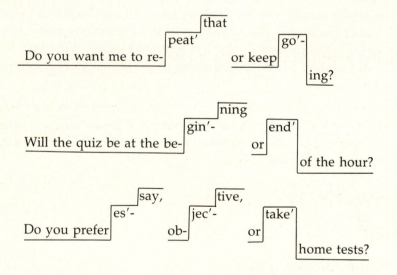

Tag Questions

A **tag question** is a phrase containing an auxiliary verb and a pronoun. It is placed at the end of a statement to make the statement into a type of question. Question tags use rising intonation to request confirmation or denial of a statement that the speaker thinks is true. Questions that have the word *right* at the end follow this pattern, because *right?* is short for *am I right?*

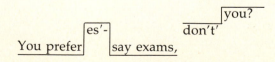

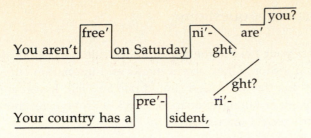

You aren't free' on Saturday ni'-ght, are' you?

Your country has a pre'-sident, ri'-ght?

Sometimes a tag question is not a real question—is not really seeking information. This type of tag is called a **comment tag.** Comment tags use falling intonation to ask the listener to agree with the speaker about the truth of the statement.

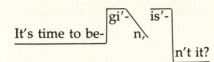

It's time to be-gi'-n, is'-n't it?

(Meaning: "I think it's time to begin.")

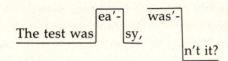

The test was ea'-sy, was'-n't it?

(Meaning: "I assume that you think the test was easy.")

EXERCISE 8: Practicing with intonation for questions

Decide what kind of question intonation is appropriate for each question below. Draw phrasal stress marks and intonation curves, as in the example below, to indicate where you think the intonation should rise and fall. If you are uncertain, check with your teacher. Then practice reading each question aloud with the correct intonation.

EXAMPLE: Can I erase' the black'board?

1. Do you think this is easy or difficult?

2. What did you say? (I can't hear you.)

3. Monday is a holiday, right?

4. Would you say the result is higher or lower than before?

5. Would you please see me after class?

6. The professor already covered this in the lecture?

7. How can we distinguish these two cases?

8. You're probably discouraged about the results of the test, aren't you? (I assume you are.)

EXERCISE 9: Practicing field-specific questions

Find the field-specific questions for your field in the appendix. Decide what kind of question intonation is appropriate for each question. Draw accent marks and intonation curves, as in Exercise 8 to indicate where you think the intonation should rise and fall. If you are uncertain about whether to use rising or falling intonation, check with your teacher. Then practice reading each question with correct intonation.

EXERCISE 10: Telling the truth

Form groups of three. One person will say a true or untrue sentence about himself or herself, making the statement as interesting as possible, such as "I have acted in several films." The other two people must decide whether the statement is true or false by asking the speaker questions for three minutes. The questions can be Wh- questions, yes/no questions, echo questions, choice questions, or tag questions, such as "What role did you play?" or "Did you play the main character?"

Each question used should be spoken with the correct intonation pattern. At the end of three minutes, each questioner should state whether he or she thinks the statement is true or false, and the person who makes the original statement should tell whether it was true or not. The game can be made more challenging by limiting the type of questions to be used.

EXERCISE 11: Preparing for the assignment

When you write questions to ask your classmates in this unit's assignment, decide what kind of intonation should be used and mark the question with the appropriate line so that you can remember to use correct intonation when you ask the question in class. If possible, ask your instructor or another native speaker to check the grammar and intonation of each question before you use it in class.

Grammar:
Responding to Negative Questions

Negative Questions

U. S. students often use negative questions and sometimes make negative statements in order to ask questions, ask for clarification, or ask for permission. Test your comprehension of negative questions in English by choosing the correct paraphrase for a *yes* or *no* answer to each question below. The way in which you answer these questions or respond to these statements in your language may be the exact opposite of what is done in English, especially if you speak Korean, Chinese, Japanese, or some other Asian language.

Question 1: "Aren't we going to review before the test?" (The student probably wants a review session before the test.)

A *no* answer in this situation means:
   a. We are NOT going to review before the test.
   b. We ARE going to review before the test.

A *yes* answer in this situation means:
  a. We are NOT going to review before the test.
  b. We ARE going to review before the test.

The correct answer for the *no* response is **a**, and the correct answer for the *yes* response is **b**.

Question 2: "So, the theorem won't work for this problem?" (The student isn't sure if the theorem will work and wants to check with the TA.)

A *no* answer in this situation means:
  a. This theorem WILL work for this problem. You CAN use it.
  b. This theorem will NOT work for this problem. You have to find another theorem.

A *yes* answer in this situation means:
  a. This theorem WILL work for this problem. You CAN use it.
  b. You're right; it will NOT work.

The correct answer is **b** in both cases.

Giving only a *yes* or *no* answer in such situations can be confusing, even for a native speaker. To be absolutely clear, it is better to give a more detailed explanation, especially if the questioner has misunderstood previous information, as in the following example:

TA statement: "We have to get through one more unit before the test on Monday."

Question: "Aren't we going to review before the test?"

Clear response: "Yes, we ARE going to review before the test. As I mentioned a few days ago, there will be a review session on Friday."

Negative Tag Questions

Tag questions can also be negative questions. If the negative is in the main clause, ignore the tag and treat the main clause as a negative statement, answering it as you did the negative statements above.

Question: "That's not right, is it?" (The student senses that there's something strange about the answer on the blackboard.)

To agree: "No. I made a mistake."

To disagree: "It **is** the correct answer. It just looks strange because it's not reduced."

If the negative is in the tag, translate the main clause into a yes/no question and answer the question directly.

Question: "This is right, isn't it?" (Translation: "Is this right?" The student thinks the answer is right, but is unsure.)

To agree: "Yes, it is (right)."
To disagree: "No, it isn't (right)."

Statements with the Intent of Questions

Often students will make statements (either positive or negative) as a way of confirming what they think is true. These do not appear to be questions because they do not have rising intonation or do not have question form. Nevertheless, you need to answer them exactly as you would answer a negative question. The following example illustrates this point:

TA:	"There are nine labs this quarter, but in figuring your grade, I will include only the eight highest scores."
Student confirmation:	"So, we don't have to do the last lab." (The student infers that the last lab is optional.)
To agree:	"Right. If you've gotten good grades on the first eight, you do not even have to come for the last one. It's simply a make-up lab."
To disagree:	"Not necessarily. It's a good idea to do the last lab because it's fairly easy and you'll probably get a good grade. That way you can throw out one of the other lab scores."

One strategy for dealing with these statements is to to avoid a confusing *yes* or *no* response. Instead, say "Right" if the original statement is true and "Wrong" (or some less direct form such as "Not necessarily" or "Not really") if the statement is false.

EXERCISE 12: Negative questions: written practice

As previously mentioned, students use negative questions for many reasons. This exercise will demonstrate some of the meanings of negative questions and will give you practice answering these questions. With a partner, answer each question with a written *no* response and *yes* response. Include a more detailed explanation to make each answer clear, as in the examples above. The first one has been done for you. When you finish, discuss your answers with the class.

1. TA: "The percentage for each grade is as follows."

    QUESTION: "Isn't the professor going to grade on the curve?" (The student thinks she would get a better grade on the curve.)

    NO: "No. The professor doesn't believe in using a curve. The grades are straight percentages."

    YES: "Yes, he **is** going to grade on the curve. The percentages I'm giving you are just approximate grades for now."

2. TA: "I'll discuss the test next week."

    QUESTION: "Don't you have them corrected yet?" (The student is anxious about her test grade.)

3. TA: "So, the answer is positive l."

    QUESTION: "Isn't the answer supposed to be a negative l instead of a positive l?" (The student has worked out the answer herself and has a different answer.)

4. TA: "So, the process is pretty complicated. Be careful."

    QUESTION: "Isn't there an easier way to solve this?" (The student is frustrated with the complexity of the problem.)

5. TA: "We still have to cover two chapters before the next test."

    QUESTION: "So, we're not going to have enough time for a review session before the test?" (The student is worried about her performance on the next test.)

6. TA: "So, you're all set to do your experiment."

    QUESTION: "Can't we do the experiment in pairs?" (The student feels more secure working with a partner.)

7. TA: "I'd like you to hand in your homework now."

    QUESTION: "Can't you let us keep our homework until we take the test?" (The student wants to use her homework to study for the test.)

8. TA: "So, we're left with 4,358."

    QUESTION: "That isn't the final answer, is it?" (The student is checking to see if the problem is finished or not.)

9. TA: "So, by using U-substitution we've solved the problem."

    QUESTION: "That's the only method that works for this problem, isn't it?" (The student wants to be able to work with the simplest method possible.)

EXERCISE 13: Practicing negative questions

Work in pairs. This time you and your partner will take turns asking each other the following questions. The answers will sometimes be positive and sometimes negative. Answer the questions truthfully. Be sure to give more than just a *yes* or *no* response. Then with your partner decide if your answer was appropriate and clear. If not, discuss how you could make it more clear. (For simplicity, all tag questions should be pronounced with rising intonation.)

1. "So, you're not going to stay in the U. S. permanently."
2. "U. S. undergrads are pretty informal in class, aren't they?"
3. "You'd like to see more of the United States before you go back to your country, wouldn't you?"
4. "Your country doesn't have a president, right?"
5. "Don't you agree that it's difficult for an ITA to make jokes in class?"
6. "So, you're not married."
7. "Most U. S. students don't have a strong background in math, do they?"
8. "Watching TV in the United States is good for improving listening comprehension, isn't it?"
9. "You're not allowed to work fulltime, are you?"
10. "Most citizens from your country have not been to the United States, right?"

Needs Assessment:
The Use of Questions in the Classroom

Knowing about the ways U. S. undergraduates ask questions will help you to field questions easily. In this needs assessment, you will be comparing the ways undergraduates use questions in class in your country with the ways they use questions in the United States.

Pre-interview Questionnaire

    Before looking at questions in the U. S. classroom, take a few minutes to answer the following questionnaire about classes in your country. (If time permits, share your information with your classmates.)

1. In your country, do students ask professors questions during class? After class? Before class?

2. Do students ask other students questions during class?

3. If students do ask questions, what kinds are most common?
   ___ about the information in the lecture
   ___ about the tests
   ___ about material that the student is confused about
   ___ about the textbook
   ___ other (Explain.)

4. If a student does not understand something, how does the student get the information?

5. If a student would like more information about a subject, how does the student get that information?

6. What do professors think of students who ask questions during class?

Interview

Now that you have thought about how students use questions in your country, find out what happens in the United States. To do this, choose one graduate TA from your department to interview. Use the following questions:

1. Who generally asks questions (for example, male students, female students, good students, poor students)?

2. When do students generally ask questions—before, during, or after class?

3. What kinds of questions do students ask? Comment on how direct and how specific they are and whether they relate to the topic being studied or to the mechanics of the class.

4. Why do students ask questions? (Possible reasons may be because they are confused, to waste class time, to show how intelligent they are, because they are interested in the subject, or to make the teacher look "stupid.")

5. If students do not ask questions, why not? In other words, how does the TA interpret a lack of questions during class?

6. If students do not ask questions, how does this TA elicit them?

UNIT 7

Presenting a Topic of General Interest

Engaging the interest of the students is central to the art of teaching.

Your assignment in this unit will be to simplify a topic for an educated audience having little background in your academic field. Choose a topic of general interest related to your field—information that you think would be interesting to almost anyone. After you speak for five minutes, you will answer questions from the audience.

How will talking to an audience that is not familiar with your topic help you become a better TA? When you are in your classroom, many of your undergraduate students will be unfamiliar with the topics in your field. One of your tasks as a TA will be to translate difficult information in the text or lectures into a form comprehensible to your students. Speaking to a general audience will help you practice this.

Your instructor may invite an audience for this presentation, or you may be able to invite colleagues, teachers, or friends. An invited audience will provide the opportunity to practice speaking to people you are not familiar with and who may be able to give you fresh insight into your strengths and weaknesses as a TA in the United States.

Thinking about what kind of information is appropriate for your audience is an important part of being an effective teacher. Preparing a presentation or lecture appropriate for a particular audience involves not only choosing an appropriate topic but choosing an appropriate level of detail and vocabulary.

Think about your own experiences as a student. Have you ever felt insulted when a professor told you information that you already knew? How do you feel when a professor speaks at a level that is above your head? In such cases the professor has misjudged your level of expertise. As a result, you tend to lose interest in the subject and probably miss most of the information.

Focus 1:
Audience Awareness

Audience awareness means being aware of, considering, and responding to your audience's needs, so that your choices of content, vocabulary, and manner of speaking are determined by the needs of your audience. During a presentation, it is important for you to keep eye contact with everyone in the group so that you can monitor their reactions and adjust your presentation to respond to their reactions.

It is important to keep in mind that your audience needs not only to understand your presentation but to be motivated by what you say. The most common method of motivating an audience in the United States is to make the listeners interested. During your presentation, you constantly ask yourself: (a) Does my audience understand what I am saying? and (b) Are they interested in what I am saying?

In **planning your presentation** you should consider the following aspects of audience awareness:

- What does your audience need or want to know?
- What does your audience already know and what do they need to add to that knowledge?
- To what level of detail will your audience be receptive?
- How can the information be presented in an interesting manner?
- Can they learn the information in any way other than your telling it to them?
- How can the information be related to your audience's own experiences?
- How can you make clear what you want the audience to learn?

During your presentation you will want to do the following:

- Move your eyes across your audience to monitor their reactions.
- If you detect a lack of understanding or interest, adjust your presentation to address the problem.
- Look for, and even ask for, questions at points in the presentation where you expect difficulty.
- Before introducing a new concept, check to see whether all the members of the audience have the background to understand the new information. If they do not, quickly review the basic information they will need.
- Avoid talking down to the audience even if they appear not to know something you think they should know.
- Occasionally ask the audience if your speech is slow enough, if your blackboard writing is clear, and if your voice can be easily heard.
- Use appropriate techniques to keep the interest of the audience: humor, interesting or surprising examples, thought-provoking questions, demonstrations, visual aids, and questioning the audience for information rather than giving it to them.

At the end of your presentation you will want to:

- Make a conclusion that highlights whatever you feel is most important for the audience to remember.
- Leave time for questions.
- Use an activity to determine whether the audience understood your most important points.
- Ask questions to make sure your audience has understood your key points.

EXERCISE 1: Giving instructions and checking to be sure your listener understands them

It is especially important that your audience understands you when they have to follow your instructions. One of the easiest ways to make sure your audience understands is to ask frequently if everything is clear. The following expressions are often used for this purpose.

"Any questions so far?"

"Is that clear?"

"Are you with me so far?"

"So far so good?"

"Did you follow that?"

"You look confused. Should I go over that again?"

Work in pairs. Each person will need a pencil and unlined paper. Sit back to back. Each person will use one set of instructions below to tell the other person how to draw an object. The person listening should close his or her book and follow the oral instructions. As you give your instructions, stop and use one of the expressions above after every step or two.

TA 1's instructions for TA 2

1. Draw an ellipse with a width of one inch and a height of one-half inch.
2. About two inches below the first ellipse, draw another ellipse exactly like the first one.
3. Connect one end of one ellipse with the same end of the other ellipse with a straight line.

4. Connect the other end of the first ellipse with the same end of the second ellipse by using a straight line.

5. Tell me the name of the object you have drawn.

TA 2's instructions for TA 1

1. Draw a circle.

2. Mark off five points on the circle that are equally distant from each other.

3. Number the points from one to five.

4. Draw a straight line from point one to point three.

5. Draw another line from point three to point five.

6. Draw another line from point five to point two.

7. Draw another line from point two to point four.

8. Draw another line from point four to point one.

9. Tell me the name of of the object inside the circle.

Now choose one or more of your own objects and give instructions to the other person to draw them.

Focus 2:
Clarity of Presentation

Classroom presentations to U. S. undergraduates are clear if they cover the information without being too long, stay focused on the topic, and contain useful information along with supporting details. Students want their instructors to focus on helping them understand the difficult parts of the course. To be focused and clear to their students, TAs must consider exactly what the students need to know, organize the information carefully, and include only useful and relevant major points and supporting details.

Graduate students who become teachers often have difficulty in giving clear and concise presentations because their experience as students was only to present information to teachers who already knew the information. Your task as a teacher, however, is to present information to students who do not know the information. When you teach undergraduates, you may need to look back to your own experience as a student to remember what kind of help beginners need.

Here are several specific ways to make your presentations clear:

- *Focus:* Keep your topic focused. Do not wander into areas that are only slightly related to your topic.

- *Conciseness:* Keep your presentation compact in length and omit information that does not reinforce important points.

- *Use of pronouns:* Use pronouns only to refer to things or concepts just mentioned.

- *Organization:* Follow your outline or notes; do not jump ahead. Let the students know if you have to go back to a point that you did not cover completely. Make your organization obvious to the students.

- *Completeness:* Include all the most important information about your topic. Be sure to provide some relevant detail or examples to support your major points.

- *Summary:* Include a summary to emphasize the major points, or conclude your presentation with a final point that relates to everything you have said.

EXERCISE 2: Improving the clarity of a presentation

Below are two excerpts of oral presentations about audience awareness given by two different international TAs. Keeping the suggestions in mind, read the excerpts carefully. Then, with a partner decide which excerpt is clearer and give three reasons for your decision.

Awareness of Your Audience 1

There are three ways to show an awareness of your audience in the United States, depending on what you want to communicate to your students and how you want to communicate it. One way is to use a lot of eye contact, which shows your students that you are aware of them. By looking at your students periodically, you can get information such as whether or not they are interested in what you are saying and how well they understand you. For example, if they are smiling and nodding, they probably understand you and enjoy your lecture.

Awareness of Your Audience 2

Showing awareness of your audience depends on what you want to communicate to your students and how you want to communicate it. Using a lot of eye contact shows your students that you are aware of them. Eye contact is very difficult for someone from my country. We prefer to look at our books when the teacher is talking.

Below are two more excerpts from the same presentation. With a partner, again read the excerpts and decide which is clearer. Give three reasons for your decision.

Awareness of Your Audience 3

So I have just told you about audience awareness and I hope that you will all try to be aware of your audiences when you teach, because I didn't learn to do this in my country and now it is hard for me to do it in the United States. So that's what I have to say about audience awareness.

Awareness of Your Audience 4

In conclusion, I would like to repeat that audience awareness is a skill, and like any other skill must be learned. At first, it may seem difficult for ITAs to learn this skill, but they can make progress by paying attention to the three ways of showing audience awareness.

Functional Language: Explaining Technical Terms

One of the roles of a teacher is to help students understand technical information by simplifying it. This role becomes even more important when the audience is completely unfamiliar with the technical details of the field. You can simplify information by:
   a. using vocabulary that your audience will understand,
   b. omitting technical details that are unimportant for this particular audience, and
   c. using broad generalizations that cover only the most important aspects of the term.
   You may feel that you are not telling all the truth or are leaving out important details. Remember, however, that if your students are completely unfamiliar with a term or concept, they will not be able to learn everything that you know about it in one class.
   To simplify technical terms, it is essential that you translate every new piece of information into common language. If a term is essential for your audience to learn, you should stop and explain it carefully before continuing. If the term itself is not important, you

may choose to use common vocabulary instead of the term. Or you can explain the term **parenthetically** (as if the explanation were in parentheses) by using one of the following structures immediately after the term.

- an **appositive**, an equivalent adjective or noun immediately following the word.

  EXAMPLE: "You need a beaker, **a container used for pouring chemicals.**"

- a **relative clause**, which is a phrase containing a subject and a verb that describes, identifies, or gives more information about a noun.

  EXAMPLE: "You use a vector, **which is a quantity having both direction and magnitude.**"

- an **or** phrase, or an explanatory phrase beginning with *or* that follows the term being explained.

  EXAMPLE: "Here *bi,* **or 2,** refers to the number of digits."

EXERCISE 3: Practicing correct pausing for parenthetical explanations

Practice reading the following examples aloud by stressing the term to be defined and by pausing before and after the definition. The parentheses indicate where the pauses should occur.

1. So, LAYPEOPLE (or people who have little or no expertise in a particular area) are often confused by technical vocabulary.
2. In the mathematical term $3x^2y^3z$, the DEGREE (the sum of the exponents of the variables in the term) is six $(2 + 3 + 1)$.
3. CONCRETE (a building material made by mixing cement and sand or gravel) is the main substance used in this process.
4. One of the most serious problems for environmentalists is WASTE (which is anything left over from a manufacturing process).
5. MACROECONOMICS (or the branch of economics that examines economic behavior on a national scale) is contrasted with MICROECONOMICS (or the branch of economics that deals with the behavior of individual industries or decision-making units).

EXERCISE 4: Practicing parenthetical explanations of terms from your field

Choose five terms from your field-specific list of terms in the appendix (or five terms you will use in your general interest presentation). Make a statement about each term and include a parenthetical definition in each statement. Practice saying each statement several times.

Assignment Preparation:
Presenting a Topic of General Interest

As a class, discuss questions 1–4. Try to give at least two answers to each question.

1. How do you know if your audience understands what you are saying? How do you know if they do not understand what you are saying?

2. What can teachers do if they think that students are not understanding what they are saying?

3. How do you know if your audience is interested in what you are saying? How do you know if they are not interested in what you are saying?

4. What can teachers do if they think that students are not interested in what they are saying?

Work with a partner who does not know much about your academic field. Discuss your respective ideas for the presentations you plan to give for this unit. Help each other answer the following questions, and use the answers to plan an interesting and clear presentation.

5. Think of a few topics in your field that might interest your partner. For each topic ask your partner:
   • Is this interesting to you?
   • What questions do you have about this topic?
   • What do you already know about this topic?

6. Is it possible to teach this topic in five minutes? Do you need to make your topic more specific or more general?

7. Which of the organizational structures discussed in Unit 3 will help you develop your information most logically and clearly?

8. How can you add interest to your presentation?

9. In your conversation with your partner, did you use any words he or she did not understand? Write them down so that you remember to explain them if you use them in your presentation.

10. What questions do you think people will ask you about your topic?

Effective teachers are personable, dynamic, and focused on student learning.

Assignment Presentation:
Presenting a Topic of General Interest

Your assignment in this unit is to simplify a topic from your field for an educated audience with little background in the field. Choose a topic of general interest related to your field—information you think would be interesting to almost anyone. Plan your lesson step by step, using the suggestions and questions below to consider your audience's needs as you plan what and how to teach them. You will speak for five minutes and then answer questions for five minutes.

1. *Invite guests.* If your instructor asks you to do so, invite friends, colleagues, or teachers to come to your class for this presentation.

2. *Choose a topic.* What topic would be interesting for people who know very little about your field? In other words, what might they enjoy hearing about? A successful, interesting topic is a question about daily life that your field can answer. For example, the field of physics can answer the question, "Why do some things float and other things sink in water?" Check the appendix for other topics that may be of general interest.

   What topic would be appropriate for your audience's level of knowledge of your field? In other words, what do they already know, and how much can you easily teach them in five minutes?

3. *Make an outline.* What specific facts do you think your audience would like to learn about the topic you have selected? What is the clearest way to organize the information?

4. *Check and revise your outline.* Can you think of any way to make your topic more interesting? For example, can you add any visual aids, demonstrations, humor, examples from your audience's experience, or techniques for actively involving the audience?

   Do you need to adjust the level of the information you are presenting? If you are not sure about their level, what questions can you ask to determine their level? Are you using any special vocabulary that a person outside of your field does not understand? If so, you need to prepare a clear definition for each word or find different words to use in explaining your ideas.

5. *Remind yourself of your audience as you speak.* What notes can you add to your outline to remind you to monitor your audience's interest and understanding? If you note disinterest or lack of understanding in your audience, what can you do about it?

6. *Practice your speech.* What patterns of emphasis and intonation can make your presentation more energetic and interesting, or make your information clearer?

7. *Prepare for questions.* What questions do you think people will ask after your presentation, and how can you clearly answer them?

Pronunciation: Emphasis

In the context of more than one sentence, **emphasis** is used to alert the listener to the important new information being given by the speaker. Emphasis is the use of extra stress on the stressed syllable of a particular word to focus the listener's attention on that word. To consider how emphasis is used in English, study the following dialog, decide which words should be emphasized, and try reading it aloud.

STUDENT:	My experiment isn't working.
TA:	Which part of the experiment isn't working?
STUDENT:	The part where you add the catalyst.
TA:	How much did you add?
STUDENT:	Two grams.
TA:	You should have used four grams.

Most native speakers of English would emphasize the following words in this dialogue:

STUDENT:	My experiment **isn't working**.
TA:	Which **part** of the experiment isn't working?
STUDENT:	The part where you add the **catalyst**.
TA:	How much did you **add**?
STUDENT:	Two **grams**.
TA:	You should have used **four** grams.

As you can see, new information is usually emphasized while old information is usually not emphasized. Speakers want their listeners to hear what is most important, so they draw attention to the new information by emphasizing it. To emphasize new information in English, speakers add extra stress to the stressed syllable of important words.

Emphasis is important in teaching because teachers often want to draw their students' attention to whatever is most important. This is illustrated in the following rule:

RULE 1: EMPHASIZE NEW INFORMATION AND DE-EMPHASIZE OLD INFORMATION

Emphasis is also often important when teachers correct wrong information in order to prevent students from learning the wrong thing. Look at the following example:

STUDENT:	The Theory of Relativity was proposed by Niels Bohr.
TA:	The Theory of Relativity was not proposed by Niels **Bohr**. It was proposed by Albert **Einstein**.

The example above also demonstrates that emphasis is important when we want to contrast two pieces of information. Thus, we need to add a second rule to our first one.

RULE 2: EMPHASIZE CONTRASTING INFORMATION

EXERCISE 5: Correcting misinformation

Practice emphasis with this circle game. The first person will read the first incorrect statement below, and the second person will correct the mistake by using emphasis. The second person will then read the second incorrect sentence, which the third person will correct by using emphasis, and so on. If you do not know the correct information, guess. If you **do** know the correct information, you can choose to give the correct information or test whether the other players are paying attention by giving the wrong information. The first sentence has been done as an example.

1. The capital city of Turkey is Istanbul.

   The capital isn't **Istanbul**. It's **Ankara**.

2. Mt. Fuji is the highest mountain in the world.

3. World War II ended in 1946.

4. Current nuclear reactors use nuclear fusion.

5. The Russians were the first to land on the moon.

6. Water consists of two atoms of carbon and one atom of oxygen.

7. The pigeon is the official symbol of the United States.

8. Buddhism is the predominant religion of India.

9. Spanish is the official language of Brazil.

10. The Olympics originated in Italy.

EXERCISE 6: Practicing emphasis by reading aloud

When teachers present a lot of information, they have to pay special attention to the use of emphasis. Using emphasis to highlight new information or to contrast pieces of information helps students know where they should pay attention.

Practice emphasizing important information by working with the paragraph below. With a partner, **circle** the word(s) in each sentence that you think should receive emphasis. Discuss your answers with the class and then try reading the paragraph with emphasis.

International teaching assistants face many challenges as they begin studying and teaching in the United States. Undergraduate students demand fluent and accurate language skills. They also expect international TAs to teach in the same way that native English-speaking TAs do. At the same time, ITAs must spend long hours trying to meet the demands of studying in a second language and culture. Is it better to think of these challenges as obstacles or opportunities? Should international TAs be required to have the same language and teaching skills as TAs from the United States? Some ITAs have found that their attitude makes a tremendous difference in dealing with these problems. The difficulties of living, studying, and teaching in a new environment can be a source of pain and anger or an opportunity to grow and develop as a human being. Which will they be for you?

EXERCISE 7: Giving longer lectures—speaking from an outline

An easy way to practice the use of emphasis is to use an outline. Most of the words that you would include in an outline are ones that you will want to emphasize because they are key words and present new information. To practice doing this, work in pairs. One person will present the information on the advantages of multiple choice tests, and the other will present the disadvantages of multiple choice tests. Before you start, underline the words you think should be emphasized.

ADVANTAGES OF MULTIPLE CHOICE TESTS

1. Better sampling of content than essay questions.
   • More questions mean more material covered.
   • Better student satisfaction with more opportunities to show what they learned.

2. Reliability can be relatively high.
   • High correlation between individuals' scores on repeated trials.

3. Ease and objectivity of scoring.
   • Usually one answer.
   • Only necessary to check letters.
   • No reading required.
   • Anyone can grade.

4. Permits analysis of item performance (how well students do on a particular question).
   • Common weaknesses among students are easy to see and can be addressed in further teaching.

5. Revision of test is easy.
   • Questions and answer choices can be tested.
   • Poor questions and answer choices can be eliminated.

DISADVANTAGES OF MULTIPLE CHOICE TESTS

1. Sometimes misused.
   • Multiple choice tests verbatim (word for word) recall only.
   • Questions often paraphrase text or lecture notes.

2. May encourage guessing.
   • High statistical probability of getting correct answer without knowing information.
   • Students may not prepare as thoroughly.

3. Difficulty in preparation.
   • Writing good alternate responses is difficult and time-consuming.
   • Writing questions that adequately cover material takes time.

Grammar: Logical Connectors

Logical connectors in English are especially useful in clarifying the logical organization of a presentation. Because of this, the grammar of logical connectors is crucial for teachers. The most common errors made by international TAs are omitting logical connectors entirely or supplying two logical connectors where only one is possible. The omission of logical connectors is especially serious because when ITAs leave them out, it is difficult for their students to identify the relationship between ideas.

EXERCISE 8: Using logical connectors correctly

Below are three case studies of ITAs at a major U. S. university, followed by statements that accurately represent the findings of the case studies or that follow from the information in the study. Read the case studies and then choose from the list of logical connectors to complete the statements. Some blanks will not have any words. Each sentence may have more than one possible answer.

Case Study #1

   This ITA had already been teaching for several quarters when he was referred to the international TA training program. When the TA instructor observed his class, she found that he had developed a rapport with his students despite his difficulties with English grammar and pronunciation. His language difficulties centered on his tendency to try to talk as fast as he could in order to convey the information quickly. He compensated somewhat by repeating the same ideas over and over, which caused him to take much more time to express his thoughts than a typical native English speaker. Tutorials centered on getting him to slow down in order to control for accuracy in pronunciation and grammar. Although he was not able to transfer this practice to his classroom presentations immediately, by the end of the term he had improved his control over the speed of his speech. He had also acquired a significant amount of cultural information about his students, which he put to good use in teaching the final classes of the term.

Choose from this list:

| because | as a result | if | so | this is because |
| but | even though | even if | then | because of this |

1. _____ the TA tried to speak quickly, _____ he made many mistakes in pronunciation.

2. _____ he would slow down, _____ he would be able to avoid making so many errors.

3. _____ he would be able to pay more attention to his speech.

4. _____ he learned to slow down only a little, _____ he did learn a lot of useful cultural information in the course.

Case Study #2

This ITA was under tremendous academic pressure when referred to the international TA training program and indicated that he had no time to prepare for his work as a TA. His first presentation was almost incomprehensible because of his poor pronunciation, his lack of fluency, and his method of preparing for the presentation as if it were an advanced graduate-level seminar. As the term progressed, he changed his presentations to a level more appropriate for first-year undergraduate students in his field. His fluency also began to improve, but his severe pronunciation problems persisted. He had some trouble with individual sounds, but his major problem was with English stress and intonation patterns. With intensive work in the tutorials, he began to show some progress. By the end of the term, he agreed that it was important for him to continue working on his English-language skills.

Choose from this list:

| by | but | as a result of | so | because of this |
| even though | even if | because | even | the reason that |

5. _____ this TA was under a lot of academic pressure, _____ he didn't have time to prepare for his work as a TA.

6. _____ his presentations were incomprehensible is _____ he prepared the presentations for advanced graduate level seminars.

7. _____ working on his pronunciation problems intensively, _____ he began to show some progress.

8. _____ his fluency improved, _____ he still had problems with stress and intonation.

Case Study #3

This ITA was scheduled to teach a recitation sometime during the following year. When she first joined the class, she spoke with a soft voice that made her difficult to understand and was hesitant to participate in discussions. Her teacher soon noticed that she was paying close attention to every bit of information about her language and teaching skills. As the class progressed, the ITA was able to point out her own errors when viewing videotapes of her teaching. Her classmates noticed that her organizational skills improved dramatically. She practiced speaking more forcefully and began to give her opinion more often during class discussions. By the end of the term, even though she still spoke too softly, she was skilled in giving presentations and answering student questions about her academic field. Her only remaining problem was mastering the word stress in terms from her field that she knew through reading but had never heard spoken.

Choose from this list:

| as a result of | then | in order to | because | if |
| by | so | even though | although | but |

9. It was difficult to understand her _____ she spoke too softly.

10. _____ she still made a few errors in her speech, _____ she became very skilled at giving presentations and answering questions about her field.

11. _____ improve the quality of her voice, _____ she practiced speaking more forcefully.

12. _____ paying attention to information about language and teaching skills, _____ she was able to point out her errors on the videotape.

Needs Assessment: TA Observation

The most important part of audience awareness is knowing who your audience is. This includes getting information about their background and what they expect from you. In teaching, TAs can improve awareness of their students by asking themselves the following questions related to various aspects of classroom audience awareness:

Awareness of student background level	Based on the material covered during previous classes, what background level do my students have for this lesson? What questions can I ask them to determine their background in this particular topic? How much variation is there between individual student levels? How can I make this material relevant to my students' lives?
Awareness of student preparation for class	Students often prepare for class by reading, solving problems, or preparing study questions. How prepared do the students seem to be for this class ? What evidence do I have to support my observation?
Awareness of student interest and motivation	How can I monitor student interest in this lesson? What things can I do or say to make the class interesting for the students? How much do the students participate in the class? What can I do to involve them in the lesson?

Awareness of student comprehension	How do I know if the students understand the content? Can I ask them questions, have them perform a task, or give them a quiz to determine their understanding? Which way would be the most efficient and effective?
Awareness of student expectations	What expectations do the students in the class have of me as their TA? In what ways am I fulfilling or not fulfilling these expectations? How do I know?

EXERCISE 9: Observation report

In order to become more aware of your U. S. undergraduate audience, observe an undergraduate class in your field taught by an experienced native English-speaking TA. If there are no native English-speaking TAs in your department, choose an international TA with excellent teaching skills. Before attending the class you should (a) ask the TA's permission to observe his or her class on a particular day and explain what your assignment is and (b) read the outline below so that you will have specific questions in mind when you attend the class.

Complete the following report during or after the observation. You will discuss your observation with your class, so include as much detail as you can to support your opinions. If possible, talk to the TA immediately after the class to get his or her reactions to your observation and to clarify any questions you may have about the class.

Your name _____ Observation date _____

Class observed _____

Format of the class: (circle one)

    lecture   discussion   recitation   lab   other: _____

Year in school of the majority of students: (circle one)

    freshman/sophomore   junior/senior   graduate

Your Observations/Inferences

Comment on the TA's:

1. Awareness of student background level

2. Awareness of student preparation for class

3. Awareness of student interest and motivation

4. Awareness of student comprehension

5. Awareness of student expectations

Your Opinions/Reactions

6. What, if anything, surprised or interested you about this class?

7. If you are currently teaching or if you have taught here or in your home country, explain the differences you noted between this class and your own teaching experience, specifically as they relate to audience awareness.

UNIT 8
Beginning a Two-Part Presentation

Previewing a unit gives the students a map of
what they are to learn.

Your assignment in this unit will be to plan a two-part presentation to present in this unit and the next. This sequence of two lessons will prepare you for teaching in a real classroom because your presentations will continue from one class to the next, just as they do in real life. This activity will help you learn how to connect one class to the next, how to divide a large amount of material into smaller units, and how to plan units longer than five minutes.

In this, the first of the two units, you will present approximately half of the material you want to cover in the two-part presentation. You will also have two other tasks. The first is to briefly preview all the material to be covered in both parts of the presentation. The second task is to end by briefly summarizing what you have covered in the first presentation and then previewing what you plan to cover in the second presentation.

In these two units you will also focus on reviewing the skills you have covered in this course. The review of past focuses will be a good way for you to assess your progress. In this unit you will review your presentation skills, and in the next unit you will review your interactive skills.

Focus:
Review of Presentation Skills

In the previous seven units you have been introduced to areas of focus designed to help you improve your presentation skills. Take a few minutes to think about each focus listed below. Indicate whether you feel you have sufficient control over each aspect of the focus. Circle the one aspect of each focus that is most important for you to keep working on after this course is finished.

PRESENTATION SKILL	GOOD CONTROL	ADEQUATE CONTROL	NEEDS IMPROVEMENT
Organization of presentation			
Overall structure			
Logical development			
Transitional devices			
Emphasis of important points			
Clarity of presentation			
Focus on topic			
Sufficient information			
Conciseness			
Use of supporting detail			
Relevance of content			
Use of practical examples			
Use of contexts familiar to students			
Use of personal or real world examples			
Connection to students' previous knowledge			
Focus on use of information			

PRESENTATION SKILL Use of blackboard and visuals	GOOD CONTROL	ADEQUATE CONTROL	NEEDS IMPROVEMENT
Appropriate choice of visuals			
Organization of visuals			
Integration of written and spoken material			
Legibility			
Correctness of spelling			
Manner of speaking			
Appropriate volume			
Appropriate speed			
Appropriate tone of voice			
Variation for intended effect			

Functional Language:
Previewing Information

When you present information, it is often helpful to tell your audience something about what they will hear. This technique is useful because it prepares them for what is coming and shows them that you have prepared. In general, there are three times during a presentation when we preview information:

- At the very beginning of a lecture or unit.
- Before each major section of the presentation.
- At the end, as a way of previewing the following class.

Previewing Upcoming Information

Students like to know what is going to be covered in a unit or a class hour. Several expressions are useful for this:

"The next (two) lecture(s) will focus on..."

"In this unit we'll be covering..."

"The next (three) class(es) will consist of..."

EXERCISE 1: Practicing previewing

Find the field-specific problem in the appendix that is closest to your academic field. Study the problem and decide what information students would need in order to do such a problem as homework. With a partner, practice using the phrases above to give students a preview of what you will cover to prepare them to do the problem.

Previewing with Rhetorical Questions

Rhetorical questions are questions used by teachers to organize the material in a lecture. They are not real questions because no answer is expected. Teachers often ask rhetorical questions when it is not possible to ask real questions for interaction, such as in a very large class. Here are examples of typical rhetorical questions.

"You may be wondering why the population decreased so dramatically during this time period. [Pause.] There are several reasons. First, ..."

"How can we measure the pressure and temperature of the gas flowing through this tube? [Pause.] One way is to attach our instruments to both the intake and the outflow valves and calculate the difference, but that doesn't tell us everything we want to know..."

"Many people want to know why the population of the world is increasing so rapidly. [Pause.] One way to understand this is to look at the phenomenon of exponential growth..."

Using rhetorical questions to organize your lecture can encourage students to take a more active role in the learning process. Here are two techniques for using your rhetorical questions more effectively:

- Pause before a rhetorical question to make it stand out and to mentally prepare students for a change in topic.
- Pause after the rhetorical question for at least three seconds in order to encourage students to think about the question before you give them the answer.

EXERCISE 2: Practicing rhetorical questions

Using your field-specific problem from the appendix, work with a partner to determine how rhetorical questions could be used to focus student attention on particular points related to the problem. Write down three rhetorical questions and your responses to each question. Check each other's questions for correct grammar. Practice asking the rhetorical questions and answers with an appropriate pause between the questions and answers. Use the following pattern:

Rhetorical Question:
[Pause]
Response:

Previewing the Following Class

Teachers can often generate interest in what will happen during the next class by telling or hinting at what is to come. Some expressions for doing this are:

"So, today we've looked at one aspect of (x). Next time we'll look at the other side of it."

"Next time we'll continue with our discussion of (x)."

"In our next class we'll talk about (x). Based on what we've discussed today, can anyone predict what will happen?"

"We've run out of time today, so the answer to our second question will have to wait until our next class. Think about it before next time and see what you come up with."

EXERCISE 3: Practicing phrases for previewing the next class

Once again work with a partner and your field-specific problem from the appendix. Decide how much information in preparation for doing the problem you will be able to cover during one class hour. Then decide how you will tell students what they will be learning during the next hour of class as they continue work in the area of your field-specific problem. Work with your partner to practice using the expressions above to preview what will happen in the next class.

Assignment Preparation:
Beginning a Two-Part Presentation

One important consideration in planning longer units is deciding how much to cover in one period. When breaking up a lesson into two or more parts, it is important to choose a convenient point at which to stop before continuing the following day. For example, if you were planning a lab, you might divide it into the following major sections:

1. Review of Theoretical Background
2. Explanation of Procedure
3. Demonstration of Experiment
4. Analysis of Data

If you had two class periods in which to cover the material, you might plan to cover the first two parts during the first class, and the last two during the second period. Of course, classes do not always work out that neatly, but it is worth a try!

Suppose that you are required to present the following material in your recitation or lab class on two subsequent days.

SUMMARY MEASURES OF FREQUENCY DISTRIBUTIONS

A measure of central tendency: The Arithmetic Mean
    definition
    calculation
    advantages and disadvantages

A second measure of central tendency: The Median
    definition
    calculation
    advantages and disadvantages

A third measure of central tendency: The Mode
    definition
    calculation
    advantages and disadvantages

Comparing the Mean, Median, and Mode

Work with a partner to plan a two-part presentation to be given in two ten-minute time periods on the two days. As you plan the presentation, answer the following questions about your presentation and make use of the presentation outline below.

1. How will you break this information up into two ten-minute presentations?
2. How will you organize the subtopics within each ten-minute presentation?

3. How much time will you devote to each subtopic within each ten-minute presentation?
4. What expressions or rhetorical questions will you use to give a preview of both presentations at the beginning of the first one?
5. What expressions will you use to preview the second presentation at the end of the first one?

DAY 1

Previewing expression for first part of presentation: _____

Time allotted

Topic 1: _____ _____

    Subtopic 1: _____ _____

    Subtopic 2: _____ _____

    Subtopic 3: _____ _____

Previewing expression for second part of presentation: _____

DAY 2

Previewing expression for second part of presentation: _____

Time allotted

Topic 2: _____ _____

    Subtopic 1: _____ _____

    Subtopic 2: _____ _____

    Subtopic 3: _____ _____

Assignment Presentation:
Beginning a Two-Part Presentation

You are to plan a two-part presentation that you will present over the next two units. Pick a topic that is easily divided into two major parts. Each part should be limited to five minutes, plus five minutes for student questions.

CONTENT (What?)	CONSIDERATION/ TECHNIQUES (How?)	TIME (How long?)
Preview of Both Presentations		
1. What general topic will you cover over the next two sessions?	How can you interest the students in your topic? How and why is the information useful to them?	

CONTENT (What?)	CONSIDERATION/ TECHNIQUES (How?)	TIME (How long?)

Body of First Presentation

2. What exactly do you want students to learn in the first presentation?

How will you tell students what you want them to learn?

3. What main points do you want to make about the general topic?

How can you know if the students are following you?

4. What examples or supporting details can you use for each main point?

How can you make your examples interesting and relevant?

Summary of First Presentation

5. What key points should you repeat in the summary?

How can you **briefly** conclude without restating the whole lecture? How can you check for what your students have learned from your presentation?

Previewing the Second Presentation

6. What are you going to cover in the second presentation? How does it relate to the first presentation?

How can you interest the students in the next class without saying too much?

Pronunciation: Enunciation

After working on your pronunciation for a number of weeks, you should have begun to see some progress. You will also have discovered that it is not possible to perfect your pronunciation by the end of the course. Until your pronunciation is perfect, you can minimize the seriousness of the problems you still have by enunciating your words clearly. **Enunciation** is the precise pronunciation of each vowel and consonant through careful movement of the parts of the mouth. Another term for enunciation is **careful articulation.**

Enunciation depends on using the parts of the mouth, especially the tongue, lips, and jaw, actively. The more your tongue, lips, and jaw move, the easier it is for listeners to understand the sounds you make. For clear enunciation you must open your mouth wide and move your lips and jaw precisely for every sound you speak. In some cultures, it is considered impolite to open one's mouth wide enough to show the teeth or tongue. In U. S. culture, it is considered impolite **not** to open one's mouth widely enough to be clearly understood. English has several expressions to describe people who do **not** enunciate:

He mumbles in his beard.

She talks to herself.

He sounds like he is talking with potatoes in his mouth.

Perhaps your native language has similar expressions. This would not be surprising, because when people cannot clearly hear the sounds a speaker makes, they become frustrated.

Even if the sounds you make are incorrect, it is helpful for them to be clearly enunciated. If people hear exactly what sounds are coming out of your mouth, they can easily repeat them and ask for clarification. In other words, if you make loud, clear mistakes, students can repeat what you said to show you what part they did not understand. Notice that clear sounds are often loud sounds. If you open your mouth enough to enunciate clearly, more sound (volume) can come out. If you are having trouble speaking loudly enough, try concentrating on opening your jaw more widely and enunciating clearly.

To illustrate the relationship between enunciation and tongue, lip, and jaw movement, close your eyes and listen as the teacher reads the following paragraph twice—the first time moving his or her mouth and jaw as little as possible, and the second time moving them as much as possible. Which style of speech would you prefer to listen to as a student?

Clear enunciation demands such active use of the facial muscles and bones that it may be compared to a sport such as gymnastics. If a person is not used to using his or her muscles, he or she will need training—warming up and practice. If practice is done correctly, the muscles will actually feel tired after practice.

EXERCISE 4: Warming up

1. Watching your mouth in a mirror, say the names of each of the vowels slowly, opening your mouth as wide as possible: *a, e, i, o, u.* Then continue talking out loud, opening your mouth the same way for each vowel in each of the words you say.

2. Hold a pencil or a pen between your teeth as you talk so that your mouth stays open at least half an inch as you speak. Keep your lips away from your pen or pencil as much as possible. This will encourage you to move your lips much more actively and precisely.

EXERCISE 5: Practicing with moving different parts of the mouth

Practice moving each important part of your mouth as much as possible.

Jaw:

- Lower your jaw (open your mouth) as wide as you can. Then close it, relax for a minute, and then open it wide again. If your throat and neck muscles are tense, make a conscious effort to keep them relaxed as you close and open your mouth again.
- Close your mouth approximately halfway and move your bottom jaw back and forth, left to right, as quickly as possible.

Lips:

- Push your lips together and as far out (in a kissing shape) as possible. Then relax them, and repeat the same process several times.
- Open your mouth and say "ah." Keeping your jaws open, bring your lips together and say "oh." Now say "ah" and "oh" in rapid succession several times, remembering to keep your jaw open.

Tongue:

- Stick your tongue out as far as possible. Raise it as high as possible and try to touch your nose. Lower it and try to touch your chin. Finally, move it from side to side as far as it will go.
- Move your tongue inside your mouth, using the tip of your tongue to draw a line first under the back of your bottom teeth and then over the back of your top teeth.

EXERCISE 6: Practicing tongue twisters

One of the best ways to practice enunciation is to say a sentence containing many similar sounds very quickly several times. Such a sentence or phrase is called a **tongue twister.** Practicing tongue twisters is a common game among children in the United States.

Read each of the following sentences or phrases four times. First read each sentence slowly to practice individual sounds, stress, and intonation. Then read it again as fast as possible. Finally read it two or more times as fast as possible without stopping.

1. She sells seashells by the seashore.
2. Peter Piper picked a peck of pickled peppers.
3. My father shovels ashes in the shipyard.
4. How much wood would a woodchuck chuck if a woodchuck could chuck wood?
5. Six thick thistle sticks.
6. Toy boat, toy boat, toy boat.
7. Rubber baby buggy bumpers.

As you can see, it is much easier to say something clearly when you say it slowly. Use this as a hint for improving your enunciation. If you have trouble enunciating each word clearly, slow down!

Grammar: Verb Form

Many ITAs are unaware of the errors they make in verb forms when speaking English. When ITAs drop the **-s** or **-ed** ending, forget to include an auxiliary or modal verb such as **is, can,** or **have,** or mix up verb forms, students have to work harder to make sense of what was said. Due to the structure of their native languages, ITAs may feel that certain aspects of the verb form in English are not necessary because the meaning can be understood from context. This may be true to some extent, but it puts an additional burden on the listener. When students are already confused about the subject matter, they may be reluctant or unwilling to pay even more attention in order to compensate for missing or incorrect verb forms.

EXERCISE 7: Making an inventory of your own accuracy in using verb forms

It will help you to learn exactly which verb forms you are not using correctly. In this exercise, you will make an inventory of the errors you make with missing verb endings or auxiliaries and incorrect verb forms.

1. From the appendix, select a topic, visual, problem, or term that you have not talked about before.

2. Make a two- or three-minute audiotape of yourself briefly explaining the topic, visual, problem, or term you have chosen. Take a few minutes beforehand to think about what you will say, and then record yourself speaking without notes as you discuss the topic, explain the visual, go over the problem, or define the term.

3. Play back the tape several times and write down exactly what you said. Transcribe every word exactly as you hear it, whether or not it is correct.

4. Underline each of the verbs in your mini-presentation. Circle the verbs that are missing an auxiliary verb or verb ending or that you think may be used incorrectly. (You may want to have your instructor check this step.)

5. Use the following chart to mark your total errors in each category and to build a profile of your ability to use verbs in English.

6. If you have made a significant number of errors in one or more categories, review a grammar text for rules related to your errors, and begin to monitor your speech for similar errors.

ERROR	EXAMPLE OF ERROR AND CORRECTION	NUMBER OF ERRORS
Main verb		
Required verb missing	There no energy. CORRECT: There *is* no energy.	
Verb endings		
Third person singular present tense verbs without required *-s* ending	It *rotate* quickly. CORRECT: It *rotates* quickly.	
Verb without required *-ed* ending	The chemicals *were heat* to 100 degrees. CORRECT: The chemicals *were heated* to 100 degrees.	
Incorrect regular past tense endings instead of **irregular past tense** verbs	The sun *shined* brightly. CORRECT: The sun *shone* brightly.	
Progressives without required *-ing* ending	The students *are take* the test today at noon. CORRECT: The students *are taking* the test today at noon.	
Auxiliaries		
Passive or **progressive** verbs without required auxiliary *be*	Today we *doing* experiment five. CORRECT: Today we *are doing* experiment five.	
Present perfect or **past perfect** verbs without required auxiliary *have*	Scientists *believed* this since the early 19th century. CORRECT: Scientists *have believed* this since the early 19th century.	
Incorrect form of verb after **modals**	They *can to do* it easily. CORRECT: They *can do* it easily.	
Total Number of Errors in Verb Form		

EXERCISE 8: Practicing verb forms

Record the same topic again, focusing on correcting one major error in verb form. Keep re-recording until you can eliminate your errors in that category. Do the same with each major error.

Needs Assessment:
Departmental Duties for TAs

If you do not already know what tasks are assigned to TAs in your department, now is the time to find out. Teaching assistants in different departments may be assigned widely differing roles. Some may only grade, duplicate materials, or take care of equipment. Others may hold office hours, meet with students individually, or answer questions in laboratories under the supervision of professors or other TAs. Still others may be in charge of recitation sessions or labs or substitute for professors as lecturers. Some TAs may take complete charge of a class and be held responsible for everything (often with the assistance of their own TA!).

Take the questionnaire below to your department. Ask your advisor, department TA supervisor, department head, fellow TA, or departmental secretary to explain what types of tasks you are expected to perform as a TA in your department. For each question, check all the answers that apply. Compare your answers with those of other ITAs in your class or other TAs in your department.

1. What types of tasks do TAs do in this department?

   ____ Grade papers ____ Hold office hours ____ Set up lab equipment

   ____ Answer questions in lab ____ Run recitations ____ Lead lab sessions

   ____ Give lectures ____ Take full responsibility for a class

2. Which of these tasks do first year TAs usually perform?

   ____ Grade papers ____ Hold office hours ____ Set up lab equipment

   ____ Answer questions in lab ____ Run recitations ____ Lead lab sessions

   ____ Give lectures ____ Take full responsibility for a class

3. What kind of support do TAs receive to help them perform these functions?

   ____ Workshops before teaching (pre-service training)

   ____ Workshops after teaching has started (in-service training)

   ____ Weekly meetings with TA coordinator

   ____ Observation by TA coordinator, professor, or experienced TA

   ____ Written information to help TAs do their jobs

   ____ Other types of university or departmental help. What are they? _____

4. If a TA is assigned to a lab, recitation, or lecture, what are his or her responsibilities?

   ____ Preparing the syllabus

   ____ Creating lab or homework assignments

   ____ Setting up or maintaining equipment

   ____ Typing or duplicating course materials

   ____ Planning and giving short presentations

   ____ Leading students in discussion

   ____ Helping students solve problems

   ____ Helping individual students during the lab or class

_____ Holding office hours or tutorials

_____ Meeting with small groups of students outside of class

_____ Creating tests and/or quizzes

_____ Administering tests and/or quizzes

_____ Making decisions about grading

_____ Other tasks not included above. What are they? _____

5. How much time will the TA position require? How much time will the TA be paid for? How much will he or she be paid? Do TAs receive any other benefits?

6. How do professors in the department evaluate TA performance? Will they visit the TA's class? If the department asks students to fill out evaluations of their TAs, will they be collected for review by the department?

7. How important is good teaching in this department? What does this department do to encourage TAs to develop their teaching skills?

8. What will happen during a TA's second and third years? Will he or she be assigned different responsibilities? Does he or she have an option to become a research assistant at a later date? Are TA assignments limited to one or two years in the department? What and who will determine the responsibilities to be assigned to the TA in the future?

Teachers show concern for their students by welcoming questions.

UNIT 9
Continuing a Two-Part Presentation

Reviewing previously taught information is an
effective way to create a context for learning
new material.

Your assignment in this unit is to plan the second half of the two-part presentation that you began in the last unit. Before you introduce the material to be covered in this presentation, you will give a short review of the previous presentation and a short explanation of the relationship between the two presentations. Then, in your conclusion, you will summarize the information presented in **both** presentations.

Review of material previously covered reminds students of what they have heard previously and provides a context for what will be covered in the current class. Beginning a presentation that builds upon previous information without reminding students of the context is like joining a group of friends in the middle of their conversation. Unless they tell you the topic of their conversation, it will probably take you some time to make sense of what they are saying, even if you understand every word. Furthermore, when you begin your class, many of your students may not have thought about the subject matter for several days. If you present new information right away, they may miss what you are saying while they try to remember what you have been discussing. Briefly reviewing what was previously covered will prompt your students to recall what was said before and to prepare for the new information they must absorb in the current class.

The focuses you will review in this unit are those related to interactive skills. Take the opportunity to polish the skills you have not yet mastered.

Focus:
Review of Interactive Skills

Many of the focus sections in the previous eight units were designed to help you improve your skills of interacting with students. Take a few minutes to think about each focus below. Indicate whether you feel you have sufficient control over each subheading covered by the focus. Circle the one aspect of each focus that is most important for you to keep working on after this course is finished.

INTERACTIVE SKILL	GOOD CONTROL	ADEQUATE CONTROL	NEEDS IMPROVEMENT
Nonverbal communication			
Posture			
Gestures			
Facial expressions			
Head movements			
Use of space			
Body movements			
Nonlanguage sounds			
Eye contact and posture with visuals			
Audience awareness			
Appropriate content			
Appropriate vocabulary			
Appropriate manner of presentation			
Monitoring of audience response			
Adjustment to audience response			
Eye contact			

INTERACTIVE SKILL	GOOD CONTROL	ADEQUATE CONTROL	NEEDS IMPROVEMENT
Interaction			
Interaction invited			
Expectation of audience participation communicated			
Friendly, nonjudgmental responses			
Encouragement of questions			
Appropriate feedback to responses from audience			
Teacher presence			
Confidence			
Rapport with audience			
Appropriate authority			
Ease of performance			
Aural comprehension			
Understanding of utterances spoken at a natural rate			
Use of listening strategies			
Negotiation of meaning through use of questions			
Method of handling questions			
Quick response			
Appropriate repetition or rephrasing of questions			
Appropriate check for comprehension			
Clarity of response to questions			
Focus on topic of question			
Direct answer			
Sufficient information			
Concise answer			

Functional Language: Reviewing Information

Review of Information Previously Covered

When beginning a presentation that continues from a previous presentation, it is important to review key terms, concepts, and other information from the previous presentation. Some useful expressions for doing this are:

"Before we go on, let's briefly review what we covered last time."

"Remember that last time we talked about..."

"Let's go over some of the key (terms/concepts/points) we covered last time."

Transition to New Information

After reviewing necessary background from the previous presentation, you also need to make some kind of transition to your current presentation to help the students see how the two parts fit together. Some useful expressions for this are:

"Remember that **last** week we talked about (x). **This** time we're going to cover (y)."

"From our **last** class we know (x). In **this** class, we'll find out why (x) is true."

"**Last** time we found out (x). In **this** class we'll go on to look at various aspects of (x)."

Summary of Information Covered Over Several Presentations

When you finish the last in a series of presentations on a particular topic, it is important to review key points for students and to give them a second opportunity to catch what they might have missed. Typical phrases for doing this are:

"So, let me summarize what we've covered in these last two weeks."

"In conclusion, the key points to review from the last few classes are:..."

"The main point to keep in mind from these last several units is..."

EXERCISE 1: Practicing expressions for review, transition, and summary

Continue working with the field-specific problem from the appendix that you worked with in Unit 8. Study the problem and decide what information should be mentioned in a review of the problem for the final exam. With a partner, practice using the phrases above to help students (a) review the problem, (b) make a transition to begin thinking about the test, and (c) summarize what aspects of this problem and others will be covered by the test.

Assignment Preparation:
Continuing a Two-Part Presentation

When continuing a two-part presentation, it is important to remember to:

1. briefly review what was covered in the previous presentation.
2. make a smooth transition into the second part of the presentation.
3. end the second part of the presentation by briefly summarizing what was covered in both presentations.

In the previous unit's assignment, you began a two-part presentation. To prepare for this unit's presentation, work with a partner and use your presentation outline from the previous unit.

- *Review:* Select an appropriate phrase from the functional language section in this unit and use it to practice giving a 30-second review of the information you covered in your presentation. Have your partner time you to be sure that you finish within the time allowed.
- *Transition:* Select an appropriate phrase from the functional language section in this unit and use it to make a 30-second transition into your topic for the next presentation. Have your partner time you to be sure that you finish within the time allowed.
- *Summary:* Select an appropriate phrase from the functional language section in this unit and use it to make a 30-second summary of what you will have covered in both of your presentations. Have your partner time you to be sure that you finish within the time allowed.

Assignment Presentation: Continuing a Two-Part Presentation

Your assignment is to review briefly the information from the first part of your presentation, make a short transition to the second part of your presentation, complete the second part of your presentation, and quickly summarize what you have covered in both presentations. Your complete presentation should be limited to five minutes, with an additional five minutes for student questions.

CONTENT (What?)	CONSIDERATION/ TECHNIQUES (How?)	TIME (How long?)
Review		
1. What terms, concepts, etc. do you need to review before you continue the presentation?	How can you review without wasting too much time?	
Transition		
2. What is the relationship between the two parts of the presentation?	How can you clearly show the relationship between the previous presentation and this presentation?	
Body of Second Presentation		
3. What exactly do you want the students to learn?	How are you going to tell the students what you want them to learn?	
4. What main points do you want to make about the general topic?	How can you know whether the students are following you?	
5. What examples or supporting details can you use for each main point?	How can you make your examples interesting and relevant?	
Summary of Both Presentations:		
6. What key points from both presentations do students need to know and remember?	How can you **briefly** summarize the key points so that students will remember them?	

Pronunciation:
-s and *-ed* Endings

Ends of Words

Many nonnative speakers of English omit the ends of words when they speak. It is important to pay attention to these final sounds because they often make a large difference in meaning. Consider the following example: The students are working in a lab with an apparatus that has several wires. You say to the students, "Take the wire and disconnect," but what you really meant to say was, "Take the wires and disconnect them." If the students have to continually ask you questions, such as whether you mean only one of the wires or all of them, they may eventually become frustrated and angry about your lack of English communication skills.

It is also important to pronounce these final sounds correctly because eliminating them can make a nonnative speaker sound like a child or an uneducated speaker of English. For example, if you say the following, your students might not respect you in the way they would if you spoke correctly. "My professor work in the lab every day, and then she grade the paper and do the research."

Voiced and Voiceless Consonants

Listen as your instructor pronounces the following words, and note what you hear:

Group 1:	Sue	pieces	faces	separate
Group 2:	zoo	pleases	phases	zero

Now, as you pronounce each of the words above, hold your fingers on the front of your neck near your vocal cords and notice what happens. You will probably observe that there is no vibration as you pronounce the sounds in Group 1, and there is a lot of vibration as you say the sounds in Group 2. The term we use for the first group is **voiceless,** and the one for the second group is **voiced**.

-s and *-es* Suffixes

It is especially important for you to know how to pronounce *-s* and *-es* suffixes. Listen as your instructor pronounces the following words and note what you hear:

Group 1:	assignment	graph	stop	pick
	assignments	graphs	stops	picks
Group 2:	lab	manual	observe	go
	labs	manuals	observes	goes
Group 3:	class	wash	match	quiz
	classes	washes	matches	quizzes

The rules for pronouncing *-s* and *-es* suffixes are as follows:

1. If a word ends in a **voiceless** consonant (Group 1), the suffix is pronounced the same as the [s] in *sit*.

2. If a word ends in a **voiced** consonant (Group 2), the suffix is pronounced the same as the [z] in *zoo*.

3. If a word ends in a [s, š, z, ž, č, or ǰ] sound (Group 3), an extra syllable [əz], as in *was*, is added.

EXERCISE 2: Pronunciation of -*s* and -*es* suffixes

In this exercise you will focus on pronouncing final -*s* and -*es* suffixes correctly. First, mark each -*s* or -*es* suffix with the correct pronunciation [s], [z], or [əz]. Then, listen as your instructor pronounces the following words and note what you hear:

1. Students (   ) must do all the experiments (   ) in the lab manual.
2. A good researcher observes (   ) closely and records (   ) the data.
3. That professor's (   ) classes (   ) are always interesting.
4. You need matches (   ) to light the burners (   ) in the labs (   ).
5. TAs (   ) should grade lab reports (   ) on time.

EXERCISE 3: Practice with -*s* and -*es* suffixes

In this exercise you will focus on pronouncing the final -*s* or -*es* suffix on plurals and third person singular verbs. Work in pairs. Each of you will define the words on one of the lists. Your partner will then repeat your answers for clarity and to correct any errors as in the following example.

EXAMPLE: astronomer/study/stars   PERSON A: What does an astronomer do?
                                    PERSON B: An astronomer studies stars.
                                    PERSON A: An astronomer studies stars. Correct.

Person A

1. biologist / study / living organisms
2. electrical engineer / try to understand / the behavior of electricity
3. mathematician / analyze / numbers and shapes
4. chemist / specialize in / the combination and behavior of elements
5. geographer / study / the earth's surface and topographical features of particular areas

Person B

1. statistician / compute / factual information
2. physicist / formulate / theories about the behavior of matter and forces
3. geologist / study / materials that make up the earth
4. computer scientist / design / programs for computers
5. mechanical engineer / plan and develop / machines

-*ed* Suffixes

The pronunciation of -*ed* suffixes is similar to that of -*s* and -*es* suffixes. Again, listen as your instructor pronounces the following words and note what you hear. See if you can discover the rules for these suffixes and compare your rules with the ones you learned in the section on -s and -es suffixes.

Group 1:	wash	pick	stop	watch
	washed	picked	stopped	watched
Group 2:	observe	transfer	transform	learn
	observed	transferred	transformed	learned
Group 3:	want	need	point	calculate
	wanted	needed	pointed	calculated

The rules for -ed suffixes are as follows:

1. Suffixes added to verbs ending in **voiceless** consonants (Group 1) are pronounced using the sound [t], as in *ten*.

2. Suffixes added to verbs ending in **voiced** consonants (Group 2) are pronounced using the sound [d], as in *dog*.

3. Suffixes added to verbs ending in [t] or [d] (Group 3) are pronounced with an extra syllable: [əd], as in *mud*.

As you can see, the rules are parallel to those for the -s and -es suffixes, which were discussed above.

EXERCISE 4: Pronunciation of -ed suffixes

In this exercise you will focus on pronouncing final -ed suffixes correctly. First, mark each -ed suffix with the correct pronunciation [d], [t], or [əd]. Then in groups of four, take turns reading the sentences with the correct pronunciation. The other members of the group should listen to and correct each reader.

1. The data is analyzed ( ).
2. Simple molecules are converted ( ) into more complex ones.
3. A thick substance is produced ( ).
4. This chemical is used ( ) as a catalyst.
5. The mixture is allowed ( ) to stand for 10 minutes.
6. This process is called ( ) conduction.
7. The reaction should be watched ( ) carefully.
8. Energy is emitted ( ) by electrons and protons.
9. The equipment should be washed ( ) after each use.
10. Light is absorbed ( ) in this process.
11. The economy may be forced ( ) into a recession this year.
12. Anyone would be pleased ( ) to receive a Nobel Prize.

EXERCISE 5: Practice with -ed suffixes

-ed suffixes are often used when speaking in the passive voice. Work with a partner and complete the following statements truthfully, paying attention to your pronunciation of -ed suffixes.

1. _____ can be detected ( ) by radar.

2. _____ can be eliminated ( ) by careful calculation.

3. _____ is determined (   ) by a barometer.

4. _____ can be simplified (   ) to 1/3.

5. _____ can be controlled (   ) by a valve.

6. _____ is affected (   ) by pressure.

7. _____ can be expressed (   ) as $x^2 - y^2$.

8. _____ is affected (   ) by temperature.

9. _____ can be plotted (   ) on a graph.

Grammar:
Verb Tense in Science and Technology

In science and technology, use of correct verb tense is especially important when describing an apparatus, explaining a visual, and discussing relevant research. Keep the following rules in mind:

1. *Describing apparatus:* When talking about a piece of temporary equipment that was constructed for a particular purpose and is no longer in use, the past tense is used. When talking about a piece of equipment that will continue to be used in the field, the present tense is used.

> The potential produced by Volta's battery *was* still weak compared to that produced by the best friction machines of the time, although it could produce considerable charge (Giancoli 1985, p. 393).

> The voltage that exists between the terminals of a battery *depends* on what the electrodes are made of and their relative ability to be dissolved or give up electrons (*ibid.*, p. 394).

2. *Explaining a visual:* When describing how the information in a visual was obtained, the past tense is used. When describing the information itself, the present tense is used.

> Faraday *did* further experiments on electromagnetic induction, as this phenomenon is called. For example, Fig. 20-2 *shows* that if a magnet is moved quickly into a coil of wire, a current is induced in the wire (*ibid.*, p. 472).

> Leonardo da Vinci's notebooks *contain* the first references to the forces present within a structure, a subject we consider as physics today, but Leonardo *was interested*, at least in part, because of the relevance to architecture and building (*ibid.*, p. 3).

3. *Discussing research:* Use the past tense to discuss the discovery of a particular principle, the present perfect to show how that discovery relates to today's thinking, and the present tense to discuss principles that are still believed to hold today.

> Copernicus's sun-centered theory of the universe... *was* not more accurate than Ptolemy's earth-centered theory for predicting the motion of heavenly bodies (*ibid.*, p. 2).

> As a result of Einstein's theory of relativity, for example, our concepts of space and time *have been* completely *changed*, and we *have come* to see mass and energy as a single entity... (*ibid.*, pp. 2-3).

Einstein's theory of relativity *gives* predictions that differ very little from the older theories of Galileo and Newton in nearly all everyday situations; its predictions *are* better mainly in the extreme case of very high speeds close to the speed of light (*ibid.*, p. 2).

EXERCISE 6: Monitoring verb tense in spontaneous speech

Choose one of the following mini-presentations to practice the use of verb tenses.

A. Select two related pieces of apparatus from your field, one with historical value that is no longer in extensive use and one that is used in current research. Write the names of the two pieces of apparatus below, think for a few minutes, and then without notes record a two- or three-minute mini-presentation that compares the two pieces of apparatus to each other in terms of their usefulness. Remember to use the past tense to refer to the piece of apparatus no longer in use and the present tense to refer to the piece of apparatus that is still used.

Apparatus 1 _____

Apparatus 2 _____

B. Choose a visual from the appendix or find a visual from your field that illustrates some kind of data. Write the name of the visual below, think for a few minutes, and then without notes record a two- or three-minute mini-presentation that explains how the data may have been collected and its importance in terms of your field today. Do not forget to use the past tense to explain how the data was collected and the present tense to talk about its current importance.

Title of the visual _____

C. Choose a famous researcher from your field. Write the name of the researcher below, think for a few minutes, and then without notes record a two- or three-minute mini-presentation that describes how the researcher made his or her contribution to your field, how this person's research helped shape current thinking in your field, and what is thought to hold true about his or her ideas in your field today. Be sure to use the past tense to describe what this researcher did, the present perfect to show how this person's research relates to current research in your field, and the present tense to describe what is still held to be true about his or her ideas in your field today.

Name of the researcher _____

Needs Assessment: Hypothesis Testing

In the needs assessment sections throughout this book, you have explored various questions about U. S. academic culture. At this point, you probably still have some unanswered questions about the U. S. classroom or about U. S. undergraduate students. To give you the opportunity to research the answers to some of your questions, you will formulate, test, and refine a hypothesis about an aspect of U. S. academic culture that is different from the academic culture of your native country. From your research in your academic field, you are probably already familiar with the concept of formulating and testing **hypotheses**: possible explanations for observed phenomena in a specific topic area.

In addition to giving you the chance to answer questions and to learn more about your students, this section may help you to break down stereotypes that could make it difficult for you to function in a U. S. classroom. Of course, stereotypes are not always wrong or bad, but the closer they are to reality, the better. The research that you will do in this section is less rigorous and scientific than that which you normally do; however, the importance of these exercises is not the nature of the research but rather in the benefits listed above.

EXERCISE 7: Forming hypotheses about U. S. undergraduates or U. S. university classrooms

Exercises 7 and 8 make use of a seven-step hypothesis refinement process described in Jorstad (1981). The first step in the process is to choose a topic for your hypothesis. Think over everything you have learned so far about the U. S. classroom and U. S. undergraduate students, and choose one area to research in more detail. Be creative. If you cannot think of anything, you can choose from the following list of topics:

1. Differences in some area of nonverbal communication, such as eye contact or use of space, between your culture and U. S. culture.
2. U. S. undergraduate degree of interest in doing well in school.
3. U. S. undergraduate degree of interest in doing well in your field.
4. U. S. undergraduate attitudes toward ITAs.
5. The reasons that U. S. universities accept so many international students.
6. U. S. undergraduate attitudes toward cheating.
7. Undergraduate student expectations of ITAs versus native English-speaking TAs.
8. The most important factors for U. S. students in making career choices.
9. Differences in greeting habits of students and teachers between your culture and U. S. culture.
10. The importance of grades in determining the future of a U. S. student.

Once you have chosen your topic, the second step in the hypothesis refinement process is to think carefully about a specific event or action that you have observed in relation to the topic. The third step is to write a hypothesis related to your observation. For example, under the topic "attitudes of U. S. students toward cheating," one observable fact is that students who are discovered to be cheating may be expelled from college. A possible hypothesis related to this phenomenon could be "Because U. S. students believe that cheating will be punished, they will attempt to hide their efforts at cheating." If you believe that the statement you have chosen could be accurate, then you may decide to use it as your hypothesis.

The fourth step is to think of four or five questions to test your hypothesis by interviewing members of your university community. Try to avoid personal questions, such as "Do you cheat on tests?," biased questions, such as "Don't you think that most people in the U. S. have a negative opinion of foreigners?," or broad questions, such as "What do you think of cheating?" Ask your instructor to check your questions for clarity, appropriateness, bias, and specificity.

After your instructor has checked your questions, go out and interview five to ten U. S. students, TAs, professors, or university staff members. Explain who you are, why you are requesting this interview, and any special directions for answering your questions. Also, make sure you keep the interview short, and thank the interviewee for his or her time. As you do your interviews, you may find some of the following expressions useful:

"I'm an international TA and I'm doing a very short interview for my TA training class. Could I have a few minutes of your time?"

"I'm investigating attitudes of U. S. students toward cheating for a class I'm taking. Could you spare a few minutes?"

"First I'll ask you a question and then I'll give you some choices. You just need to tell me which choice fits you best. OK?"

"OK. That does it. Thanks a lot. I really appreciate it!"

"That's all. Thanks for helping me."

EXERCISE 8: Refining your hypothesis and reporting your results

Record in writing or by tape recorder the results you get from each of your interviewees. Then complete the remaining steps of hypothesis refinement by responding to the following list of questions and instructions as you prepare for the class discussion in the next unit.

1. Why did you choose your hypothesis? Before your interviews, did you think that your hypothesis would be confirmed?

2. Describe the U. S. students, TAs, professors, or university staff members that you interviewed. Who were they (sex, age, profession, etc.)?

3. Which of your questions were most useful in testing your hypothesis?

4. Summarize the interviewees' answers to your questions.

5. Analyze your data. What conclusions can you draw about this aspect of U. S. culture? Is your sample of U. S. students, TAs, professors, or university staff members large enough for you to be relatively sure of your conclusions?

6. If necessary, refine your hypothesis; that is, based on your results, write a new hypothesis that more accurately reflects U. S. culture.

7. How do the results of your hypothesis-testing compare with what you would expect to get if you were able to interview members of a university community in your own country?

8. What implications do your results have for you as an ITA in a U. S. university classroom?

9. In one paragraph, summarize your hypothesis, your findings, and the conclusions you have drawn from your findings.

10. Be ready to discuss your hypothesis, findings, and conclusions as part of the assignment in Unit 10.

UNIT 10

Leading a Discussion

Involving students in discussion helps them apply concepts to their own experience.

Your assignment in this unit is to lead a portion of a discussion on "The implications of cultural differences for the success of international TAs." During different parts of the discussion you will lead the discussion, be a time-keeper, make sure that each contribution to the discussion is verbally responded to by someone in the group, and make sure that the contributions to the discussion are synthesized into an answer to the discussion question.

The assignment will give you a structured experience of how discussion of a topic can help students to understand, integrate, and internalize information. U. S. teachers often avoid telling students authoritatively, "This is the truth. Learn it." Instead, they elicit reactions and relevant experiences by saying, "This is what someone in the field has found to be true. Is it true in your experience? Does it make sense in light of what you have found to be true?"

This U. S. cultural concept of discussion reflects a number of values that are different from many other cultures, possibly including your own. An assumption of most U. S. educators is that individual differences in knowledge, experience, and opinion contribute to learning; if we were all alike and had the same information, it would be very difficult to find resources for learning new things. A second assumption of U. S. educators, revealed by the frequent use of discussions in class, is that the primary role of a teacher in the United States is not to be an authority and dispense new information, but to be a collaborator with the students and facilitate their acquisition of new understanding. This view of the teacher's role rises out of an underlying philosophy that the goal of education is to learn **how** to think, not just to learn a set of facts.

This unit offers you an opportunity to synthesize the cultural learning you have done in the needs assessment sections throughout this book. In the focus section of this unit, you will also have a chance to review the language learning you have done, just as you did with your presentation and interactive skills in the past two units.

Focus 1: Fluency

Fluency means speaking a language smoothly and without hesitation. Speaking English fluently includes:

1. speaking in phrases rather than one word at at time,
2. pausing between phrases but not in the middle of phrases,
3. speaking without false starts (the repetition of a word or words as one tries to think of what words to say next), and
4. speaking with the regular rhythm resulting from using American English phrasal stress patterns.

The degree to which a person is fluent even in his or her own language varies according to a number of factors:

1. *Topic:* Speaking about an unfamiliar topic often decreases a person's fluency.
2. *Audience:* Speaking in front of a large audience in a formal setting is usually more stressful than speaking to a small group of friends, and causes a decrease in fluency.
3. *Physiological or psychological state of the speaker:* The ability to communicate fluently often decreases when a person is tired or under stress.
4. *Lack of vocabulary:* Ignorance of the exact, appropriate word when trying to communicate an idea may interfere with fluency.

5. *Speed:* Trying to express ideas too fast can interfere with fluency because the speaker does not have enough time to choose his or her words carefully or to organize the information clearly.

6. *Concern about correctness:* Being overly concerned about using the perfect word or perfect grammar may cause loss of fluency because of a focus on form rather than content.

7. *Reading a presentation aloud versus saying something in one's own words:* Even a native speaker of a language has difficulty reading a text aloud with expression. This difficulty is even more exaggerated when the speaker is unfamiliar with the material or in a stressful situation such as giving a lecture.

8. *Presenting a large amount of material without notes or a plan:* Giving lectures without notes may interfere with fluency because organization, vocabulary, and examples require careful planning.

9. *Speaking in spontaneous situations:* Speaking without planning, such as when answering questions, often interferes with fluency because the speaker has to think of the concepts as well as how to say them.

Because the factors above affect one's ability to communicate fluently in a second language, lack of practice is not the only reason that you may have fluency problems in English. It is a good idea to keep these factors in mind to avoid discouragement if your fluency is not up to your expectations on a particular day.

Identifying the reason for your fluency problems may help solve them. The chart below lists the most common factors interfering with fluency and suggests ways nonnative speakers can deal with these problems. Many of these suggestions have been mentioned in previous units.

Problem	Suggested Solution
1. Unfamiliarity with topic	Practice beforehand with a friend or audiotape yourself.
2. Unfamiliarity with audience	Over-prepare to increase confidence in presenting your content.
	Get as much exposure to new audiences as possible. (The more times you have experienced this, the more confident you will feel.)
	Start with something to break the ice, or break down any barrier between you and your audience, such as a story, anecdote, or interesting question.
3. Tiredness	Get plenty of rest beforehand.
4. Nervousness	Breathe deeply before and while speaking.
5. Lack of vocabulary	Paraphrase what you mean.
	Use gestures or visuals to communicate.
	Give an example.
6. Speed	Try to speak slowly.
	Focus on saying one thought group at a time.
7. Concern about correctness	Focus on the content instead of on using the correct grammar.
	Avoid repeating a phrase while you think of the correct grammar. Start speaking only after you have thought of the entire phrase, or pause briefly and then continue speaking. For example, do not say: "I have to... I have

Problem	Suggested Solution

to... I have to design one tomorrow." Instead, say: "I have to [pause] design one tomorrow."

Tape record yourself speaking about a topic before presenting it. Then critique yourself as you review the tape, and try to think of a better way to express your ideas.

8. Need to write out presentation — Use your own words instead of reading a written presentation.

9. Lack of preparation — Use notes to help you organize and to allow you to focus on the content instead of on the organization.

10. Difficulty with questions — Use hesitation devices such as "Just a minute, let me think."

Predict questions and possible answers.

Follow the steps for fielding questions: speak within three seconds, rephrase the question, give a concise answer, and check for comprehension.

EXERCISE 1: Practicing vocabulary strategies

One of the biggest obstacles for second language learners in achieving fluency in English is a lack of vocabulary. Keep in mind that you will never learn all the words in the English language because even native speakers do not know all of them. Instead, focus on trying to communicate your ideas when you cannot think of the exact word. That way, you will sound fluent even when you do not have all the exact words.

Look at the vocabulary strategies listed below. In each case, a speaker could not think of the exact word in parentheses, so he or she paraphrased:

1. Analysis — Break the object down into its parts.

   (a toaster) — "I can't think of the word, but it has two openings where you put in bread to cook, a long electrical cord, something on one end that you push down to make it work, and a piece of metal to adjust the temperature."

2. Illustration — Draw a diagram to describe the object.

   (a spring) — "I don't know how to say this in English, but I can draw it for you."

 "It's like this."

3. Cause and effect — Describe what causes a phenomenon or what results from it.

   (gravity) — "I'm not sure what the word is, but this is what makes objects fall toward the earth."

4. Example	Give an example of what you're talking about.
(stereotype)	"I'm talking about a way of looking at a group of people. For example, we tend to believe that all Spaniards play the guitar and dance flamenco."
5. Comparison and contrast	Talk about how the object is similar to or different from something else.
(a sweet potato)	"I don't know what it's called in English, but this vegetable is similar to a potato in shape and how it is grown, but is different from a potato because it is usually deep orange and has a sweet taste."
6. Definition	Use a definition to describe what you mean.
(a shopkeeper)	"The word I'm looking for means a person who owns and works in a small store."
7. Opposites	If you can't think of the word, use its opposite.
(sad)	"I'm not exactly sure of the word, but it means that a person is unhappy."
8. Description	Give the size, color, shape, material, function, or other aspects of the object.
(a razor)	"I'm talking about a small object with a handle that is made of metal or plastic. One part of it is flat and silver colored and is very sharp. It's used to take the hair off a person's face or body. Can you tell me the word in English?"
9. Nonverbals	Use your body to demonstrate what you mean.
(to shrug one's shoulders)	"I don't know how to say it, but it looks like this:"

Work in pairs. Each of you has a list of five words. Use one of the strategies above to try to get your partner to say the word on your list without telling what what the word is.

EXAMPLE: (genes) "These are like blueprints for a house, but for living things. They are used to give instructions to the body for what the organism will be like."

TA 1	1. transportation		**TA 2**	1. atmosphere
	2. discouraging			2. persuade
	3. risk			3. rotation
	4. disaster			4. corruption
	5. recycle			5. resist

EXERCISE 2: Eliminating false starts and stops

It can be very confusing and annoying to an English speaker if you begin sentences that you do not finish or if you make several attempts to say a word or to express an idea. The following example illustrates this problem:

"The pu-pur-purpose of this exper-experiment... It's important to do this exper-experiment for many purpo-reasons."

An effective way to handle this problem is to: (a) finish the sentence and then rephrase what you mean, or (b) indicate what you are doing by using a phrase such as:

"Let me start over."

"Let me start again."

"Let me begin again."

To practice making your speech smoother, tape record yourself answering one of the questions from your field-specific list in the appendix. Try to focus on finishing each sentence without making any false starts. If you do need to start again, be sure to use one of the phrases above.

EXERCISE 3: Eliminating fillers

Many learners of English and even native speakers use **fillers:** words or sounds that indicate you are thinking of what to say next—the correct word or how to finish your thought group. Some common fillers are:

"um"	"um-m-m"	"Ya (you) know"
"uh"	"uh-h-h"	"Ya (you) see"
"the"	"the-uh-uh"	"I mean"

Fillers do not help your listeners' understanding. If you cannot think of what to say before you finish a thought group, avoid using fillers; pause and do not say anything.

Another technique to eliminate fillers is to draw out the first word of your thought group until you can think of the rest of the words in that thought group. Look at the following example:

"C-o-m-e back tomorrow / a-f-t-e-r you finish your report."

To practice thinking in English and avoiding fillers, work in groups of three or four. Each member of the group should take one of the topics below to talk about for two minutes without stopping. These topics were chosen because they are difficult to elaborate upon. When the speaker cannot think of a word or has not finished a thought group, he or she should use one of the strategies above, pausing or drawing out the first word of the thought group. The other members of the group should listen and give the speaker feedback on how well he or she did.

Topics:	insects	chairs	the letter K
	truth	boxes	ink

Focus 2:
Comprehensibility

Comprehensibility means using language in such a way that your audience can understand your intended meaning. Some major components in making your information comprehensible to your listener are pronunciation, grammar, fluency, and vocabulary. Serious problems in any of these four areas will interfere with your overall comprehensibility.

Comprehensibility consists of the ability to produce speech at two levels: (a) the sounds are clear enough that your audience could repeat your words; and (b) the meaning that the audience understands is the same as the meaning you intended to give.

EXERCISE 1: Self-assessment of English language skills

In the previous eight units you were introduced to ways to improve your language skills. Assess your current spoken-English skills by taking a few minutes to think about each skill below. Indicate whether you feel you have sufficient control over each subheading covered by the skill. Circle the one aspect of each skill that is most important for you to work on.

Language skill	Good control	Sufficient control	Needs improvement
Pronunciation			
Individual sounds	_____	_____	_____
Stress	_____	_____	_____
Intonation	_____	_____	_____
Enunciation	_____	_____	_____
Intelligibility	_____	_____	_____
Fluency			
Phrasing	_____	_____	_____
Pauses	_____	_____	_____
Smooth rhythmic patterns	_____	_____	_____
Grammar			
Accurate form	_____	_____	_____
Appropriate usage	_____	_____	_____
Vocabulary			
Word choice	_____	_____	_____
Form of words (derivations)	_____	_____	_____
Appropriate level of formality	_____	_____	_____

EXERCISE 4: Reviewing compensation strategies

Decide whether pronunciation, fluency, grammar, or vocabulary is most difficult for you. Think of ways to compensate for your weaknesses; that is, think of how you can use your strengths to make up for your weaknesses in that area. If you need help, refer to the following chapters of this book for specific strategies. Review the appropriate section, choose two strategies that you can use, and then list them:

Grammar	Unit 2 (Grammar: Compensation Strategies)
Fluency	Unit 10 (Focus 1: Fluency)
Vocabulary	Unit 10 (Focus 1, Exercise 1: Vocabulary Strategies)
Pronunciation	Unit 2 (Pronunciation: Compensation Strategies)

EXERCISE 5: Practicing compensation strategies

Choose a visual from the appendix or from another source to describe to a partner. Give your partner instructions for how to draw the visual without looking at it. Your partner can ask questions if he or she needs clarification. When you finish, compare your partner's drawing to the original visual, and then ask your partner to assess your performance by answering the following questions:

1. How easy or difficult was it to understand the instructions?

   ____ easy   ____ somewhat difficult   ____ difficult

2. If you had difficulty, which area caused the most problems?

   ____ pronunciation   ____ grammar

   ____ fluency   ____ vocabulary

3. How effectively did the speaker use compensation strategies?

   ____ ineffectively   ____ effectively   ____ very effectively

Assignment:
Leading a Discussion

Your assignment in this unit is to:

- take part in a discussion on "The implications of cultural differences for our success as international TAs";
- lead a portion of the discussion that will focus on the hypothesis regarding one specific cultural difference that you tested in the last unit; and
- lead group feedback, using the Discussion Evaluation Form from the appendix after your portion of the discussion. Each ITA will have an equal portion of time to lead his or her part of the discussion and elicit feedback on that portion.

For each portion of the discussion:

1. one participant will initiate and lead the discussion (the *initiator*),
2. one participant will be a *time-keeper*,
3. one participant will make sure that each contribution to the discussion is verbally responded to by someone in the group (the *gatekeeper*), and
4. one participant will make sure that the contributions to the discussion are synthesized into an answer to the discussion question (the *synthesizer*).

To lead your portion of the discussion, first prepare a brief one-minute summary of what your hypothesis was, whether the data you collected confirmed or negated your hypothesis, and what conclusions you drew about your hypothesis. Second, prepare a list of three to five **open-ended questions** to elicit the other group members' reactions to both your findings and your conclusions. Open-ended questions do not limit possible answers. Thus, yes/no questions and choice questions are not open-ended questions because the first type limits the possible answers to *yes* or *no* and the second type limits the answers to whatever alternatives were given in the question. Open-ended questions typically begin with *why* or *how*. Examples of open-ended questions are:

"How have your experiences confirmed or negated my hypothesis?"

"Why or why not?" (after a question such as, "Do you think the conclusions I drew from my data are valid or invalid?")

To set up the discussion, the class should divide into groups of four and decide in what order the four participants will speak. The three participants who are not leading the discussion assume the remaining roles of time-keeper, gatekeeper, or synthesizer.

When you are the leader, you begin the discussion with a brief summary of your hypothesis-testing process and then elicit the other participants' reactions with one of your prepared open-ended questions. For the rest of your allotted time, all four members of your group should discuss:

1. experiences relating to the hypothesis,

2. conclusions that can be drawn from everyone's experiences, and

3. how the information shared about the hypothesis can help each of you to be more effective teaching assistants.

Two minutes before the end of the allotted time for a given hypothesis, the time-keeper should warn the group members that they have two minutes to conclude the discussion. The last two minutes should be spent synthesizing a group answer to the question "What are the implications of the cultural difference (about which the leader formed his or her hypothesis) for our success as international TAs?" After each discussion of a given hypothesis, the group should evaluate the discussion process, using the Discussion Evaluation Form in the appendix.

Needs Assessment: What Happens After the International TA Program?

The course is almost over, and you are probably thinking about what will happen after you leave it. In this section, you will have the chance to plan for what will happen in your future career as an ITA and as an instructor in your own country.

Working as an ITA in the United States

In this course you have had support from your instructor and from the other ITAs in the program. After you finish the course, you may need new sources of support and information if problems arise or when you have questions about teaching. To prepare for these situations, try to answer the following questions. In some cases, you will need to interview people in your department.

1. After I finish this program, where can I take:

   a. administrative problems, such as departmental policies?
   b. pedagogical concerns, such as the best way to teach a concept?
   c. personal problems, such as financial difficulties?

2. If I need feedback on my teaching, who could observe me and provide feedback on specific problems? How can I find out if my university or department provides either of the following options?

   a. Free services to assist TAs by giving them advice on specific classroom problems. (Some will even observe TAs' classes and provide confidential feedback.)
   b. A mentoring system that matches ITAs with native English-speaking TAs. If nothing like this exists in my department, how could I find a TA from the United States to be

my mentor? (A peer relationship with another TA helps both to gain insight into each other's cultures.)

3. How can I best monitor my own performance as an ITA? By audiotaping my classes? By videotaping them? By keeping a journal?

4. How can I continue learning about U. S. classroom culture? Consider the following possibilities:

   a. How can I know more about my undergraduate students, their background in the subject, their interests, and their expectations of me as their TA? (Would it be helpful for me to interview some U. S. undergraduate students to find out what they expect of their TAs?)

   b. Does my department have standardized feedback evaluation forms to give my students before midterm and at the end of the term? If not, can I write my own form and administer it?

   c. One way to learn more about U. S. classroom culture is to use professors as potential models for teaching. A useful tool for doing so is called DIE, an acronym for Description-Interpretation-Evaluation (Wendt 1984). In the description step, the observer simply describes what he or she **sees** or **hears.** In step 2, interpretation, the observer says what he or she **thinks** the observed phenomenon means. In step 3, evaluation, the observer reacts to the observed phenomenon by describing how he or she **feels** about it. To apply this technique, consider the following questions, being careful not to make any judgments until completing the process.

   • What techniques do professors in my department use to teach their classes?

   • What do I think they want to accomplish by using those techniques?

   • Do I believe these techniques are effective in helping students learn, and do I want to adopt them?

Working as a Teacher in Your Own Country

If you intend to return to your own country and to teach there, you will have to readjust to your own culture, just as you had to adjust to U. S. culture when you came here. You may want to start thinking about how you will make that readjustment because it will affect the decisions you make while you are here. You may find some difficulty during the readjustment period. Experts in cross-cultural communication say that the best way to prepare for your return home before you actually get there is to think about what it will be like. To begin this process, answer the following questions and be prepared to discuss them with other members of your class. (Note: This book is **not** advocating that you employ a U. S.–style teaching approach in your country. It is important to come to an informed and well-thought-out decision that is entirely yours.)

EXERCISE 6: Making choices about your teaching style in your home country

You have several options regarding the way you teach when you go back to your country. List some of the pros and cons of each alternative listed below:

• teach the way you taught before you came to the United States (or the way you have observed others teach in your home country);

• teach the way you learned to teach here; or

• introduce in your own country some of the teaching methods you learned here.

You may have some apprehension about how to make that choice when you return home. The following suggestions may help you decide what teaching style you should use. You might observe several classes before beginning to teach so that you can see what the norm is. If you taught in your native country before coming here, you may be surprised how much or how little teaching has changed there since you left. If you have never taught in your home country, it is still a good idea to observe current teaching practices before you teach. Then, if teaching styles between your home country and the United States are radically different, you will be in a better position to decide what to do.

It is also important to look at the student population. Do they seem satisfied with how they are taught? Do you feel that they are learning as much as they can? How willing or resistant to change do they and your country's educational system seem to be?

EXERCISE 7: Easing your adjustment from one teaching style to another upon returning home

For each alternative listed above, list the kinds of things you can do to help your students or yourself adjust to the changes you make. For example, if while teaching in your country you decide to introduce some of the ways that you learned to teach while in the United States, it might be a good idea tell students what you will do and explain why you are doing it.

Where Can You Go from Here?

Keep Working on Your English Language Skills

1. *Grammar*
   Write your own grammar practice exercises by photocopying newspaper, magazine, or textbook passages and crossing out every fifth or seventh word after writing the word on a separate piece of paper. A few days later, after you have forgotten the exact words that were used in the passage, look at your copy with the deleted words, and try to fill in the blanks with words that fit grammatically into the sentence. Finally, compare the words you filled in with the words that were originally used in the written passage. If you did not choose exactly the same word, try to determine if the word you used is nonetheless a grammatical choice. If you are unsure, ask a native speaker of English. You may want to work on specific grammatical points by crossing out all verb endings, for example, or prepositions, or auxiliary verbs.

2. *Pronunciation*
   • Practice difficult words: As you plan lessons, pick out words with difficult sounds in them and practice them before you teach. Periodically review any feedback forms from this class on which your teacher wrote words that you have had trouble pronouncing.
   • Imitate native speakers of English: As you listen to TV or radio, imitate the sounds and intonation of the speakers. If you have access to audiotapes or videotapes, play one sentence at a time and imitate the way it was spoken.
   • Find out if your university has any language laboratories with audiotape or videotape collections for English practice.

3. *Vocabulary*
   • The best way to expand your vocabulary is to read as much and as widely as possible. Do not check the dictionary for every word you do not understand, but try to guess its

meaning from the context. If you see the same unfamiliar word many times, check its exact meaning and try to learn it.

- Use some consistent system to keep track of new words. You may want to record the words in a small notebook or a set of small cards. At the end of each day, look up each new word in a dictionary, write down a simple definition, and try to use it in a sentence. Every day, review your lists of words. If you review often enough, you will begin to recognize the words when you hear them again, later you will understand them as they are used, and eventually they will be so familiar that you will be able to use them in your own speech.
- Spend time before and after class talking with your students. Ask them about the slang and everyday expressions students use. Try using this informal vocabulary at other times when you speak with your students outside of class.

4. *Listening*

When you do not have a chance to talk to live individuals, listen to English as much as possible on radio and TV. When you cannot understand what was said, try to:
- figure out what must have been or could have been said.
- analyze the reason you did not understand.
- try to figure out what would help you understand the same kind of language next time.

Keep Working on Your Teaching Skills

1. Continue to get as much feedback as possible on your teaching. You may do this informally, by talking to your students individually, or by formal feedback forms at midterm and at the end of the term.

2. Set up an exchange observation system with another ITA to give you both a chance to continue working on the issues you have discussed in this course.

3. Audiotape yourself regularly. As you listen to the tape, imagine yourself as one of your students in order to identify your most troublesome areas.

Keep Working on Your Intercultural Communication Skills

1. Use your own observational skills to spot cultural differences between your culture and the culture of your present environment. When you observe something happening that seems strange, look for possible cultural reasons for why it happened or why it was done that way.

2. Check the courses offered by the speech and communication department in your university. Many speech and communication departments offer classes in intercultural communication.

Appendices

Appendix I: Feedback Forms

Giving Feedback

Feedback, positive comments as well as constructive criticism on your presentations, is an important component of this course. Your instructor will be giving you weekly feedback on your presentations using the Instructor's Feedback Form in the following section. This form lists the focuses for each unit that will be tested at the end of the course. This weekly feedback from your instructor will give you a clear idea of your strengths and weaknesses and of your progress throughout the course.

Another major source of feedback is **peer feedback,** classmates critiquing one another. This critiquing enables you to help each other improve and is good preparation for learning how to evaluate yourself.

Each unit in this book has a separate peer feedback form with questions related to the focuses for that unit. As you listen to each presentation, answer the questions on separate sheets of paper or on photocopies of the page. After the presentation, your instructor may ask you to give oral feedback to your peers based on what you have written or to hand in your written feedback for your classmates to look at in tutorials.

Giving feedback may differ from culture to culture. In the culture of the United States, it is important to give both positive and negative feedback. Also, it is best to look at the person you are critiquing and to comment directly. In other words, it is better to say ''You did a good job of making your topic interesting'' instead of ''He or she did a good job of making the topic interesting.'' This makes the communication much more personal.

Instructor Feedback Form

Assignment: _____

ITA: _____ Date: _____

I. Comments on Language Skills:

   A. Pronunciation

   B. Grammar

   C. Fluency

   D. Comprehensibility

II. Comments on Teaching Skills: Circle class focuses and individual focuses for this presentation.

   A. Organization of presentation

   B. Clarity of presentation

   C. Relevance of content

   D. Use of blackboard and visuals

   E. Manner of speaking

   F. Nonverbal communication

   G. Audience awareness

   H. Interaction

   I. Teacher presence

   J. Aural comprehension

   K. Method of handling questions

   L. Clarity of response to questions

III. Instructor's Overall Impression:

          Good | **Needs Work**

Peer Feedback Form for Introducing Yourself

Unit 1: INTRODUCING YOURSELF   Speaker: _____

Date: _____   Topic: _____

1. Did you find the speaker's self-introduction easy to understand? Explain why or why not.

2. How did the speaker conclude? Was it an appropriate conclusion? Do you have any suggestions for other ways to conclude?

3. What suggestions for improvement can you give the speaker?

Peer Feedback Form for Introducing a Syllabus

Unit 2: INTRODUCING A SYLLABUS   Speaker: _____

Date: _____   Topic: _____

1. Content: Did the speaker include too much information? include too little information? Give suggestions, if appropriate.

2. Potential communication problems: Did the speaker discuss language difficulties by acknowledging them rather than by apologizing? make a favorable impression on you?

3. Nonverbal communication: Was the speaker's nonverbal communication effective? distracting? List any behaviors that added to the presentation.

   List any behaviors that detracted from the presentation.

4. Teacher presence: Did the speaker show concern? interest? openness? confidence?

5. Would you want to be in this person's class? Why?

Peer Feedback Form for Explaining a Visual

Unit 3: EXPLAINING A VISUAL   Speaker: _____

Date: _____   Topic: _____

1. Was the visual easy to see?

   Clearly labeled?

   Well-chosen for the purpose?

2. Did the speaker follow each of the recommended steps in explaining a visual?

   Title, name, or purpose

   Overall layout or organization

   Terms or symbols

   One or more examples

   Trends or obvious features

   Predictions based on information given

   Emphasis of important points

3. Write down any organizational cues you heard the speaker use:

4. What was best about the speaker's presentation?

5. What is the most important thing for the speaker to improve?

Peer Feedback Form for Defining a Term

Unit 4: DEFINING A TERM   Speaker: _____

Date: _____   Topic: _____

1. Did you find the speaker's definition easy to understand? Explain why or why not.

2. How did the speaker make the topic relevant to your experience?

3. Give the speaker feedback about what you understood by filling in the following outline:

    Term: _____

    Definition: _____

    Examples: _____

    _____

    _____

    _____

    _____

4. Did the speaker use: appropriate volume?

    appropriate speed?

    appropriate tone of voice?

    appropriate variation for comprehensibility?

Peer Feedback Form for Teaching a Process

Unit 5: TEACHING A PROCESS   Speaker: _____

Date: _____   Topic: _____

1. Comment on this speaker's choice of a process to teach. Was the choice very good? adequate? inappropriate? Make suggestions for improvement.

2. Comment on the method that this speaker chose to present the information. Was the method very good? adequate? inappropriate? Make suggestions for improvement.

3. Rate this speaker's ability to interact with students (to lead them to the correct answer in a supportive way). Was the interaction very good? adequate? unsatisfactory? Make suggestions for improvement.

4. Rate this speaker's ability to respond to incorrect student answers in an appropriate way. Was the response very good? adequate? unsatisfactory? Make suggestions for improvement.

5. Rate this speaker's ability to understand the members of the class or to compensate appropriately when he or she did not understand. Was the speaker's ability to understand (or compensate for not understanding) very good? adequate? unsatisfactory? Make suggestions for improvement.

Peer Feedback Form for Fielding Questions

Unit 6: FIELDING QUESTIONS   Speaker: _____

Date: _____   Topic: _____

Circle Yes or No in each category.

	1	2	3	4	5	6	7	8

1. Did the speaker:

   a. respond within 3 seconds?

	1	2	3	4	5	6	7	8
a. respond within 3 seconds?	Yes	Yes	Yes	Yes	Yes	Yes	Yes	Yes
	No	No	No	No	No	No	No	No
b. restate the question?	Yes	Yes	Yes	Yes	Yes	Yes	Yes	Yes
	No	No	No	No	No	No	No	No
c. answer clearly and concisely?	Yes	Yes	Yes	Yes	Yes	Yes	Yes	Yes
	No	No	No	No	No	No	No	No
d. check to see if the question was answered?	Yes	Yes	Yes	Yes	Yes	Yes	Yes	Yes
	No	No	No	No	No	No	No	No

2. What was the best feature of this speaker's method of handling questions?

3. What one thing could help this speaker handle questions more effectively?

Audience Feedback Form for Presenting a Topic of General Interest

Unit 7: PRESENTING A TOPIC OF GENERAL INTEREST   Speaker: _____

Date: _____   Topic: _____

1. Was the topic interesting to you?

   Yes ____   No ____   Somewhat ____
   Comments:

2. Did the speaker seem aware of you and your reactions as he or she spoke? For example, did he or she make appropriate eye contact, or respond to any of your facial expressions?

   Yes ____   No ____   Somewhat ____
   Comments:

3. Did you understand the content of the presentation?

   Yes ____   No ____   Somewhat ____
   Comments:

4. Did the speaker present the right amount of information: enough but not too much?

   Yes ____   No ____   Somewhat ____
   Comments:

5. Did you easily understand the speaker in terms of vocabulary, pronunciation, grammar, volume and speed of speech?

   Yes ____   No ____   Somewhat ____
   Comments:

6. Was the presentation well organized, with an introduction, conclusion, and clear flow of ideas?

   Yes ____   No ____   Somewhat ____
   Comments:

7. Did the speaker handle the audience's questions well and give appropriate answers?

   Yes ____   No ____   Somewhat ____
   Comments:

8. What was the best aspect of this speaker's presentation?

9. What could the speaker do to improve his or her teaching or language skills?

Peer Feedback Form for Beginning a Two-Part Presentation

Unit 8: BEGINNING A TWO-PART PRESENTATION

Speaker: _____

Date: _____

Topic: _____

Each speaker has completed a self-assessment of his or her presentation skills. As you listen to the speakers, indicate your perceptions of their skills so that they can compare their self-assessment with your assessment.

Presentation Skill	Good Control	Sufficient Control	Needs Improvement
Organization	_____	_____	_____
Clarity of presentation	_____	_____	_____
Relevance of content	_____	_____	_____
Use of blackboard and visuals	_____	_____	_____
Manner of speaking	_____	_____	_____

Answer the following questions as you listen to each speaker's presentation.

1. Are you clear about what the speaker wants you to learn from the first part of the presentation?

2. Are you clear about what will be covered during the second part of the presentation?

3. What did you like best about this presentation?

4. What is the main thing the speaker should work on for the next presentation?

Peer Feedback Form for Continuing a Two-Part Presentation

Unit 9: CONTINUING A TWO-PART PRESENTATION   Speaker: _____

Date: _____   Topic: _____

Each speaker has completed a self-assessment of his or her interactive skills. As you listen to the speakers, indicate your perceptions of their skills so that they can compare their self-assessment with your assessment.

Interactive Skill	Good Control	Sufficient Control	Needs Improvement
Nonverbal communication	_____	_____	_____
Audience awareness	_____	_____	_____
Interaction	_____	_____	_____
Teacher presence	_____	_____	_____
Aural comprehension	_____	_____	_____
Method of handling questions	_____	_____	_____
Clarity of response to questions	_____	_____	_____

Answer the following questions as you listen to each speaker's presentation.

1. Did the speaker help you remember what was covered in the last presentation?

2. Did the speaker make a clear transition between the review of the previous presentation and this presentation?

3. Did the speaker effectively summarize the key points from both presentations?

4. What did you like best about this presentation?

5. What is the main thing the speaker should work on in the future?

Discussion Evaluation Form
Unit 10

Since the success of a group discussion depends on the contributions of every member, this feedback form will be used to discuss orally how each member feels the group as a whole performed. The questions should be answered after each portion of the discussion, so that the group has three chances to improve its satisfaction with the discussion. At the end of each portion, the leader should take a vote on how many members chose each answer to questions 1 through 8, and write that number in front of the answer. After considering everyone's answers, the group should answer questions 9 and 10 and then continue with the next portion.

1. I felt comfortable expressing my ideas and opinions in this discussion.

    ____ sometimes   ____ always   ____ rarely

2. I learned ____ in this discussion.

    ____ a lot   ____ some   ____ very little

3. The quality of my participation in this discussion was

    ____ very good   ____ average   ____ poor

4. We used the time

    ____ very well   ____ pretty well   ____ poorly

5. The hypothesis discussed was

    ____ very clear   ____ pretty clear   ____ unclear

6. Each question or comment offered got a verbal response from someone in the group

    ____ every time   ____ most of the time   ____ rarely

7. Our comments ____ help(ed) to answer the discussion question.

    ____ significantly   ____ somewhat   ____ did not

8. ____ contributed to the success of this discussion.

    ____ Everyone   ____ Only three members   ____ Only two members

9. The initiator did a(n) ____ job of leading this discussion.

    ____ very good   ____ average   ____ poor

10. The timekeeper did

    ____ very well   ____ only average   ____ poorly

11. The gatekeeper did

    ____ very well   ____ only average   ____ poorly

12. The synthesizer did

    ____ very well   ____ only average   ____ poorly

13. Aspects of our behavior that I think made this discussion successful:

14. Aspects of our behavior that I would like to change in order to make our next discussion more successful:

Appendix II: The ITA Test

Information for ITAs

The ITA Test may be given as a final examination for this course. If so, ITAs will be asked to present five minutes of information for an undergraduate lab, recitation, or lecture in their field and then to answer questions from a panel of instructors on the information they have presented. The members of the panel will be from one or more of the following groups: ITA instructors, representatives from ITAs' departments, university administrators, and/or undergraduate students. Instructors will provide ITAs with one or two pages of field-specific textbook material from which to teach or will guide them in selecting their own material.

If the ITA Test is used for final ITA evaluations, its results will be used in conjunction with the recommendations of instructors to determine whether ITAs should begin teaching and whether they need to take any additional training in English language classroom communication skills. ITAs have been preparing for the ITA Test as they used this textbook throughout the term. If they have done the assigned work, have used English whenever possible outside of class, and have developed their skills for teaching in a U. S. university, they can expect to perform well.

The ITA Test was inspired by Iowa State University's TEACH Test and the Educational Testing Service's SPEAK Test and Test of Spoken English (TSE). The creators of the TEACH Test, Roberta Abraham and Barbara Plakans, and the Educational Testing Service have graciously given permission to use aspects of their tests here. The procedure, scoring scale, and descriptors for this test were developed with the assistance of Karin Smith and other members of the staff of the University of Minnesota TA English Program. The ITA Test makes use of a 300-point scale to allow for comparisons with the TSE or the SPEAK Test, but the creators of the ITA Test do not wish to imply that an individual score on the ITA Test is in any way equivalent to the same individual's score on the TSE or the SPEAK Test.

Information for Instructors

At the close of the term, this textbook recommends evaluating each ITA through the use of the ITA Test. This test is representative of the tasks that ITAs must perform in labs, recitations, and lectures in that it requires ITAs to present information from their field and answer questions about the information. It also reflects the format of the majority of videotaped teaching tasks that ITAs perform while using this textbook.

TEST ADMINISTRATION

A panel should be convened consisting of one or more of the following groups: ITA instructors, departmental faculty, university administrators, or undergraduate students. Individual ITAs should sign up ahead of time for fifteen-minute slots: five minutes for presentation, five minutes to answer questions, and five minutes in which the panel will fill out the score sheet for the test. The group may want to appoint a gatekeeper or traffic manager to welcome ITAs and help them follow the procedures of the test. The gatekeeper may be designated as responsible for questions, to allow other panel members to concentrate on rating the test. Alternatively, if there are undergraduate students participating on the panel, their responsibility may be to ask the questions. Each of the ten-minute tests should be videotaped for review at a later date.

ITA PREPARATION

ITAs should either (a) be given one or two pages of written material specific to their field that is suitable for a five-minute teaching task or (b) be asked to find such material themselves by photocopying a page from a current introductory textbook. Panel members attending the test should be given a copy of what each ITA will teach so they may prepare questions to ask the ITA regarding the material presented.

SCORING

Panel members should review the following scale for scoring the test and then participate in one or more sessions to practice scoring the test using sample videotapes of ITA presentations. The scoring scale contains descriptors that specify the degree to which ITAs are able to control the use of language, teaching, and interactive skills in their presentation and question-answering session. Each ITA should be scored by the same number of panel members. The group may decide not to allow each ITA's instructor to evaluate his or her own student. It is important for panel members not to begin rating from the beginning of each presentation. Instead, taking notes in the margin before selecting a rating for each category allows the panelist to score his or her overall impression rather than only a first impression. Because rating something as subjective as classroom communication skills is difficult, problems of inter- and intra-rater reliability will occur. For this reason, it is important for the raters to work together before the test to agree on exactly how they will interpret the descriptors for the categories of the test and how the scores will be averaged.

NOTE

The scoring rubric for the entire ITA Test (page 173) and the presentation language skills (page 174) have been adapted from SPEAK® materials with permission of Educational Testing Service, the copyright owner.

Test results using an adaptation of an ETS testing instrument should in no way be construed as confirming or denying the validity of the original test on which it was based, or as possessing any validity of the original test. Furthermore, the test scores obtained from an ETS scoring scale used with an adaptation of an ETS scoring rubric cannot be assumed to be equivalent to scores obtained from the original, ETS-developed test and scoring rubric.

ITA RECOMMENDATIONS

Following the test, panel members should meet to review the test scores and determine final recommendations for each ITA regarding future teaching responsibilities and training requirements. The group will determine a passing score or score range for the test. Panel members may also be asked to consider in their final recommendations the ITAs' level of performance during the training program in conjunction with their performance on the test. ITAs taking the test may receive their actual test scores or only recommendations based on the test and on their performance during the training program.

ITA Test Score Sheet

ITA: _____

Rater: _____ Date: _____

I. Presentation Language Skills   Comments

Pronunciation	0 .5 1 1.5 2 2.5 3
Grammar	0 .5 1 1.5 2 2.5 3
Fluency	0 .5 1 1.5 2 2.5 3
Comprehensibility	0 .5 1 1.5 2 2.5 3

TOTAL FOR PRESENTATION LANGUAGE SKILLS _____
(Out of 12)

II. Teaching Skills

Organization of presentation	0 .5 1 1.5 2 2.5 3
Clarity of presentation	0 .5 1 1.5 2 2.5 3
Relevance of content	0 .5 1 1.5 2 2.5 3
Use of blackboard and visuals	0 .5 1 1.5 2 2.5 3
Manner of speaking	0 .5 1 1.5 2 2.5 3
Nonverbal communication	0 .5 1 1.5 2 2.5 3
Audience awareness	0 .5 1 1.5 2 2.5 3
Interaction	0 .5 1 1.5 2 2.5 3
Teacher presence	0 .5 1 1.5 2 2.5 3
Aural comprehension	0 .5 1 1.5 2 2.5 3
Method of handling questions	0 .5 1 1.5 2 2.5 3
Clarity of response to questions	0 .5 1 1.5 2 2.5 3

TOTAL FOR TEACHING SKILLS _____
(Out of 36)

III. Interactive Language Skills

Pronunciation	0 .5 1 1.5 2 2.5 3
Grammar	0 .5 1 1.5 2 2.5 3
Fluency	0 .5 1 1.5 2 2.5 3
Comprehensibility	0 .5 1 1.5 2 2.5 3

TOTAL FOR INTERACTIVE LANGUAGE SKILLS _____
(Out of 12)

IV. Evaluator's Overall Impression

No Teaching Yet Continue training	Office Hours/Tutoring Continue training	Classroom Teaching Continue training	Classroom Teaching No further training
0 1 2 3	4 5 6 7	8 9 10 11	12 13 14 15

TOTAL OVERALL IMPRESSION _____
(Out of 15)

TOTAL RAW SCORE _____ × 4 = **TOTAL SCORE** _____
(Out of 75)   (Out of 300)

ITA Test Descriptors

I. PRESENTATION LANGUAGE SKILLS

Pronunciation

3 - Nativelike stress and intonation patterns. Accurate pronunciation and clear enunciation of individual sounds. Almost always intelligible.

2 - Minor problems with stress and intonation. General accuracy in pronunciation of most individual sounds. Some difficulty with enunciation, but is generally intelligible.

1 - Major problems with stress and intonation. Difficulty with the pronunciation of some individual sounds. Poor enunciation. Occasionally unintelligible.

0 - Nonnative stress and intonation patterns, poor pronunciation of individual sounds, or lack of enunciation cause general unintelligibility.

Grammar

3 - Accurate grammatical form and appropriate use of structures. Occasional errors that might be made by a native speaker.

2 - Occasional difficulty with accurate grammatical form and appropriate use of structures. Minor errors that do not interfere with meaning.

1 - Frequent difficulty with accurate grammatical form and appropriate use of structures. Major errors that sometimes interfere with meaning.

0 - Constant difficulty with accurate grammatical form and appropriate use of structures. Only memorized phrases can be easily understood.

Fluency

3 - Very few nonnative pauses. Smooth and nativelike rhythmic patterns that never interfere with intelligibility.

2 - Some nonnative pauses. Some difficulty with smooth and nativelike rhythmic patterns, which causes occasional interference with intelligibility.

1 - Numerous nonnative pauses. Much difficulty with smooth and native-like rhythmic patterns, which causes frequent interference with intelligibility.

0 - Nonnative pauses and halting rhythm cause constant interference with intelligibility.

Comprehensibility

3 - Completely comprehensible. Only a few errors in pronunciation, grammar, fluency, or vocabulary.

2 - Generally comprehensible. Some errors in pronunciation, grammar, fluency, or vocabulary that occasionally interfere with intelligibility.

1 - Somewhat comprehensible. Major errors in pronunciation, grammar, fluency, or vocabulary that often interfere with intelligibility.

0 - Generally incomprehensible due to very little ability in pronunciation, grammar, fluency, or vocabulary.

II. TEACHING SKILLS

Organization of presentation

3 - Organization appropriate for topic. Logical development and sequencing of ideas effectively convey information. Successful use of transitional devices. Important points are signaled overtly, through repetition, or by pauses. Supplies preview and summary of material presented.

2 - Organization may not be completely appropriate for topic. Logical development and sequencing of ideas may be somewhat loose. Some transitional devices may be missing or ineffectively used. Important points not always signaled. Attempts preview and/or summary of material presented.

1 - Organization inappropriate for topic. Logical development and sequencing of ideas not readily apparent. Few transitional devices. Ineffective signaling of important points. Little or no attempt at preview or summary of material presented.

0 - No organization; ideas confused and disconnected. No transitional devices, and no signaling of important points. No preview or summary.

Clarity of presentation

3 - Stays focused on topic. Appropriate amount of information for the objectives of the presentation and the needs of the audience. Concise yet substantial. Effective use of supporting detail to develop topic.

2 - May occasionally stray from topic. Amount of information may not be completely appropriate for the objectives of the presentation and the needs of the audience. May lack substance or conciseness. Use of supporting detail to develop topic may not be effective.

1 - Often strays from topic. Some information conveyed, but presentation is too brief, too long, or has little substance. Insufficient use of supporting detail.

0 - Rarely focuses on topic. Little information conveyed. No conciseness or substance. No supporting detail.

Relevance of content

3 - Information clearly connected to familiar contexts, personal experiences, or practical examples. Information related to materials previously learned, and clear explanation given of why and how the content is useful.

2 - Information may be inadequately connected to familiar contexts, personal experiences, or practical examples to illustrate the concepts under discussion. Information not always related to material previously learned, and little explanation given of why and how the content is useful.

1 - Information only minimally connected to familiar contexts, personal experiences or practical examples which illustrate the concepts under discussion. Fails to sufficiently relate subject matter to material previously learned and no explanation of why and how the information is useful.

0 - Information not related to contexts familiar to the student. No examples. No reference to material previously learned or to the usefulness of the information.

Use of blackboard and visuals

3 - Well-chosen, well-organized, and easy to read material on board or in visuals. Board work and visuals complement the information in the presentation and are smoothly integrated into it.

2 - Material on board or in visuals generally well-chosen, adequately organized, legible, and integrated into the presentation. Occasional problems with speaking to the blackboard, blocking the students' view of the visuals, illegibility, misspellings, organization of material, or choice of visual content.

1 - Minimal use of the board or visuals to convey information, or visual material is disorganized, illegible, or poorly chosen. Speaking to the blackboard interferes with comprehensibility; or body position makes visual support difficult to see.

0 - No visuals. Their use would enhance presentation.

Manner of speaking

3 - Volume, speed, and tone completely appropriate. Manner of speaking varied as needed to maximize comprehensibility and put audience at ease.

2 - Volume, speed, and tone may not always be appropriate. Volume may be too loud or too soft; speed too rapid or slow. Tone may convey attitudes not intended. Despite problems, manner of speaking does not make audience uncomfortable or detract from the presentation.

1 - Volume, speed, or tone inappropriate for the situation. Volume, speed, or tone make the audience uncomfortable or detract from the presentation.

0 - Volume, speed, or tone completely inappropriate for the presentation and audience.

Nonverbal communication

3 - Nonverbal behavior completely appropriate. Posture, gestures, facial expressions, use of space, and use of non-language sounds coincide with and reinforce verbal communication.

2 - Nonverbal behavior generally appropriate for the situation and does not detract from verbal communication, but minor problems may occur with posture, gestures, facial expressions, use of space, or use of non-language sounds.

1 - Inappropriate nonverbal behavior detracts from verbal communication. Posture may be too rigid or too relaxed. Gestures, facial expressions, or head movements may be unusual or awkward. May stand too near or too far from the audience or move around the room too little or too much. May display nervous movements or use non-language sounds that reflect nervousness.

0 - Extensive occurrence of nonverbal behaviors that are inappropriate for the situation.

Audience awareness

3 - Content, vocabulary, and manner of presentation appropriate for audience. Consistently monitors audience's verbal and nonverbal responses and adjusts presentation accordingly. Good eye contact with audience.

2 - Content, vocabulary, and manner of presentation generally appropriate for audience, but does not always monitor audience verbal and nonverbal responses to make necessary adjustments to presentation. Acceptable eye contact with audience.

1 - Content, vocabulary, or manner of presentation somewhat inappropriate for audience. Little monitoring and minimal adjustment for audience response to presentation. Minimal eye contact with audience.

0 - Content, vocabulary, or manner of presentation are inappropriate for audience. No monitoring of audience verbal and nonverbal response. Virtually no eye contact with audience.

Interaction

3 - Invites interaction and clearly communicates expectations regarding audience participation. Friendly, nonjudgmental response to audience. Encourages questions and provides appropriate feedback.

2 - Attempts to interact with audience but may not clearly communicate expectations of audience participation. Manner may be somewhat unfriendly or judgmental. Encourages questions but may not always provide appropriate feedback.

1 - Limited interaction with audience. Seems somewhat unapproachable and does not clearly communicate expectations regarding audience participation. Difficulty with encouraging questions and providing appropriate feedback .

0 - Behavior discourages interaction. Does not communicate expectations regarding audience participation, and does not provide appropriate feedback to audience responses. Discourages questions.

Teacher presence

3 - Behavior demonstrates confidence, poise, rapport with audience, and ease of performance. Assumes leadership position without authoritarian bearing.

2 - Behavior demonstrates confidence and poise, but may have some difficulty in establishing rapport with the audience or performing effectively. May not assume a leadership position, but behavior does not alienate listeners or detract from presentation.

1 - Behavior occasionally makes audience uncomfortable. May occasionally appear to be nervous, hesitant, overly authoritarian, condescending, or indifferent to audience needs.

0 - Behavior makes audience uncomfortable. Appears to be nervous, lacking in confidence, hostile, unapproachable, or unconcerned about audience needs.

Aural comprehension

3 - Able to understand audience utterances spoken at a natural rate, even when not clearly related to context. May require occasional repetition or clarification, but not extensive adjustments by others.

2 - Able to understand most audience utterances in context. May not immediately understand rapidly spoken or rambling discourse, but uses listening strategies to identify main ideas and clarifies mis-understandings through negotiation with the speaker.

1 - Able to understand sentence level audience utterances when clearly related to context, but comprehension is uneven. Frequently misunderstands and requires others to adjust utterances extensively by repeating, rephrasing, or slowing down. Often unable to clarify misunderstandings through negotiation with the speaker.

0 - Unable to understand sentence level audience utterances even after repetition.

Method of handling questions

3 - Responds quickly. Repeats or rephrases questions when appropriate. Checks for comprehension when appropriate.

2 - May take too long to respond. May not repeat or rephrase questions when appropriate. May not check for comprehension when appropriate.

1 - Takes too long to respond. Does not repeat or rephrase questions. Does not check for comprehension.

0 - Does not respond to questions.

Clarity of response to questions

3 - Always focuses on question and answers it directly. Concise yet substantial. Contains appropriate amount and quality of information.

2 - May occasionally stray from topic of question. May lack substance or conciseness, include an excess amount of information, or approach topic too indirectly.

1 - Responds to question but does not address it adequately. Strays from topic or provides a response that is too brief, has little substance, or is too indirect.

0 - Does not respond to question or response contains little information pertinent to question.

III. INTERACTIVE LANGUAGE SKILLS

Descriptors for all language skills in this section are identical to those for the Pronunciation, Grammar, Fluency, and Comprehensibility of Presentation Language in section I.

IV. OVERALL IMPRESSION

0–3 - No teaching yet; continue training.

4–7 - Office hours or tutoring; continue training.

8–11 - Classroom teaching; continue training.

12–15 - Classroom teaching; no further training.

Appendix III: Field-Specific Materials

BIOLOGY

BIOLOGY VISUALS

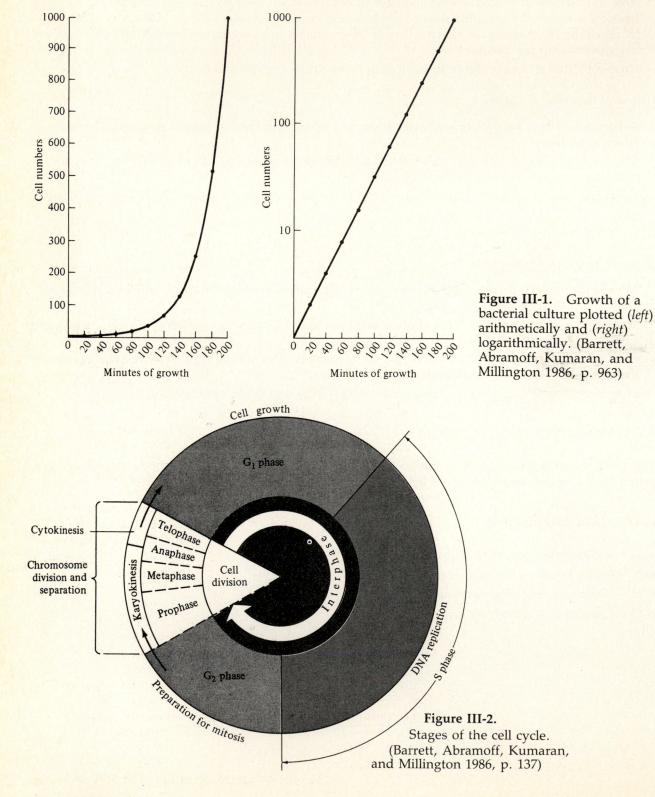

Figure III-1. Growth of a bacterial culture plotted (*left*) arithmetically and (*right*) logarithmically. (Barrett, Abramoff, Kumaran, and Millington 1986, p. 963)

Figure III-2. Stages of the cell cycle. (Barrett, Abramoff, Kumaran, and Millington 1986, p. 137)

BIOLOGY TERMS

active transport
aerobic oxidation
algae
allele
amino acid
anaerobic oxidation
angiosperm
animal behavior
antibody
artery
asexual reproduction
bacteria
biome
blood vessel
brain
cancer
capillary
carbohydrate
cardiac cycle
catabolism
cell division
cell membrane
cell organelles
cellular differentiation
cellular respiration
centriole
chloroplast
chromosome
cilia
coelom
coenzyme
cytokinesis
defense mechanism
digestion
disaccharide
DNA
double helix
ecological succession
ecology
ecosystem
electron microscope
embryo
endocrine gland
endocytosis
endoplasmic reticulum
enzyme
enzyme-substrate
epigenesis
erythrocyte
eukaryotic cell
evolution
excretion
exocytosis
facilitated diffusion

fertility control
fertilization
flagella
food chain
fossil
fungi
gamete
gas exchange
gastrointestinal activity
gene
genotype
germination
glucose
glycolysis
gogli complex
gymnosperm
habituation
heredity
heterotroph
histology
hormonal control
hormonal coordination
immune system
immunodeficiency
imprinting
inheritance
internal clock
invertebrate
ionic regulation
Krebs cycle
latent learning
leaf
leukocyte
lichen
Linnaeus
lipid
lower animals
lymph
lysosome
macrophage
meiosis
membrane permeability
Mendel's laws
metabolism
microfilament
microtubule
mitochondria
mitosis
monera
monosaccharide
muscular contraction
mutation
natural selection
nerve impulse

nervous system
neuron
nucleic acid
nutrition
operant conditioning
organic evolution
organism
osmoregulation
osmosis
oxygen diffusion
parturition
passive transport
peroxisome
phagocytosis
phenotype
phloem
phosphoglyceride
photoperiodism
photosynthesis
phylogenetic tree
phylum
plant
plant cell wall
plasma membrane
plastid
platelet
pollution explosion
polypeptide
polysaccharide
prokaryotic cell
protein
protist
protozoa
ribosome
RNA
root pressure
ruminant
sex determination
sex linkage
sexual reproduction
slime mold
social behavior
species
steriod
striated muscle
symbiosis
taxonomy
vacuole
vascular cambrium
vascular plant
vascular tissue
vertebrate
virus
xylem

(Barrett, Abramoff, Kumaran, and Millington 1986)

BIOLOGY PASSAGES

"One of the great scientific generalizations is that of the cell theory, or cell doctrine, which states that all organisms are composed of microscopic units called cells. Modern biologists view the cell as the unit of life's structure, function, origin, and development. Cells can be regarded as the simplest units of life and, indeed, can survive and multiply for an indefinite period of time apart from the organisms from which they were taken. The same cannot be said of any cell part."

(Barrett, Abramoff, Kumaran, and Millington 1986, p. 33)

"Exceptions to the broadly stated cell theory—according to which all organisms are composed of cells and all cells have a nucleus—have long been recognized. For example, bacteria, while possessing DNA, lack organized nuclei. Should they thus be considered noncellular, or are they composed of one cell? Both alternatives contradict the cell theory. Moreover, some tissues are essentially cells with more than one nucleus. Despite these exceptions, the cell theory remains one of the fundamental unifying biological principles."

(*ibid.*)

BIOLOGY QUESTIONS

1. I've heard that camels don't need water because they get it from biochemical reactions. I was wondering if you could explain how.
2. You said that adding a hydrogen atom is the most common form of reduction. So, is removing a hydrogen atom an oxidation?
3. Could you go over again the reasons why plants produce oxygen and carbohydrates?
4. If plant roots can get water by osmosis, why do they have to get ions from the soil?
5. I always get mitosis and meiosis mixed up. Could you remind me which is which?

(All but number 5 from Barrett, Abramoff, Kumaran, and Millington 1986)

BIOLOGY TOPICS OF GENERAL INTEREST

1. The difference between algae and fungi: common types of algae and fungi we see in our everyday lives.
2. The difference between RNA and DNA: which one is associated with the double helix.
3. Why whales and bats are classified as mammals.
4. The significant ways in which human beings differ from other primates.

BIOLOGY PROBLEM

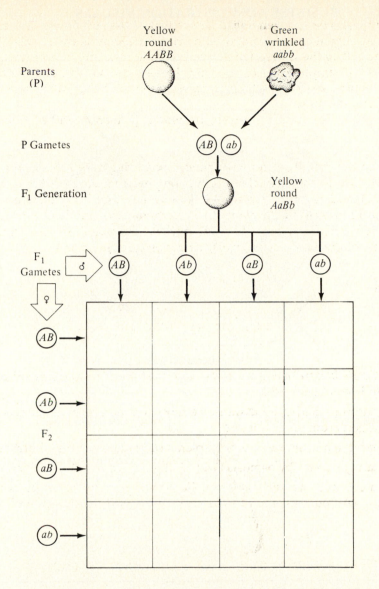

Figure III-3. Fill in the Punnett Square for a dihybrid cross
between pea plants with yellow, round seeds and plants
with green, wrinkled seeds. Round and yellow
are dominant over wrinkled and green, respectively.
(Barrett, Abramoff, Kumaran, and Millington 1986, pp. 601, 603)

BUSINESS ADMINISTRATION VISUALS

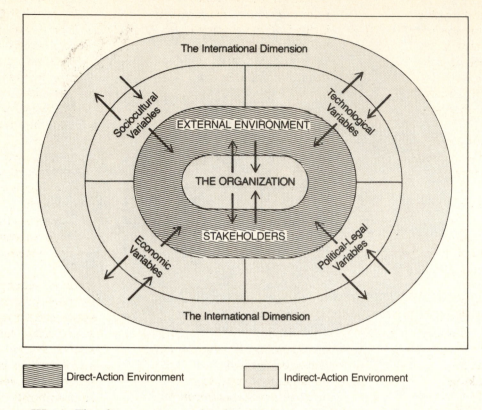

Figure III-4. The direct-action and indirect-action environments of an organization. (Stoner and Freeman 1989, p. 84)

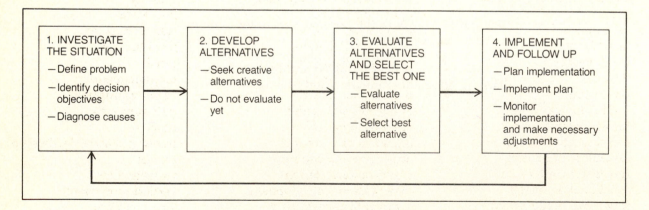

Figure III-5. The rational problem-solving process. (Stoner and Freeman 1989, p. 166)

BUSINESS ADMINISTRATION TERMS

affirmative action
annual objectives
arbitration
behavior modification
break-even analysis
budgetary control
budgeting process
bureaucracy
business-unit strategy
capacity planning
case study
change agent
charismatic leadership
collective bargaining
committee
communication barrier
company
competitive edge
conflict-reduction method
conflict-stimulation method
control process
control system
coordination mechanism
coping skills training
corporation
decentralization
decision making
delegation
demotion
discipline
division of work
downsizing
dysfunctional conflict
entrepreneurship
environmental analysis
environmental constraint
ethics
executive
financial control
fixed budget
flextime
forecasting
formal authority
formal organization
franchising
functional authority
functional conflict
functional manager
functional organization
functional strategy
general manager
goal formulation
grapevine chain

group norms
heuristic principles
human resource audit
human resource management
individual development
industry analysis
information system
informational role
innovation
innovative leadership
institutionalizing strategy
internal constraint
international management
interpersonal role
job description
job design
job enrichment
job satisfaction
job specialization
key-performance area
lateral relationship
leadership
level of strategy
line authority
management development
management level
management process
management-labor conflict
manager selection
managerial responsibility
managerial role
managing conflict
matrix organization
motivation
multinational enterprise
nonprogrammed decision
operating budget
operational control
operational planning
operationalizing strategy
opportunity finding
organization chart
organizational career
organizational change
organizational conflict
organizational culture
organizational design
organizational development
organizational structure
performance appraisal
plant closure
portfolio framework

position description
post-action control
pre-action control
problem solving
problem-finding process
process consultation
product manager
product/market organization
productivity
productivity management
programmed decision
promotion
qualitative forecasting
radial movement
rational decision making
recruitment
resistance to change
resource analysis
reward system
risk
scientific management
selection process
self-managed work groups
semivariable costs
single-use plan
social responsibility
source of power
staff authority
stakeholders
standing plan
strategic formulation
strategic partnership
strategic planning
strategic-control point
strategy implementation
synergy
task force
task-technology
team building
threat
top management
training program
trait approach
transfer
transformational leadership
trustee
variable costs
vertical movement
vice-president
whistleblowing
work behavior
work-flow layout

(Stoner and Freeman 1989)

BUSINESS ADMINISTRATION PASSAGES

"As a company grows, the number of work units and subunits increases, and layers of supervision are added. Managers and subordinates alike become further removed from the eventual results of their actions. They need a clear understanding of how their activities fit into the larger picture of what the organization is and does. Most organizational structures are too complex to be conveyed verbally. To show the organization's structure, managers customarily draw up an organization chart, which diagrams the functions, departments, or positions of the organization and shows how they are related. The separate units of the organization usually appear in boxes, which are connected to each other by solid lines that indicate the chain of command and official channels of communication."

(Stoner and Freeman 1989, p. 265)

"Not every organization welcomes such charts. For example, Robert Townsend, the former president of Avis, suggested that organization charts are demoralizing, because they reinforce the idea that all authority and ability rest at the top of the organization. Most organizations, however, do develop these charts and find them helpful in defining managerial authority, responsibility, and accountability."

(*ibid.*)

BUSINESS ADMINISTRATION QUESTIONS

1. I didn't quite get what you said about the major factor for the current success of Japanese and Korean multinationals.
2. Could you go over the criteria a manager would use to decide on individual versus group problem-solving?
3. I was wondering if you could talk about what each major type of financial statement has before the test.
4. The book says job design is the "structure of individual jobs." What does *structure* mean here?
5. I don't get exactly how entrepreneurship creates economic growth and change. Could you explain it again?

(all from Stoner and Freeman 1989)

BUSINESS ADMINISTRATION TOPICS OF GENERAL INTEREST

1. How we can motivate workers, such as government employees or professors with tenure, who have a high level of job security.
2. What quality circles are and what their effect is on plant productivity.
3. What kinds of employer approaches can minimize employee burnout.
4. The best way to make decisions in the face of uncertainty.

(all from Stoner and Freeman 1989)

BUSINESS ADMINISTRATION PROBLEM

Case Study: The Use and Abuse of Joyce Roberts

Joyce Roberts, 29 years old, was a middle-level manager at Amalgamated Products Inc. (API). For the last nine months, she had been on special assignment to a key marketing-staff function at corporate headquarters, working directly with the Marketing Vice-President, Bernard Peach, even though there were two levels of management between them. Peach had come to Roberts' boss and told her not to give her any other assignments—that Roberts was to work directly for Peach. In order to communicate more closely, Peach had Roberts install a high-tech phone system in her office and gave Roberts access to an executive secretary.

API was a staid company, facing a number of changes in its external environment. It was highly centralized, and a number of key managers complained that the company was overly bureaucratic. Many older managers, like Roberts' boss (and her bosses' boss) were looked upon as "dead wood" incapable of operating in the new environment. Nevertheless, change was normally a slow process at API, and on a number of matters Roberts found herself in direct conflict with her boss even though she was acting on Peach's direct orders. She was unsure how much resentment was building up beneath the surface, but she found working directly with Peach, occasionally mentioned as a future CEO, exhilarating—even if she was frustrated by being caught in the middle of larger bureaucratic struggles.

Peach and Roberts worked together closely on a high-profile revamping of API's products, and by all measures the project promised to be quite successful. Two days before the presentation to API's Executive Committee, Peach dispatched Roberts to the resort where the meeting was to be held in order to double- and triple-check all of the arrangements. When Peach arrived, he called Roberts' room at 3 A.M. and together they checked the slide projector to be sure that the tops of the slides were straight when projected.

After the presentation, the committee adopted most of the recommendations, and two days later Bernard Peach was promoted to Group Vice-President—Asia. Joyce Roberts went into her office to find two memos on her desk. The first was the announcement that Bernard Peach had been promoted and had already left for his new job. The second was a handwritten note from her boss to talk about her performance problems over the last six months. Roberts wondered what she should do.

Source: This case was prepared by R. Edward Freeman, Olsson Professor of Business Administration, The Darden School, University of Virginia. It is based on an actual situation, but all names and some facts are disguised.

Case Questions:
1. What are the sources and uses of power in this case?
2. What problems does Joyce Roberts now have?
3. What advice would you give Roberts?

(Case study and questions from Stoner and Freeman 1989, p. 325)

CHEMISTRY VISUALS

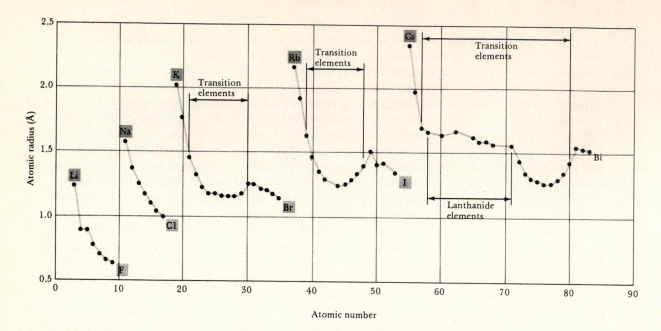

Figure III-6. Atomic radii versus atomic number. The noble gases are not included in this graph because there is no simple way of relating their radii to those of the other elements on the basis of solid-state structure determinations. Gaps in the graph are due to lack of experimental data. (Brown and LeMay 1988, p. 207)

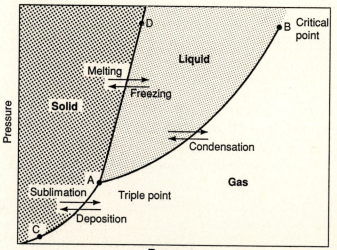

Figure III-7. General shape for a phase diagram of a system exhibiting three phases: gas, liquid, and solid. (adapted from Brown and LeMay 1988, p. 371)

CHEMISTRY TERMS

activation energy
alcohol
aldehyde
alkali metal
alkane / alkene / alkyne
allotrope
aluminum
amide / amine
amorphous solid
amphoterism
aqueous solution
atomic mass
atomic number
balanced equation
binary oxide
boiling point
bomb calorimetry
bond energy
bond polarity
bonding molecular orbital
buffer solution
carbon dioxide
carboxylic acid
catalysis
catalyst
chromium
colligative property
colloid
combustion analysis
compound
concentration
conjugate acid
conjugate base
continuous spectrum
copper
corrosion
covalent bonding
critical temperature
desalinization
dialysis
diatomic molecule
diffusion
dilution
dipole moment
direction of reaction
dissolution
double bond
dynamic equilibrium
effusion
electrode potential
electrolysis
electrolyte solution
electron configuration
electron shell

electron spin
electronegativity
element
elementary reaction
endothermic process
enthalpy
entropy
equilibrium concentration
equivalence point
ester
ether
exothermic process
first order reaction
formula weight
free-energy function
freezing-point depression
gas density
halide
halogen
heat capacity
heat of formation
heat of reaction
heterogeneous catalysis
homogeneous catalysis
hybrid orbital
hydrogen bonding
hydrolysis
hydrophobic
hydrophylic
ideal gas
inorganic compound
internal energy change
ionic bond
ionization energy
iron
isotope
joule
ketone
kinetic-molecular theory
law of conservation of mass
limiting reactant
line spectrum
magnetic quantum number
manometer
mass number
mass spectrometer
meniscus
metalloid
metal oxide
metathesis reaction
mixture
molality
molarity
mole fraction

molecular geometry
molecular weight
multiple bond
net ionic equation
neutralization
nickel
nitric acid
nitrogen
nonbonding electron
normal melting point
nucleic acid
octet rule
organic compound
orbital overlap
osmosis
oxidant
oxidation number
oxidation-reduction reaction
oxidizing agent
oxygen
ozone
periodic table
pH scale
phase diagram
photodissociation
photoelectric effect
photoionization
polar covalent bond
polymer
polyprotic acid
precipitation
protein
proton
quantum theory
radiant energy
reaction
reducing agent
second-order reaction
silicon
single displacement reaction
solubility
solution stoichiometry
specific heat
spectrum
substrate
sulfurous acid
surface tension
thermal conductivity
titration
triple bond
valence electron
vapor pressure
vaporization
viscosity

(Brown and LeMay 1988)

CHEMISTRY PASSAGES

"Every substance has a unique set of properties, or characteristics, that allow us to recognize it and to distinguish it from other substances. Properties of matter can be grouped into two categories: physical and chemical. Physical properties are those properties that we can measure without changing the basic identity of the substance. Physical properties include color, hardness, density, melting point, and boiling point. Chemical properties describe the way a substance may change or 'react' to form other substances. A common chemical property of iron is its ability to combine with oxygen in the presence of water to form a red-brown substance that we call rust (an oxide of iron)."

(Brown and LeMay 1988, p. 4)

"Matter can undergo changes of two basic types: physical changes and chemical changes. Physical changes are processes in which a material changes its physical appearance but not its basic identity. The evaporation of water is a physical change. When water evaporates, it changes from the liquid state to the gas state, but it is still water; it has not changed into any other substance. All changes of state are physical changes. In chemical changes, also called chemical reactions, substances change not only in physical appearance but also in basic identity; that is, one substance is converted into another. For example, hydrogen burning in air undergoes a chemical change in which it is converted to water."

(*ibid.*, pp. 4–5)

CHEMISTRY QUESTIONS

1. I don't get the difference between a reactant and a reagent. Could you explain it again?
2. How can you separate substances when their boiling points are less than 30 degrees apart?
3. When I buy shampoo in the store sometimes I see a pH value on the bottle. Could you go over again what PH value is and explain how people can choose which pH value is best for their hair?
4. I'd like to know what the phase rule is and how it's used to figure out the number of degrees of freedom.
5. I don't really understand why human blood is a buffer solution.*

CHEMISTRY TOPICS OF GENERAL INTEREST

1. Why salt causes snow to melt and cars to rust.
2. Why acid rain is such a danger to living creatures in lakes and rivers.
3. Some people think hot water freezes faster than cold water. Is this true? Why or why not?
4. Why ethyl alcohol is drinkable and methyl alcohol is poisonous.

*from Brown and LeMay 1988

CHEMISTRY PROBLEM

Sample Exercise

Calculate the molarity of a solution made by dissolving 23.4 g of sodium sulfate (Na_2SO_4) in enough water to form 125 mL of solution.

Solution to Sample Exercise

$$Molarity = \frac{moles\ Na_2SO_4}{liters\ soln}$$

$$Moles\ Na_2SO_4 = (23.4\ g\ Na_2SO_4) \left(\frac{1\ mol\ Na_2SO_4}{142\ g\ Na_2SO_4} \right) = 0.165\ mol\ Na_2SO_4$$

$$Liters\ soln = (125\ mL) \left(\frac{1\ L}{1000\ mL} \right) = 0.125\ L$$

$$Molarity = \frac{0.165\ mol\ Na_2SO_4}{0.125\ L\ soln} = 1.32\ \frac{mol\ Na_2SO_4}{L\ soln} = 1.32\ M$$

Problem:

Calculate the molarity of a solution made by dissolving 5.00 g of $C_6H_{12}O_6$ (MW = 180 amu) in sufficient water to form 100 mL of solution.

(Brown and LeMay 1988, p. 87)

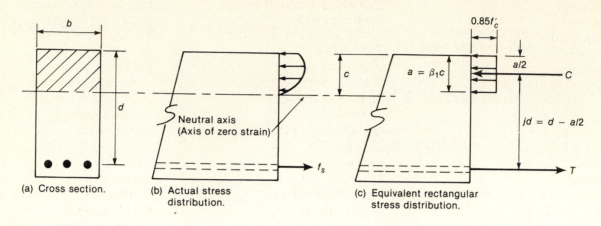
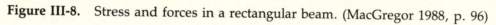

Figure III-8. Stress and forces in a rectangular beam. (MacGregor 1988, p. 96)

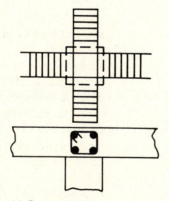

(a) Beam stirrups.

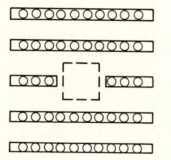

(c) Bar and stud stirrups.

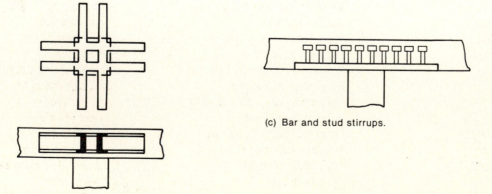

(b) Shear heads.

Figure III-9. Shear reinforcement in slabs. (MacGregor 1988, p. 502)

allowable stress design
alternate design procedure
anchorage
arch action
axial load
axially loaded column
axle steel
B-region
balanced reinforcement
balanced steel ratio
bar anchorage
bar cut-off point
beam-column joint
bearing
bending
bent-up bars
biaxial bending
bond strength
bond stress cracking
braced frame
bracket
buckling load
building code
bundled bar
camber
capacity reduction factor
carry-over factor
cement
centroid
clear span length
coefficient of friction
column capital
column-footing joint
compression failure
compressive strength
compressive stress block
continuous beam
continuous frame
crack width
cracking moment
creep coefficient
curing temperature
cylinder strength
D-region
deep beam
deflection
detailing
discontinuity region
double curvature
doubly reinforced
dowel
ductility
durability
eccentricity of load

effective depth
effective flange width
effective length of column
effective moment of inertia
elastic analysis
elastic definition equation
elastic stress field
embedment length
equivalent frame method
Euler buckling load
factored load
factored resistance
fan yield line
fatigue
flange
flexural bond stress
flexural stiffness
flexure
footing
girder
gross section
hanger reinforcement
heat of hydration
hinge
hook
hoop
horizontal earthquake force
horizontal shear transfer
imposed deformation
inclined crack
inflection point
influence area
interaction diagram
joint
joist
L-shaped section
lap slice
limit states design
live load
load deflection behavior
load transfer
microcrack
modular ratio
modulus of elasticity
modulus of rupture
moment curvature diagram
moment of inertia
moment redistribution
neutral axis depth
nominal strength
one-way slab
overreinforced section
P-delta effect

pattern loadings
pile-cap
plastic centroid
plasticity truss model
point of inflexion
progressive collapse
pull-out test
punching shear
radius of gyration
reinforced concrete
reinforcing bar
service load
shear crack
shear force
shear stress
shrinkage
simple support
single curvature
soil pressure
spacing
spandrel
spiral pitch
spiral reinforcement ratio
splice
spread footing
standard bend point
steel yield
stirrup
strain compatibility solution
strain distribution
strength reduction factor
stress block
stress-strain curve
strip footing
T beam
tapered beam
tensile strength
tension failure
thermal expansion
tie spacing
tied column
tolerance
torsion
transformed section
triaxial strength
truss model
two-way slab
ultimate strain
unbraced frame
underreinforced section
waffle slab
working stress design
yield line analysis

(MacGregor 1988)

CIVIL ENGINEERING PASSAGES

"Loads may be described by their variability with respect to time and location. A permanent load remains roughly constant once the structure is completed. Examples are the self-weight of the structure, and soil pressure against foundations. Variable loads such as occupancy loads and wind loads change from time to time. Variable loads may be sustained loads of long duration, such as the weight of filing cabinets in an office, or loads of short duration, such as the weight of people in the same office. Creep deformations of concrete structures result from the permanent loads and the sustained portion of the variable loads. A third category is accidental loads, which include vehicular collisions, and explosions."

(MacGregor 1988, p. 27)

"Loads are frequently classed as static loads if they do not cause any appreciable acceleration or vibration of the structure or structural elements, and as dynamic loads if they do. Small accelerations are often taken into account by increasing the specified static loads to account for the increase in stresses due to such accelerations and vibrations. Larger accelerations such as those that might occur in highway bridges, crane rails, or elevator supports are accounted for by multiplying the live load by impact factors. In some cases, dynamic analyses are used to compute the maximum forces."

(*ibid.*)

CIVIL ENGINEERING QUESTIONS

1. I'm still not sure I get how the ratio of water to cement is related to the strength of concrete. Does it have something to do with porosity?
2. Could you go over some of the reasons for using compression reinforcement in beams?
3. How do you tell a flexural crack from a shear crack? Could you give us some more examples?
4. How come the ACI Code has requirements for minimum bar spacing?
5. Which of the factors you mentioned the other day are the most important in affecting the shrinkage of concrete?

(all from MacGregor 1988)

CIVIL ENGINEERING TOPICS OF GENERAL INTEREST

1. What factors can cause bridges to collapse.
2. How highways are banked to create better driving conditions.
3. The types of construction that cause soil erosion and the types of construction that can help prevent it.
4. How buildings in earthquake-prone areas should be constructed.

CIVIL ENGINEERING PROBLEM

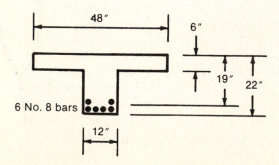

Figure III-10. Analysis of moment capacity based on strain compatibility: compute ϕM_n For the beam shown in the figure. Use $f'_c = 3750$ psi and $f_y = 60,000$ psi. (MacGregor 1988, p. 166)

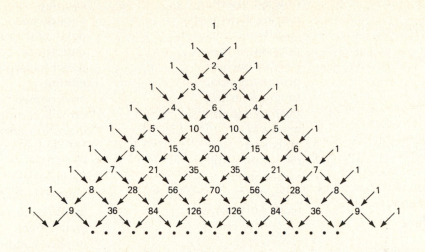

Figure III-11. The top of Pascal's triangle of binomial coefficients.
(Kruse 1989, p. 407)

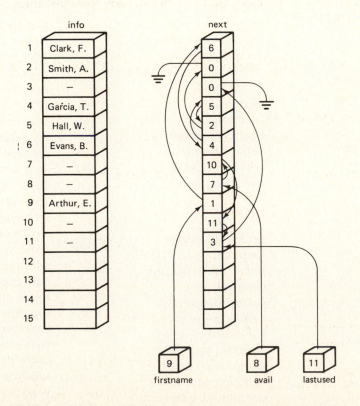

Figure III-12. The array and stack of available space.
(Kruse 1989, p. 275)

COMPUTER SCIENCE TERMS

Pascal

algorithm
algorithm development
array
array implementation
arrays of arrays
average-case analysis
backtracking
big Oh notation
binary search
binary search tree
binary trees
breadth-first algorithm
chaining
circular queue
coding
collision resolution
concurrency
contiguous implementation
contiguous insertion sort
contiguous storage
data abstraction
data structure
data type
debugging
declaration
depth-first algorithm
divide and conquer sorting
documentation
doubly linked list
driver
dynamic memory allocation
Eight-Queens Puzzle
factorials
fibonacci numbers
file window
format
graph traversal
hash function
heapsort
hierarchical records
information hiding
inverted table
iteration
jagged table
linked implementation
linked lists
linked queues
linked stacks
lower bounds
main program
mergesort
minimax method

multidimensional array
one-dimensional analysis
open addressing
ordered insertion
parsing statements
partitioning
popping entries
priority queues
processing nodes
program testing
pushing entries
quicksort
radix sort
re-entrant program
recursion
refinement
rectangular array
sequential search
shell sort
simple operation
simulation
sparse table
specifications
stack
storage area
string operation
stubs
text editor
text file
topological sorting
Towers of Hanoi
tree-structured programs
treesearch
treesort
triangular table
type declaration
variant records
window operation
with statement

COBOL

arithmetic verbs
assumed decimal point
binary table lookup
class test
COBOL notation
coding form
cohesion
collating sequence
compilation error
completeness check
compound test
condition name tests

consistency check
copy statement
corresponding option
coupling
data division
data-validation program
date check
direct lookup
editing
environment division
error detection
execution error
file section
flowchart
hard coding
hierarchy chart
identification division
if statement
implied conditions
indexes
input-loaded table
level numbers
microcomputer
nested *ifs*
next sentence
numeric test
occurs clause
operators
performing sections
picture clause
program maintenance
pseudocode
reasonableness check
report writer
sequence check
sequential file maintenance
sequential table lookup
sign test
size error option
span of control
stepwise refinement
stop run
structured design
subprogram
subscript
times option
top-down development
two-level break program
two-level table
usage clause
value clause
working-storage section
Yourdon structure chart

(Kruse 1989 and Grauer 1985)

COMPUTER SCIENCE PASSAGES

"In computer programs designed to be used by many people, the procedures performing input and output are often the longest. Input to the program must be fully checked to be certain that it is valid and consistent. Errors in input must be processed in ways to avoid catastrophic failure or production of ridiculous results. The goal, often unattainable, is *fail-safe* programs, that is, programs that will not fail no matter what input they receive. The procedures for input from the user should be designed to be as forgiving as possible, since people make many mistakes. For many applications, the input should be echoed back and the user given a chance to correct any errors before processing proceeds."

(Kruse 1989, p. 52)

"After all the subprograms have been assembled into a complete program, it is time to check out the completed whole. One of the most effective ways to uncover hidden defects is called a *structured walkthrough.* In this activity, the programmer shows the completed program to another programmer, or a small group of programmers, and explains exactly what happens, beginning with an explanation of the main program followed by the subprograms, one by one. Structured walkthroughs are helpful for three reasons. First, programmers who are not familiar with the actual code can often spot bugs or conceptual errors that the original programmer overlooked. Second, the questions that other people ask can help you to clarify your own thinking and discover your own mistakes. Third, the structured walkthrough often suggests tests that prove useful in later stages of software production."

(*ibid.*, p. 60)

COMPUTER SCIENCE QUESTIONS

1. Could you talk about the basic order of steps a programmer goes through in trouble-shooting a program?
2. How do computer languages differ, for example, COBOL and FORTRAN? How does a person know which language to use for a certain situation?
3. I have a question about AI. Suppose we have a computer that can understand Korean literature and history, better than any human being. Can we say the computer has intelligence?
4. If you're computing the weekly pay for a factory worker who will get time and a half only if he works more than 40 hours, how can you program the computer to do this?
5. Why is it important to know whether or not a graph has a Eulerian Walk, and how do you know if it has one or not?

COMPUTER SCIENCE TOPICS OF GENERAL INTEREST

1. What artificial intelligence (AI) means and the current problems AI scientists are working on.
2. How computers make decisions.
3. How personal computers differ from mainframe computers.
4. The function of a microchip in a computer.

In the nineteenth century, a game called the **Towers of Hanoi** appeared in Europe, together with promotional material (undoubtedly apocryphal) explaining that the game represented a task underway in the Temple of Brahma. At the creation of the world, the priests were given a brass platform on which were 3 diamond needles. On the first needle were stacked 64 golden disks, each one slightly smaller than the one under it. (The less exotic version sold in Europe had 8 cardboard disks and 3 wooden posts.) The priests were assigned the task of moving all the golden disks from the first needle to the third, subject to the conditions that only one disk can be moved at a time, and that no disk is ever allowed to be placed on top of a smaller disk. The priests were told that when they had finished moving the 64 disks, it would signify the end of the world. Our task is to write a computer program that will type out a list of instructions for the priests. We can summarize our task by the instruction

     Move (64, 1, 3, 2)

which means

   Move 64 disks from needle 1 to needle 3 using needle 2 as temporary storage.

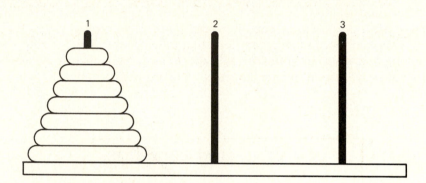

Figure III-13.   The Towers of Hanoi.

(Kruse 1989, p. 350)

ECONOMICS VISUALS

	Number of firms	Products differentiated or homogeneous	Price a decision variable	Free entry	Distinguished by	Examples
Perfect competition	Many	Homogeneous	No	Yes	Price competition only	Wheat farmer Textile firm
Monopoly	One	A single, unique product	Yes	No	Still constrained by market demand	Public utility Beer in Taiwan
Monopolistic competition	Many	Differentiated	Yes, but limited	Yes	Price and quality competition	Restaurants Hand soap
Oligopoly	Few	Either	Yes	Limited	Strategic behavior	Automobiles Aluminum

Figure III-14. Characteristics of different market organizations.
(Case and Fair 1989, p. 54)

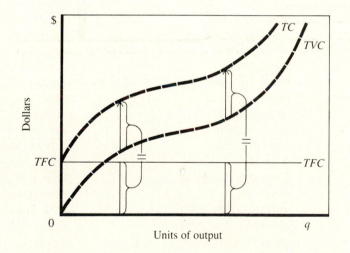

Figure III-15. Total cost equals fixed cost plus variable cost.
(Case and Fair 1989, p. 192)

ECONOMICS TERMS

accounting
advertising
allocation of resources
allocative process
antitrust laws
asset value
balance of payments
balance sheet
book value
borrowing
budget constraints
business cycle
capital
capital accumulation
capital markets
choice
collusion
comparative advantage
competition
competitive equilibrium
competitive input markets
competitive output decisions
competitive supply
constant returns to scale
constrained choice
consumer
consumer choice
consumer loss
consumer surplus
consumption
consumption demand
contraction of firms
cost
decision variable
decision-making unit
decreasing returns to scale
demand
demand curve
depreciation
depression
developing nations
diminishing marginal utility
discounting
downward-sloping demand
economic growth
economic region
economic systems
economic value
efficiency of competition
elasticity
equilibrium
excess demand
excess supply
exchange rates

excise tax
expansion of firms
factor demand curve
Federal Reserve
firm
firm behavior
fiscal policy
fixed costs
forecasting
foreign exchange
future income
general equilibrium
GNP
household
household behavior
imperfect competition
imperfect markets
income distribution
income statement
income tax
increasing returns to scale
indifference curve
inflation
input market
interest
interest rate
international economy
international trade
investment
labor income
labor markets
labor supply
labor supply curve
land markets
leisure
long-run decisions
loss
macroeconomics
marginal cost curve
marginal revenue
market
market constraints
market failure
maximizing profit
microeconomics
monetarism
money market
money supply
monopolistic competition
monopoly
monopsony
natural monopoly
normative economics
oligopoly

open economy
opportunity cost
output
output market
past income
perfect competition
positive economics
poverty
present value
price
price elasticity of demand
price rationing
private sector
production functions
production technology
profit
profit equation
profit-making firms
property income
public finance
public goods
public policy
public sector
quantity
recession
redistribution
regulation
rent
rent-seeking behavior
salaries
sales
saving
scarcity
shift of demand
shift of supply
short-run decisions
short-run costs
stock market
substitution effects
supply
supply curve
supply-side economics
tariffs
taxation
total costs
total revenue
unemployment
unemployment rate
unions
variable costs
variable factor of production
venture capital
wage change
wages

(Case and Fair 1989)

ECONOMICS PASSAGES

"What happens in an economy is the outcome of thousands of individual decisions. Households must decide how to divide up their incomes over all the goods and services available in the marketplace. Individuals must decide whether to work or not to work, whether to go to school, and how much to save. Businesses must decide what to produce, how much to produce, how much to charge and where to locate. It is not surprising that economic analysis focuses on the process of decision making."

(Case and Fair 1989, p. 4)

"Nearly all decisions involve trade-offs: there are advantages and disadvantages, costs and benefits, associated with every action and every choice. A key concept that recurs again and again in analyzing the decision-making process is the notion of opportunity cost. The full 'cost' of making a specific choice includes what we give up by not making the alternative choice. That which we forgo when we make a choice or a decision is called the opportunity cost of that decision."

(*ibid.*)

ECONOMICS QUESTIONS

1. Would you mind going over again how you determine the equilibrium price if you know the demand and supply schedule for a particular product?

2. A few weeks ago you discussed changes in supply and demand under conditions of perfect competition. What happens if there's a monopoly?

3. I'm still not sure I completely understand the concept of profit maximization. Could you calculate the profit maximization for a firm with a certain number of workers?

4. I read in the paper that the English get twice as many bushels of wheat per acre as do we Americans, but we get twice as many bushels per worker as the English do. Does this have something to do with the Product Transformation Curve?

5. Could you explain the difference between diminishing marginal returns and decreasing returns to scale? I know that they're different, but I don't quite get how.

ECONOMICS TOPICS OF GENERAL INTEREST

1. The strongest currency on the world market and why.

2. How economic conditions differ in developing countries from those in developed countries.

3. Economic principles individuals can apply to their daily lives.

4. How the principles of supply and demand affect the price and availability of new cars on the market today.

ECONOMICS PROBLEM

Figure III-16. Assume that widgets can be produced using two different techniques, A and B. The table to the right provides data on the total input requirement of each at four different output levels.

	Q = 1		Q = 2		Q = 3		Q = 4	
	K	L	K	L	K	L	K	L
A	5	2	8	4	11	5	15	5
B	3	3	6	5	8	7	11	10

a. If labor is $2.00 per unit and capital is $3.00 per unit, which is the minimum cost of producing one widget? Two widgets? Three widgets? Four widgets?

b. Graph cost of production as a function of output. (Put output on the X axis and cost on the Y axis.)

c. How much did it cost to go from an output of one to an output of two? To go from an output of two to three? From three to four?

(Case and Fair 1989, p. 180)

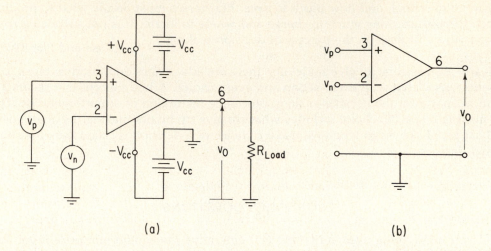

(a)   (b)

Figure III-17. Schematic diagram of the op-amp: (a) model showing supply
voltages and signal inputs with connection to ground reference;
(b) commonly used simplified symbol for modeling the op-amp.
(Del Toro 1986, p. 50)

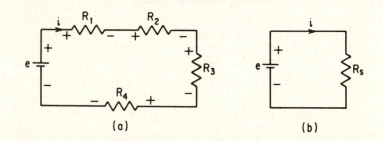

(a)   (b)

Figure III-18. Resistances in series: (a) original configuration;
(b) equivalent circuit. (Del Toro 1986, p. 73)

ELECTRICAL ENGINEERING TERMS

accelerometer
accumulator
actuator
adder
Ampere's law
amplitude demodulation
amplitude detection
asynchronous circuit
average power
balanced three-phase circuit
binary logic
block diagram
bode diagram
Boltzmann relation
Boolean algebra
breakpoint frequency
capacitance
capacitance parameter
circuit analysis
circuit differential equation
circuit element
closed-loop control
combinational logic circuit
complete response
complex impedance
conduction property
control instructions
controlled source
controller
conversion factor
Coulomb's law
D-C generator analysis
D-C motor analysis
decibel
decoder
demultiplexer
dependent source
differential operator
diffusion current
digital logic gate
digital system
diode detector
drive amplifier
dynamic response
eddy-current loss
electric circuit
electromagnetic induction
electromagnetic torque
emitter-coupled logic
emitter-follower amplifier
encoder
equivalent circuit
error-rate control
Faraday's law

feedback control system
ferromagnetic material
first order circuit
flip-flop
flux density
forced solution
forcing function
Fourier series
frequency response
ground reference
half-stepping
half-wave rectifier
hysteresis
hysteretic angle
impulse response
independent current source
independent voltage source
induced voltages
inductance
inductance parameter
instantaneous power
insulated-gate FET
integral error control
integrated circuit
Karnaugh map
Kirchhoff's laws
Laplace transform
linear equivalent circuit
logic gate
magnetic circuit
magnetic force
magnetic quantity
magnetism
magnetization curve
mathematical transform
mesh current
microprocessor
multiplexer
mutual inductance
network analysis
network reduction
no-load test
node-pair voltage
Ohm's law
open-loop control
operation instructions
operational amplifier
operational impedance
output-rate control
parallel combination
partial-fraction expansion
periodic function
permeability
permittivity

phasor diagram
phasor representation
potential energy barrier
power factor
power-factor control
random access memory
RC circuit
read only memory units
required switching sequence
relay
reluctance force
resistance
resistance parameter
resonance
revolving magnetic field
right-hand rule
RL circuit
RLC circuit
rotating field
second-order circuit
semiconductor
semiconductor diode
semiconductor triode
series
series-parallel circuit
servomechanism
sign sensitivity
silicon-controlled rectifier
single-phase motor
sinusoidal function
sinusoidal input
starter
steady-state response
step response
stepper motor
subtractor
synchronous generator
synchronous motor
tachometer generator
three-phase induction motor
three-phase voltage system
thyristor drive
torque-speed characteristic
transfer instructions
transformer
transient solution
transistor
transistor amplifier
translator logic
undamped response
unit-impulse function
valence electron
voltage regulation
voltage source

(Del Toro 1986)

ELECTRICAL ENGINEERING PASSAGES

"Very often in circuit analysis it is necessary to deal with several elements in a closed-loop circuit which exhibit the property of dissipating heat. In the powerline circuits which supply electrical energy to homes and commercial establishments, for example, several resistive elements are frequently combined to carry the same current. Thus in a circuit which supplies electrical power to a lamp, three resistances are found: the internal resistance of the distribution transformer located beneath the street, the lamp resistance, and the resistance of the wires used to conduct the electrical power to the lamp. Similarly, radio and television circuits as well as industrial electronic circuitry employ series combinations of various resistors to achieve specific desirable objectives. To analyze such circuits properly we must know how to treat resistances in series."

(Del Toro 1986, p. 73)

"All current-carrying conductors and resistors involve a heat loss which occurs at a rate given by I^2R. At first this heat is stored in the body of the material, thereby bringing about a temperature rise. As soon as the body temperature exceeds the ambient temperature, however, heat is transferred to the surrounding medium. Eventually a point is reached where the heat is transferred at the same rate that it is produced. Consequently, heat ceases to be stored in the material, and temperature no longer rises. The ability of a resistor to transfer heat necessarily depends on the area exposed to the surrounding medium. If the power-dissipating capability of a resistor or rheostat is inadequate for a specified rating it can easily burn out."

(*ibid.*, p. 34)

ELECTRICAL ENGINEERING QUESTIONS

1. I've been wondering about how and why TV antennas influence the clarity of a TV picture. Could you explain it?
2. I have a question about adding resistors—if you add two resistors together, each having resistance R1, what is the resulting resistance?
3. Could you talk about under what conditions you should use series circuits, parallel circuits or a combination of the two?
4. Could you describe what kinds of materials are used to make semiconductors?
5. Is the resistance at the input terminals of an idealized op-amp really infinite?*

ELECTRICAL ENGINEERING TOPICS OF GENERAL INTEREST

1. Why compact disk players are superior to LP record players.
2. How computers use electronic components to process information.
3. How speakers turn electronic signals into sound waves.
4. How a light bulb works.

ELECTRICAL ENGINEERING PROBLEM

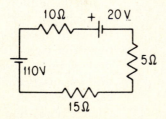

Figure III-19. For the circuit shown in the figure, find the current that flows and the potential difference across each resistor. (Del Toro 1986, p. 21)

*from Del Toro 1986

INDUSTRIAL ENGINEERING

INDUSTRIAL ENGINEERING VISUALS

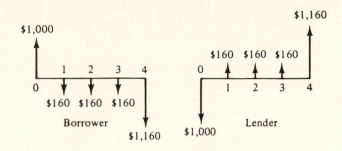

Figure III-20. Cash flow diagrams.
(Thuesen and Fabrycky 1989, p. 38)

Compounding Frequency	Number of Periods per Year	Effective Interest Rate per Period	Effective Annual Interest Rate
Annually	1	18.0000%	18.0000%
Semiannually	2	9.0000	18.8100
Quarterly	4	4.5000	19.2517
Monthly	12	1.5000	19.5618
Weekly	52	0.3642	19.6843
Daily	365	0.0493	19.7142
Continuously	∞	0.0000	19.7217

Figure III-21. Effective annual interest rates for various
compounding periods at a nominal rate of 18%.
(Thuesen and Fabrycky 1989, p. 57)

INDUSTRIAL ENGINEERING TERMS

abandonment decision
accelerated cost recovery
actual dollars
adjustment of cost data
after-tax analysis
after-tax cash flow
allocating indirect costs
allowance for errors
amortized cost concept
annual equivalent amount
annual percentage rate
asset
balance sheet
benefit
benefit-cost analysis
bond
book value
borrowed money
break-even analysis
budget constraint
capital assets
capital gains
capital losses
capital recovery factor
capital recovery with return
cash flow
compound interest
compound-amount factor
constantly increasing costs
consumer goods
continuous compounding
continuous payments
conversion factor
corporation
cost accounting
cost estimating method
cost-effectiveness
currency exchange
decision criteria
decision rule
decision trees
depletion
depreciable asset
depreciation
depreciation method
design
deterioration
disbenefit
discrete compounding
discrete payments
earning power of money
economic life
economy of operations

effective interest rate
engineering economy
engineering proposal
equal-payment series
equivalence calculations
estimating indirect costs
exchange
expectation variance
factory overhead
federal income tax
financing method
first cost
fixed cost
frequent compounding
future-worth amount
gain
general accounting
general welfare
geometric gradient factor
growth-free rate
Hurwicz rule
implied salvage value
income tax
income tax rate
incremental cost
incremental investment
index
indirect cost
individual
inflation rate
installation cost
interest formula
interest rate
internal rate of return
interpolation
investment
investment credit
irreducibles
judgement in estimating
Laplace rule
lender
life-cycle cost
linear programming model
load distribution
loading to normal capacity
loan
location
loss
lot size
maximax rules
maximin rules
measure of deflation
measure of inflation

minimax regret rule
minimum-cost analysis
Monte Carlo analysis
multiple alternatives
net benefits
nominal interest rate
obsolescence
opportunity cost
par value
payback period
payoff matrix
permanent facilities
personnel
present-worth amount
probability theory
procurement operations
producer goods
production activities
profit
project balance
public activities
purchasing power
queuing system
range of estimates
rate of return
removal cost
replacement alternatives
replacement analysis
retained earnings
retirement decision
risk analysis
rollback procedure
schematic illustration
sensitivity analysis
service life
simple interest
single factor
sinking fund factor
state income tax
straight-line depreciation
tax credit
temporary facilities
time value of money
total investment
uniform gradient factor
unit of production
unused value
utility
value
variable demand
waiting-line operation
wear and tear
working capital

(Thuesen and Fabrycky 1989)

INDUSTRIAL ENGINEERING PASSAGES

"Engineers are confronted with two important interconnected environments, the physical and the economic. Their success in altering the physical environment to produce products and services depends upon a knowledge of physical laws. However, the worth of these products and services lies in their utility measured in economic terms. There are numerous examples of structures, machines, processes, and systems that exhibit excellent physical design but have little economic merit."

(Thuesen and Fabrycky 1989, p. 4)

"The usual function of engineering is to manipulate the elements of one environment, the physical, to create value in a second environment, the economic. However, engineers sometimes have a tendency to disregard economic feasibility and are often appalled in practice by the necessity for meeting situations in which action must be based on estimates and judgment. Yet today's engineering graduates are increasingly finding themselves in positions in which their responsibility is extended to include economic considerations."

(*ibid.*, p. 5)

INDUSTRIAL ENGINEERING QUESTIONS

1. What's the difference between interest and an interest rate?
2. I don't really get the connection between the balance sheet and the profit and loss statement. Could you go over it again?
3. How exactly does inflation affect depreciation charges?
4. Could you do a problem comparing the interest on $1,000 for 10 years at 12% simple interest versus the same amount compounded annually?
5. What are some of the problems we have to watch out for when we try to determine if a cost is fixed or variable?

(all but number 1 from Thuesen and Fabrycky 1989)

INDUSTRIAL ENGINEERING TOPICS OF GENERAL INTEREST

1. How cultures differ in the ways they organize and motivate factory workers.
2. A comparison of quality and efficiency in factories, when one person performs one factory job all day and when one person performs a variety of tasks throughout the day or week.
3. What system an industry should use to decide what quantities of different types of products it should produce.
4. What a country can do when one of its industries begins to fall behind similar industries in other countries due to the age of factories, problems with the labor force, dramatic changes in the market, or a scarcity of raw materials.

INDUSTRIAL ENGINEERING PROBLEM

For an interest rate of 10% compounded annually, find:

(a) How much can be loaned now if $2,000 will repaid at the end of 4 years?

(b) How much will be required 6 years hence to repay a $50,000 loan made now?

(Thuesen and Fabrycky 1989, p. 71)

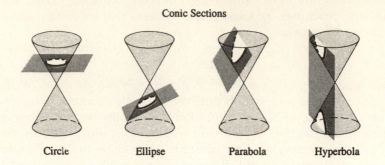

Figure III-22. Four types of conic sections. (Angel 1988, p. 390)

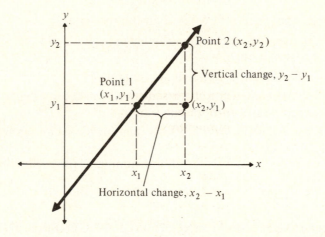

Figure III-23. Determining the slope of a line passing through two points: (x_1, y_1) and (x_2, y_2). (Angel 1988, p. 105)

MATHEMATICS TERMS

Algebra

absolute value
addition
addition property
antilogarithm
arithmetic
arithmetic sequence
arithmetic series
associative property
asymptote
binomial formula
binomial theorem
braces
brackets
Cartesian coordinate system
coefficient
collinear
commutative property
completing the square
complex fraction
complex number
compound inequality
conic section
conjugate axis
constant
counting numbers
Cramer's rule
cross multiplication
degree of a polynomial
denominator
determinant
discriminant
distance formula
distributive property
division
domain
double negative property
element of a set
ellipse
equals / is equal to
even roots
exponent
exponential function
factoring by grouping
factoring formula
finite sequence
foci of an ellipse
formula
fraction
fractional expression
function
functional notation
geometric figure
geometric sequence

geometric series
graph
hyperbola
hyperbolic
hypotenuse
identity property
imaginary number
inequality
infinite geometric series
infinite sequence
inverse function
inverse property
linear equation
linear inequality
logarithm
logarithmic equation
logarithmic function
major axis of an ellipse
midpoint formula
minor axis of an ellipse
monomial
multiplication
multiplication property
multiplying radicals
negative exponent rule
nonlinear system
nth term
numerator
one variable
operation
origin
parabola
parallel lines
parentheses
perpendicular lines
point-slope form
polynomial
polynomial function
principal diagonal
priority of operations
product rule
property
proportionality
Pythagorean theorem
quadratic equation
quadratic formula
quadratic function
quotient rule
radical
radical equation
radius
rational exponent
rational expression

real number
reduction
root
scientific notation
second-degree inequality
secondary diagonal
sequence
series
set
simplifying radical
slope of a line
slope-intercept form
square root function
subset
subtraction
synthetic division
third-order system
trinomial
two variables
vertex of a parabola
word problem
zero exponent rule

(Angel 1988)

Calculus

antiderivative
cardioid
chain rule
cosecant
cosine
cotangent
differential
differentiate
differentiation
equilateral triangle
factorial
integrate
integration
integration by parts
isoceles triangle
limit
Maclaurin series
orthogonal
parameter
partition
polar coordinates
rectangular coordinates
remainder
secant
sine
tangent
trigonometric function
u-substitution

MATHEMATICS PASSAGES

"To solve equations we use the addition and multiplication properties to isolate the variable on one side of the equal sign. The addition property states that the same number can be added to both sides of an equation without changing the solution to the original equation. Since subtraction is defined in terms of addition, the addition property also allows us to subtract the same number from both sides of an equation."

(Angel 1988, p. 41)

"The multiplication property states that both sides of an equation can be multiplied by the same nonzero* number without changing the solution. Since division is defined in terms of multiplication, the multiplication property also allows us to divide both sides of an equation by the same nonzero number. To solve an equation we will often have to use a combination of properties to isolate the variable. Our goal is to get the variable all by itself on one side of the equation."

(*ibid.*, p. 41)

MATHEMATICS QUESTIONS

1. I don't understand what a limit of a function is. Could you please give the definition and tell us when we have to use it and how we use it?
2. Can you please explain in simple terms what a continuous function is? I'm really confused about it.
3. The other day you mentioned the Binomial Theorem, but I still really don't know what it is. Could you explain it again and tell us when we have to use it?
4. Could you please explain the difference between an ellipse, a hyperbola and a parabola?
5. Are the set of cardinal numbers and the set of natural numbers the same? And where do the real numbers fit in? How are they different from the natural numbers?

MATHEMATICS TOPICS OF GENERAL INTEREST

1. How to calculate the probability of getting a pair of sixes when you throw two dice.
2. What functions in real life can be accurately described only by someone who knows calculus.
3. How Binomial Distribution can be used to calculate the probability that a family with five children has exactly three boys given that five baby girls are born for every four baby boys.
4. How students can use mathematics at the end of the term to predict the grade they must get on the final exam in order to get an A for the course.

MATHEMATICS PROBLEM

Mrs. Sanders and her daughter Teresa jog regularly. Mrs. Sanders jogs at 5 miles per hour, Teresa at 4 miles per hour. Teresa begins jogging at noon. Mrs. Sanders begins at 12:30 P.M. and travels the same straight path.

(a)   Determine at what time the mother and daughter will meet.

(b)   How far from the starting point will they be when they meet?

(Angel 1988, p. 58)

*The word *nonzero* was not included in the original paragraph.

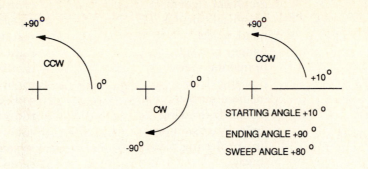

Figure III-24. Positive arc, negative arc, and arc by starting, ending, and sweep angles. Information necessary for drawing an arc is the beginning angle or point, the ending angle or point, and sweep angle. (Luzadder and Duff 1989, p. 73)

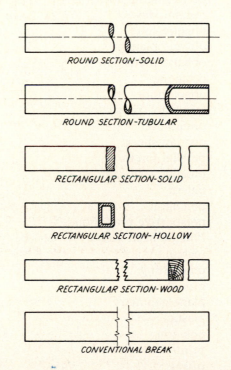

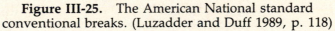

Figure III-25. The American National standard conventional breaks. (Luzadder and Duff 1989, p. 118)

MECHANICAL ENGINEERING TERMS

alignment chart
alloy
aluminum
anchor bracket
anchor clip
angle block
angle bracket
angular prospective
angular tolerance
auxiliary view
axonometric projection
bearing of a line
bilateral auxiliary view
Bow's notation
brass
bronze
CADD
CADD strategies
cam
cast iron
centering bearing
chamfer
clockwise
computer aided design
computer drafting
cone pulley
control housing cover
coordinate axes
coordinate plane projection
copper
counterclockwise
curved boundary
cut-off clip
cutting gear teeth
cylindrical fit
design process
dimensioning practices
double-curved surface
dovetail bracket
drafting technique
drilled flange
edge view
ejector clip
electric windings
electrical insulation
electronic drawing
empirical equation
engineering construction
engineering drawing
fastener
feeder bracket
fillet
force couple
frustum of a pyramid

gear cover
geometric surface
geometric tolerance
graphical algebra
graphical calculus
hand wheel
hanger bracket
horizontal view
housing cover
inclined surface
isometric drawing
limit dimensioning
line-projecting plane
linkage
locating slide
manual drawing equipment
moment of a vector force
mutilated block
noncoplanar force
noncurrent vector forces
nonintersecting lines
nonisometric lines
normal view
oblique cone
oblique plane
oblique projection
octagon
offset guide
one-plane projection
orientation
overlay sheet
parallel forces
parallel vector forces
patent
pentagon
perspective projection
Phillips head screw
piercing point
pipe fitting
pipe thread
plane geometry
plastic
polygon
printed circuit layout
prism
process model
production drawing
profile view
prototype
pump cover
pyramid
qualitative chart
quantitative chart
radial bearing

reaming
rectangular right pyramid
reference plane
reproduction
resistance welding
resultant of parallel forces
right circular cylinder
riveting
robot
rod support
rod yoke
rubber
runout
screw threads
sectional view
sheet-metal connector
shifter link
SI metric system
sketching
skew lines
slant height
slotted guide link
solid cylinder
solid geometry
space diagram
space relationships
spatial graphics
spiral of Archimedes
spoke
spring
steady brace
steel
string polygon
structural drawings
support anchor
surface texture
tangent arc
three dimensions
tolerance of form
tolerance of location
topographic map drawing
transition piece
triangulation
true length of a line
true-length diagram
truncated cone
two dimensions
two-piece elbow
unilateral auxiliary view
vector addition
vector diagram
vector geometry
welding

(Luzadder and Duff 1989)

MECHANICAL ENGINEERING PASSAGES

"Using CADD, a three-dimensional model of the design is kept as a mathematical description in the memory of the computer; thus allowing the designer to see any and all views of the design and how the design operates. This is a fundamental change in the way a designer works. Previously, a designer had to translate the mental conception or mathematical model into a two-dimensional diagram before the object could be made. With CADD, it is the three-dimensional model that is translated as needed into two-dimensional diagrams for documentation and communication."

(Luzadder and Duff 1989, p. 71)

"When the cutting plane cuts an object lengthwise, the section obtained is commonly called a *longitudinal section;* when crosswise, it is called a *cross section.* It is designated as being either a *full section*, a *half section*, or a *broken section*. If the plane cuts entirely across the object, the section represented is known as a full section. If it cuts only halfway across a symmetrical object, the section is a half section. A broken section is a partial one, used when less than a half section is needed."

(ibid., p. 149)

MECHANICAL ENGINEERING QUESTIONS

1. Some cars use diesel-powered engines. I'd like to know how a diesel-powered engine is different from a gasoline-powered one, and what difference it makes in how the car runs.

2. In my readings on stress, I've run across a term called margin of safety. Could you please explain exactly what that term means?

3. Could you go over how we can tell whether a drawing indicates a clockwise revolution or a counterclockwise revolution of an object about its axis? I think you said it's related to the view, but I forgot how.*

4. What are the different types of internal combustion engines? I mean, how are they classified, and what makes them different from each other?

5. When mechanical engineers are designing engines and they want to make them more fuel-efficient, what do they do? What I mean is what aspects of the engine do they concentrate on?

MECHANICAL ENGINEERING TOPICS OF GENERAL INTEREST

1. How convection can be used to cool food quickly.

2. How a refrigerator and an air conditioner work.

3. How robots are used in today's industry and how they will be used in the future.

4. New methods of pollution control we can expect in the near future.

MECHANICAL ENGINEERING PROBLEM

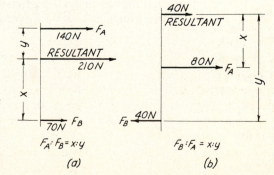

Figure III-26. In the figure, the resultant of parallel forces has been determined arithmetically. Now use the graphical method to determine the location of the line of action for the resultant.
(Luzadder and Duff 1989, p. 203)

*from Luzadder and Duff 1989

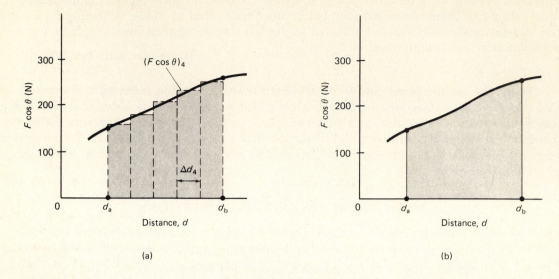

Figure III-27. Work done by a force F can be calculated (a) by taking sum of areas of the rectangles; (b) area under the curve of $F \cos \Theta$ vs. d. (Giancoli 1985, p. 97)

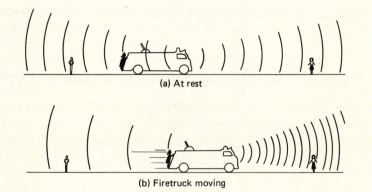

Figure III-28. (a) Both observers on the sidewalk hear the same frequency from the firetruck at rest. (b) Doppler effect: observer toward whom the firetruck moves hears a higher-frequency sound, and observer behind the firetruck hears a lower frequency. (Giancoli 1985, p. 341)

PHYSICS TERMS

absolute pressure
absolute zero
acceleration
adhesion
air resistance
alloy
alpha particle
alternating current (AC)
AM radio wave
ampere
angular momentum
Archimedes' principle
atmospheric pressure
axis of rotation
battery
Bernoulli effect
beta particle
Boyle's law
breeder reactor
Brownian motion
buoyant force
capillary action
center of gravity
center of mass
centrifugal force
centripetal acceleration
centripetal force
chain reaction
chemical cell
coherent radiation
cohesion
component vector
condensation nucleus
conduction
conservation of energy
conservation of momentum
constructive interference
contact force
continuous spectrum
convection
converging lens
correspondence principle
coulomb
deceleration
density
destructive interference
dew point
diffraction
diffusion
direct current (DC)
dispersion
diverging lens
Doppler shift
efficiency

elasticity
electric circuit
electric dipole
electric force field
electrical conductor
electrical insulator
electrical potential
electrical resistance
electromagnetic spectrum
electromagnetic waves
electroscope
emission spectrum
energy / mass relation
entropy
escape velocity
first postulate of relativity
fluorescence
FM radio wave
force field
gamma ray
gravitational field lines
gravitational force
half-life
incoherent radiation
inertial frame of reference
inertial mass
instantaneous speed
intensity
internal energy
iridescence
kinetic energy
kinetic friction
latent heat of fusion
latent heat of vaporization
laws of thermodynamics
length contraction
longitudinal wave
magnetic declination
magnetic force field
magnetic inclination
metastable state
moment of inertia
momentum
net force
net vector
nuclear fission
nuclear fusion
nuclear reactor
ohm
orbital
parallel circuit
Pascal's principle
perfectly elastic collision
perfectly inelastic collision

phosphorescence
photoelectric effect
photon
polar molecule
polarization
positron
potential energy
quantum number
quark
radiation
radioactive nuclei
refraction
relative humidity
relative speed
resonance
resultant vector
rotating frame of reference
rotational inertia
second postulate of relativity
secular equilibrium
selective reflection
selective transmission
semiconductor
series circuit
shock wave
short circuit
specific heat
spectroscope
spring constant
static charge
static friction
sublimation
superconductor
surface tension
terminal speed
thermal equilibrium
time dilation
torque of a force
total internal reflection
trajectory
transformer
transverse wave
ultrasonic wave
unstable atom
vacuum
vapor pressure
virtual image
viscosity
volt
watt
wave amplitude
wave frequency
wave mechanics
wavelength

(Bolemon 1989)

PHYSICS PASSAGES

"Until the present century, no one could divide an atom into smaller parts, to uncover its inner structure. But today physicists can explore atoms in a variety of ways. They can scatter radiation (X rays, visible light, or heat rays, for example) from matter to see how much is reflected or absorbed or if the matter changes the radiation in some way. They can break atoms up and use their pieces as projectiles to pierce other atoms, see what comes out, and work backward to find out what must have happened. These investigations have shown what atoms are like."

(Bolemon 1989, p. 169)

"Any atom is made up of three kinds of particles so tiny we cannot see them by any means. We call these particles electrons, protons, and neutrons. An atom that these three particles build occupies a roughly spherical volume, but its outer boundary isn't as well-defined as the surface of a billiard ball is. That's because the sphere is not a solid ball of matter but instead is almost entirely empty space! That sphere represents a volume where the lightweight electrons move. The electrons' behavior in (and out of) atoms is actually rather bizarre.... For the present you might think of electrons and their motion as physicists did early in this century before the whole picture was revealed. Imagine electrons to be planetlike particles whirling at superhigh speeds about a speck at the atom's center called the nucleus. That speck is the home of the protons and neutrons, particles almost 2000 times as massive as electrons."

(*ibid.*)

PHYSICS QUESTIONS

1. So what exactly is the net effect of leaving the refrigerator door open? When you explained it last time, I didn't get your final conclusion.

2. Could you explain the concept of momentum again? You lost me.

3. How come sound seems to travel more clearly in cold weather than in warm weather? At least, that's what it seems to me.

4. Last week you gave us the definition of harmonic motion, but I still don't get it. Could you give us a simple example?

5. Could you please explain again what the Doppler Effect is and how it can be applied to changes that we notice as a train passes by?

PHYSICS TOPICS OF GENERAL INTEREST

1. Why friction is sometimes helpful and sometimes a problem.
2. Why water remains in an open container without spilling when swung around in a circle at the end of a rope.
3. Why deserts get hot while islands at the same latitude remain cool.
4. Why some things float and other things sink in water.

PHYSICS PROBLEM

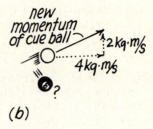

Figure III-29.   The vector momentum of a cue ball is shown
in the figures (a) and (b) before and after a collision
with the 3-ball. Ignoring any effects of friction with the table,
what is the momentum of the 3-ball after the collision?
(Bolemon 1985, p. 93)

PSYCHOLOGY VISUALS

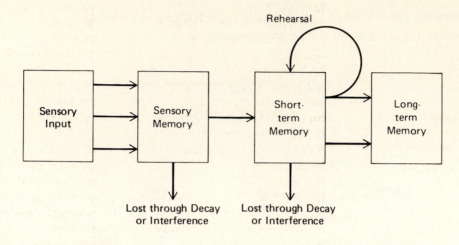

Figure III-30. Atkinson and Shiffrin's multiprocess view of human memory. (Worchel and Shebilske 1989, p. 225)

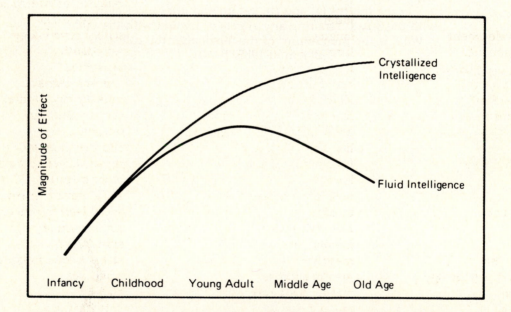

Figure III-31. The graphic shows fluid intelligence (general mental skills, such as the ability to make inferences or deductive reasoning) first increases and then decreases with age, while crystalized intelligence (specific mental skills, such as one's vocabulary) steadily increases. (Worchel and Shebilske 1989, pp. 265, 267; Brim and Kagan, 1980, pp. 469, 471)

PSYCHOLOGY TERMS

abnormal behavior
accepting
achievement
adjusting
adjustment
adolescence
affiliation
aggression
alcoholism
anorexia nervosa
antisocial personality
anxiety
artificial intelligence
autonomic nervous system
behaviorism
body language
brain
brain damage
bulimia
burnout
chemical regulators
child development
classical conditioning
clinical psychology
coercive sex
cognition
cognitive development
cognitive dissonance
cognitive learning theory
cognitive map
concept formation
conditioned response
constant stimuli
counseling
conversion disorder
daydream
death
decision making
depressant
depression
depth perception
developmental psychology
discrimination
distorted speech
dream
drug addiction
drug-induced state
elderly
electrical regulators
emotion
endocrine system
experimental psychology
extrasensory perception
extrinsic motivation

family commitments
fear
first operant response
functionalism
generalized anxiety disorder
geometrical illusion
Gestalt therapy
hallucinogen
higher-order conditioning
human development
human language
human sexual behavior
human sexual response
humanism
hunger
hypnosis
imaginal thought
innate emotional expression
insanity
insight
intelligence
intelligence testing
interference
intrinsic motivation
IQ
judgment
language control center
language development
late adulthood
latent learning
learning
life-span
limbic system
linguistic relativity
long-term memory
love
maladaptive behavior
mania
manic disorder
meditation
memory
mental abilities
middle adulthood
mood disorder
moral development
motor development
multiple personality
near-death experience
nervous system
neural impulse
neurobiological correlates
neuron
obesity

occupational commitments
operant behavior
opponent-process theory
panic disorder
paranoia
perception
personal space
personality
personality development
personality trait
persuasibility
phobia
physical abilities
physical growth
physiological pattern
physiological psychology
prenatal development
problem solving
propositional thought
psychoanalysis
psychoanalytic psychology
psychogenic amnesia
psychokinesis
retention
reticular activating system
schizophrenia
school psychology
self-identity
sensation
sensory changes
sensory deprivation
sensory memory
sex role
short-term memory
signal-detection theory
sleep disorder
social development
social learning theory
somatic theory
spinal cord
state of consciousness
stimulant
stress
structuralism
subjective pattern
suicide
thirst
thought
trace decay
violence
visual illusion
work stress
young adulthood

(Worchel and Shebilske 1989)

PSYCHOLOGY PASSAGES

"The human personality is wonderfully complex and the various theories offer different perspectives in the effort to understand it.... Psychoanalytic theory suggests that we can best understand human behavior by identifying internal forces that are set into action during infancy and childhood. Humanistic theories argue that we can understand personality by looking at the 'good side' of people and examining how the desire for self-fulfillment guides behavior. Learning theories add that our quest to understand personality must take into account external events; these theories also suggest that personality changes throughout life, as well as present situations, are at least as important as past events in directing behavior."

(Worchel and Shebilske 1989, p. 490)

"These different theories influence the direction of research.... For example, an investigator guided by psychoanalytic theory will focus his or her attention on early childhood experiences, whereas a researcher who adopts a learning perspective will study external variables that occur in the person's present environment. Although the different methods of study uncover different characteristics of the personality, we cannot conclude that one method is more correct than the others; each has a purpose and helps us understand personality. And each theory offers insight into the nature of psychological disorders and helps chart treatment programs for those disorders."

(*ibid.*)

PSYCHOLOGY QUESTIONS

1. I read that an important concept in social learning theory is learned helplessness, but I don't understand what it means.
2. I'm getting the four elements of classical conditioning mixed up. In Pavlov's dog salivation experiment, what exactly are the US (unconditioned stimulus), UR (unconditioned response), CS (conditioned stimulus), and CR (conditioned response)?
3. Is the Cognitive Theory the one that psychologists currently believe best explains depression? If so, why?*
4. Whenever I hear about Post-Traumatic Stress Disorder, it's usually about Vietnam Vets. Can anyone else have it?
5. I was wondering if you could talk about how you make sure you get conditioned responses when you're using classical conditioning.*

PSYCHOLOGY TOPICS OF GENERAL INTEREST

1. The difference between clinical depression and feeling depressed.
2. The factors that can influence a person who is learning another language.
3. The difference between psychosis and neurosis.
4. What we know about how colors in the environment influence individual behavior.

*from Worchel and Shebilske 1989

PSYCHOLOGY PROBLEM

Identify the unconditioned stimulus (US), the unconditioned response (UR), the conditioned stimulus (CS), and the conditioned response (CR) in the following experiment by Delamater, LoLordo, and Berridge (1986).

Before conditioning, these experimenters observed that rats make distinct facial expressions when they are given sugar or quinine with water but not when they are given an auditory signal with water. The expression in response to sugar was described as an ingestive reaction. The expression in response to quinine was described as an aversive reaction. During one conditioning period, they paired an auditory signal with the presentation of sugar water. During another conditioning period, they paired an auditory signal with the presentation of quinine. After conditioning with sugar, the auditory signal plus water produced ingestive facial responses. After conditioning with quinine, the auditory signal plus water produced aversive facial responses.

(Worchel and Shebilske 1989, p. 191)

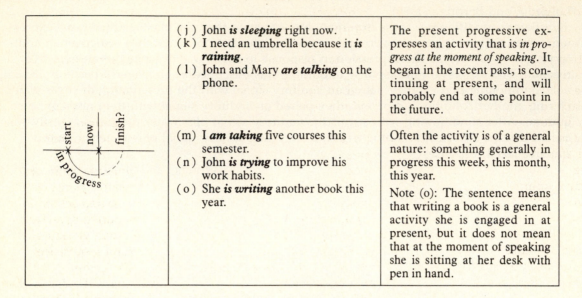

	(j) John *is sleeping* right now. (k) I need an umbrella because it *is raining*. (l) John and Mary *are talking* on the phone.	The present progressive expresses an activity that is *in progress at the moment of speaking*. It began in the recent past, is continuing at present, and will probably end at some point in the future.
	(m) I *am taking* five courses this semester. (n) John *is trying* to improve his work habits. (o) She *is writing* another book this year.	Often the activity is of a general nature: something generally in progress this week, this month, this year. Note (o): The sentence means that writing a book is a general activity she is engaged in at present, but it does not mean that at the moment of speaking she is sitting at her desk with pen in hand.

Figure III-32. Present progressive verb phrase in English. (Azar 1989, p. 11)

	Form of the passive: **be** + *past participle*.
ACTIVE: (a) Mary **helped** the boy. PASSIVE: (b) The boy **was helped** by Mary.	In the passive, *the object* of an active verb *becomes the subject* of the passive verb: "the boy" in (a) becomes the subject of the passive verb in (b). (a) and (b) have the same meaning.
ACTIVE: (c) An accident **happened**. PASSIVE: (d) (none)	Only transitive verbs (verbs that are followed by an object) are used in the passive. It is not possible to use verbs such as **happen**, **sleep**, **come**, and **seem** (intransitive verbs) in the passive. (See Appendix 1, Chart A-1.)

	ACTIVE			PASSIVE	
simple present	Mary	**helps**	John.	John	**is helped** by Mary.
present progressive	Mary	**is helping**	John.	John	**is being helped** by Mary.
present perfect	Mary	**has helped**	John.	John	**has been helped** by Mary.
simple past	Mary	**helped**	John.	John	**was helped** by Mary.
past progressive	Mary	**was helping**	John.	John	**was being helped** by Mary.
past perfect	Mary	**had helped**	John.	John	**had been helped** by Mary.
simple future	Mary	**will help**	John.	John	**will be helped** by Mary.
be going to	Mary	**is going to help**	John.	John	**is going to be helped** by Mary.
future perfect★	Mary	**will have helped**	John.	John	**will have been helped** by Mary.

★The progressive forms of the present perfect, past perfect, future, and future perfect are very rarely used in the passive.

Figure III-33. Forming the passive verb voice in English. (Azar 1989, p. 120)

active voice
adjective
adjective clause
adverb
adverbial clause
affirmative
agreement
apostrophe
appositive
article
auxiliary verb
capitalization
causative verb
cause and effect
clause
collective noun
comma
command
comparative
complex sentence
compound sentence
conditional sentence
conjunction
conjunctive adverb
continuous tense
contraction
coordinating conjunction
correlative conjunction
count noun
dangling modifier
definite noun
degree of certainty
dependent clause
direct speech
double negative
ellipsis
expletive
expression of quantity
fragment
frequency adverb
future perfect
future perfect progressive
future progressive
future time
generic noun
gerund
habitual past
imperative sentence
impersonal pronoun
incomplete sentence
indefinite noun
indefinite pronoun
independent clause
indirect object

infinitive
infinitive phrase
information question
inseparable phrasal verb
interrogative sentence
intransitive verb
inverted word order
irregular past participle
irregular plural noun
irregular verb
linking verb
main clause
main verb
meaning
modal
modal auxiliary
modifier
modification
necessity
negation
negative question
noncount noun
nonprogressive verb
noun
noun clause
object
object of a preposition
object pronoun
parallel structure
paraphrase
participial adjective
participial phrase
participle
particle
passive voice
past habit
past participle
past perfect progressive
past perfect verb
past progressive
past tense
past time
perfect verb
perfect progressive verb
period
permission
personal pronoun
phrasal verb
plural
polite request
possessive
possessive noun
possessive pronoun
predicate

prefix
preposition
prepositional phrase
present participle
present tense
progressive
prohibition
punctuation
quantity
question
question word
quotation mark
quoted speech
reduction
reflexive pronoun
relative clause
repeated action
reported speech
restrictive clause
run-on sentence
semicolon
separable phrasal verb
sequence of tenses
simple form
simple future
simple past
simple present
simple sentence
singular
spelling
stative verb
subject
subject pronoun
subject-verb agreement
subjunctive
subordinate clause
subordinating conjunction
suffix
suggestion
superlative
tag question
tense
time clause
transition
transitive verb
two-word verb
uncountable noun
usage
verb form
verb of perception
verb tense
word choice
word order
yes/no question

(Azar 1989)

SECOND LANGUAGE PASSAGES

"The modal auxiliaries in English are: can, could, had better, may, might, must, ought to, shall, should, will, would. Modal auxiliaries generally express a speaker's attitudes, or 'moods.' For example, modals can express that a speaker feels something is necessary, advisable, permissible, possible, or probable; and, in addition, they can convey the strength of these attitudes. Each modal has more than one meaning or use."

(Azar 1989, p. 68)

"The present perfect expresses the idea that something happened (or never happened) *before now, at an unspecified time in the past.* The exact time it happened is not important. If there is a specific mention of time, the simple past is used: *I saw that movie last night.* The present perfect also expresses the *repetition of an activity before now.* The exact time of each repetition is not important. The present perfect also, when used with **for** or **since**, expresses a situation that *began in the past and continues to the present.*"

(*ibid.*, p. 29)

SECOND LANGUAGE QUESTIONS

1. I'm going to your country next summer on vacation. In your opinion, what parts of the culture do I need to know in order to avoid offending people or making a fool of myself?
2. I'm having a hard time with the pronunciation of cognates. Are there any rules you can give me that would make it easier?
3. Can you explain what the subjunctive is and how to know when you should use it?
4. Can you give me any rules of thumb about when I should use the informal *you* and when I should use the formal *you*? Sometimes it's clear, for example, when speaking to someone you just meet who is very old, but it's really confusing for me otherwise.
5. Can you give me some tips on the best way to learn and remember new vocabulary? I have a terrible memory.

SECOND LANGUAGE TOPICS OF GENERAL INTEREST

1. A grammatical form in the language you teach that is different from English in a particularly interesting way.
2. How people usually apologize in the culture you teach.
3. The one work of literature that most typifies the culture you teach and why.
4. The typical family structure in the culture you teach.

Figure III-34.   Participial adjectives.

--The problem confuses the students. (a) It is *a **confusing** problem*.	The present participle conveys an active meaning. The noun it modifies does something. In (a): The noun "problem" does something; it "confuses." Thus, it is described as a "confusing problem."
--The students are confused by the problem. (b) They are ***confused** students*.	The past participle conveys a passive meaning. In (b): The students are confused by something. Thus, they are described as "confused students."
--The story amuses the children. (c) It is *an **amusing** story*.	In (c): The noun "story" performs the action.
--The children are amused by the story. (d) They are ***amused** children*.	In (d): The noun "children" receives the action.

Complete the sentences with the present or past participle of the verbs in italics.

1. The class *bores* the students. It is a _____**boring**_____ class.

2. The students *are bored by* the class. They are _____**bored**_____ students.

3. The game *excites* the people. It is an _____ game.

4. The people *are excited by* the game. They are _____ people.

5. The news *surprised* the man. It was _____ news.

6. The man *was surprised by* the news. He was a _____ man.

7. The child *was frightened by* the strange noise. The _____ child sought comfort from her father.

8. The strange noise *frightened* the child. It was a _____ sound.

9. The work *exhausted* the men. It was _____ work.

10. The men *were exhausted*. The _____ men sat down to rest under the shade of a tree.

(Azar 1989, p. 144)

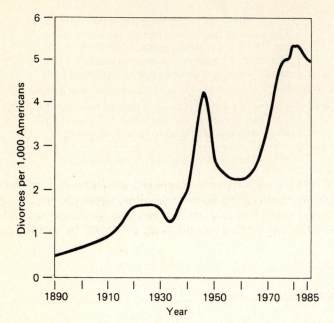

Figure III-35. The divorce rate for the United States, 1890–1987. (Macionis 1989, p. 6)

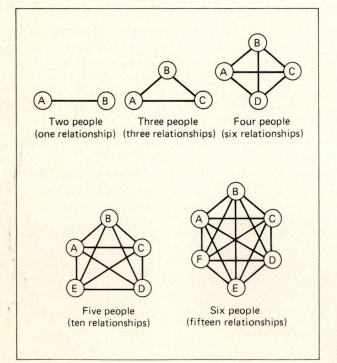

Figure III-36. Group size and relationships. (Macionis 1989, p. 183)

SOCIOLOGY TERMS

abuse
achieved status
adolescence
adult socialization
adulthood
ageism
age-sex pyramid
aggregate
alienation
annihilation
anticipatory socialization
ascribed status
assimilation
bereavement
biological explanation
blue-collar jobs
bureaucracy
caste
category
child rearing
childhood
class consciousness
classless society
competition
conglomerate
constraint
correlation
corruption
counterculture
criminal recidivism
criminal justice system
cross-cultural perspective
crowd dynamics
cult
cultural ecology
cultural integration
cultural relativity
cultural transmission
culture shock
deductive logical thought
delinquency
demography
dependent variable
deviance
deviant subculture
disabled
discrimination
elderly
empirical evidence
environmental pollution
ethics
ethnicity
ethnocentrism
ethnomethodology

family life
feminism
gender
group conformity
group leadership
historical perspective
human development
human freedom
human intelligence
hypothesis
ideology
immigration
income
independent variable
individual
inductive logical thought
industrial capitalism
inequality
ingroup
institution
institutional support
interview
life cycle
life expectancy
limitation
longevity
lower class
mass media
mass society
medical care
meritocracy
middle class
migration
minority group
mob
mobility
modern society
monarchy
mores
mortality
myth
network
nonverbal communication
occupational prestige
old age
oligarchy
one-parent family
outgroup
panic
participant observation
patriarchy
peer group
personality
pluralism

political party
political system
population growth
poverty
prejudice
primary group
psychological explanation
public opinion
qualitative research
quantitative research
racism
reference group
reliability
religion
religious affiliation
resocialization
revolution
riot
role conflict
rumor
sample
scientific evidence
secondary group
secularization
segregation
self
sexism
social change
social class
social control
social experience
social function
social interaction
social isolation
social mobility
social movement
social stratification
socialization
sociobiology
sociocultural evolution
special-interest group
status
stigma
technology
underdevelopment
upper class
urbanization
validity
violence
wealth
white-collar jobs
working class
workplace

(Macionis 1989)

SOCIOLOGY PASSAGES

"In industrial societies, people first live within a family of orientation—the family into which a person is born, and which provides intensive early socialization. Later in life, a person lives within a family of procreation—a family within which people have or adopt children of their own. In most societies of the world, families result primarily from marriage, which is a socially approved relationship involving both economic cooperation and sexual activity. As we shall see, patterns of marriage show striking variation around the world. At present in the United States, however, marriage can unite only one male and one female. The importance of marriage as the basis for procreation is evident in the traditional attachment of the label of illegitimacy to children born out of wedlock. However, this norm has weakened considerably in recent years."

(Macionis 1989, p. 370)

"Careful operationalization of variables is the first step in carrying out useful measurement in social research. But the quality of measurement in science is based on two other considerations, the reliability and the validity of the measurement process. **Reliability** is *the quality of consistency in measurement*. If the social class of the same person were measured several times (by the same or different researchers) and each time the same value was assigned, this measurement would be considered to be reliable. A process of measurement that is not reliable is of little use in sociology—just as a scale that gave inconsistent readings of weight would be useless to a physicist."

(*ibid.*, p. 33)

SOCIOLOGY QUESTIONS

1. I've heard that there's been a recent increase in the aged population. How come?
2. What would **you** say are the typical causes of social disorder in third world countries?
3. I'd like to know more about your country's main social problems? Are they different from ours and if so, why?
4. What do you see as possible solutions to the problems of way too many old people compared to the number of young people that countries with successful population control, like China, will have to face?
5. Can you talk about some of the pros and cons of using surveys as a research method?

SOCIOLOGY TOPICS OF GENERAL INTEREST

1. The effects of population control on a society.
2. How methods of child rearing can affect the behavior of adults in a society.
3. What possible roles religion can take in human society.
4. How the degree of ethnocentrism in a particular culture can affect the behavior of individuals toward other members of other cultures.

SOCIOLOGY PROBLEM

In evaluating research outcome, it is important to ask the following question: Does the study design fully support the conclusion?

As part of its advertising campaign, a major aspirin manufacturer refers to a study that claims that people who use their product, increase fluid intake, and get plenty of sleep recover from the common cold significantly faster than cold sufferers who do not. Citing these results, they encourage cold sufferers to purchase and use their product for relief from the common cold.

Based on your knowledge of research design, how would you evaluate the manufacturer's assertion that their product provides relief from the common cold? Identify the problem and evaluate the conclusion drawn by the manufacturers.

STATISTICS

STATISTICS VISUALS

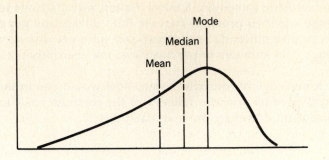

Figure III-37. Frequency distribution is skewed to the left.
(Levin and Rubin 1989, p. 51)

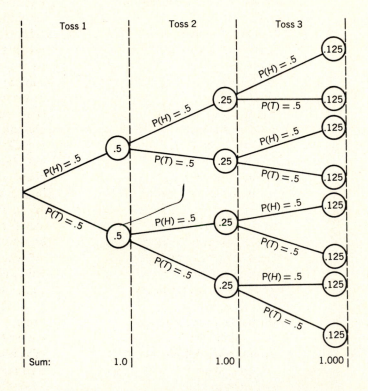

Figure III-38. Completed probability tree showing
the possible outcomes and their respective probabilities
for three tosses of a fair coin.
(Levin and Rubin 1989, p. 100)

STATISTICS TERMS

a priori
addition rule
analysis of variance
analytical study
ANOVA
arithmetic mean
association
autocorrelation
bar graph
binomial distribution
cell
central limit theorem
central tendency
chi-square test
class interval
classical probability
coefficient
conditional probability
confidence interval
contingency table
correlation
correlation matrix
counting rules
critical value
cross-classification table
cross-tabulation
cyclical relative
decile
degree of freedom
dependent variable
determination
difference score
discrete quantitative data
discrete random variable
dispersion
dot chart
dummy-variable model
empirical rule
enumerative study
equality of variance
error sum of squares
error variance
expected value
explained variation
explanatory variable
exponential distribution
exponential smoothing
extrapolation
factor
factorial
finite population
frequency distribution
frequency histogram
given value

goodness of fit
graphical technique
histogram
homogeneity of variance
homoscedasticity
hypothesis testing
independent variable
inference
inferential statistics
influence analysis
interaction
interquartile range
interval scaling
joint event
joint probability
least-squares method
level of significance
linear relationship
linear trend model
mathematical expectation
mean
measure of dispersion
measure of variation
median
midrange
missing value
mode
multicollinearity
multiple determination
multiple regression
multiplication rule
mutually exclusive
net regression coefficient
nominal scaling
nonparametric method
normal approximation
normal distribution
normality assumption
null hypothesis
objective probability
one-tailed test
operational definition
ordered array
ordinal scaling
p-value
paired difference t-test
paired sample
parabolic
parametric method
partial determination
Pearson product-moment
percentile
periodic effect
permutation

pie chart
Poisson distribution
polygon
population parameter
population variance
prediction
principle of parsimony
probability distribution
proportion
quadratic trend model
qualitative data
quantile
quantitative data
quartile
questionnaire
randomized block design
randomized design
range
regression coefficient
regression diagnostics
rejection region
related population
relative efficiency
sample size
sample variance
sampling distribution
scatter diagram
shape of the curve
significance
simple probability
skewness
standard deviation
standard error
statistical inference
stepwise regression
subjective probability
summary table
supertable
t distribution
t test
table of random numbers
tabulation
treatment
Tukey's T method
two-tailed test
type I error
type II error
u-shaped distribution
unequal variance
unexplained variation
uniform distribution
variable
variance

(Berenson and Levine 1989)

STATISTICS PASSAGES

"There are many ways to sort data. We can simply collect and keep them in order. Or if the observations are measured in numbers, we can list the data points from the lowest to the highest in numerical value. But if the data are skilled workers (such as carpenters, masons, and iron workers) required at construction sites, or the different types of automobiles manufactured by all automakers, or the various colors of sweaters manufactured by a given firm, we will need to organize them differently. We will need to present the data points in alphabetical order or by some other organizing principle. One useful way to organize data is to divide them into similar categories or classes and then count the number of observations that fall into each category. This method produces a frequency distribution."

(Levin and Rubin 1989, p. 8)

"Information before it is arranged and analyzed is called *raw data*. It is 'raw' because it is unprocessed by statistical methods. The purpose of organizing data is to enable us to see quickly all the possible characteristics in the data we have collected. We look for things such as the range (the largest and smallest values), apparent trends, what values the data may tend to group around, what values appear most often, and so on. The more information of this kind that we can learn from our sample, the better we can understand the population from which it came, and the better we can make decisions."

(*ibid.*, pp. 8–9)

STATISTICS QUESTIONS

1. I'm still confused about the Least Square Method. How about giving us a **simple** example to show how it's used?

2. When talking about a normal distribution, what if some point x lies exactly on the line for the mean of the distribution? What is the value of z?*

3. For a normal distribution, does the mean always lie between the mode and the median?

4. If we have two populations that are normal and we take samples from them, why isn't the ratio of all possible sets of the two sample variances also normally distributed?†

5. Under what conditions would a large sample not be a good idea? For example, do they decrease the standard error?*

STATISTICS TOPICS OF GENERAL INTEREST

1. The kinds of things that occur in normal distribution and the kinds of things that don't.

2. How a basic knowledge of statistics can help a common person in his or her daily life.

3. How newspapers and television set up public opinion polls and their accuracy.

4. The extent to which statistical evidence can be used to show cause and effect.

STATISTICS PROBLEM

Use the coefficient of variation to show which of the following employees shows less variability in output rate of analyses. Suppose that each day laboratory technician A completes 40 analyses with a standard deviation of 5. Technician B completes 160 analyses per day with a standard deviation of 15. Which employee shows less variability?

(Levin 1986, p. 131)

*from Levin and Rubin 1983
†from Levin 1987

Subtechnical Terms Applicable to All Scientific Fields

abolishment/abolition
   to abolish
absolute/absolutely
abstract/abstraction
acceleration/deacceleration
   to accelerate/to deaccelerate
accurate/accuracy
addition/additional/additionally
   to add
adjacent/adjacency
administration/administrative
   to administer
advantage/advantageous/disadvantage/disadvantageous
affected
   to affect
aggregate/aggregation
alignment
   to align
alternate/alternative/alternatively
   to alternate
altitude
ambiguity/ambiguous/unambiguous
analogy/analogue
analysis/analytic/analytical/analyst
   to analyze
angle/angular
answer/answerable
   to answer
apparatus
application/applicant/applicable
   to apply
appropriate/appropriately/appropriateness
approximate/approximately
   to approximate
arbitrary/arbitrarily
area
arithmetic/arithmetical/arithmetically
ascent/descent
   to ascend/to descend
assertion
   to assert
assumption
   to assume
atmosphere/atmospheric
attainment/attainability
   to attain
attributable
   to attribute
authenticity/authentic/authentically
   to authenticate
author/authority/authoritative
   to author

auxiliary
average
   to average
avoidable/unavoidable
   to avoid
awkwardness/awkward/awkwardly
axis/axes/X axis/Y axis
balance/imbalance
   to balance
band
   to band
base/basic/basically/basis
behavior
   to behave
biology/biological
boiling
   to boil
calculation
   to calculate
cancelation
   to cancel
capital/capitalist/capitalism/capitalization
   to capitalize
category
   to categorize
causal/causality
   to cause
certain/certainty/uncertainty
character/characteristic
   to characterize
chart
   to chart
circle/semicircle/circular/circulation
   to circle/to circulate
circumference
claim
   to claim
class/classical/classification
   to classify
cold/cool
   to cool
column/columnar
communication/communicative
   to communicate
comparison/comparable
   to compare
compensation/compensatory
   to compensate
competition
   to compete
complication
   to complicate

composition/component/composite
  to compose
compression/compressibility
  to compress
computation/computational
  to compute
concave
concentrate/concentration
  to concentrate
concept
  to conceptualize
concreteness/concrete/concretely
condition/conditional
  to condition
conduction/conductivity/conductor/conductive
  to conduct
cone/conical/conically/conicity
  to be conical
connection
  to connect
consecutive/consecutively
consequent/consequently/consequence
conservation/conservative
  to conserve
consideration/considerable/considerably
  to consider
constant/constantly
construct/construction/constructive
  to construct
container/containment/containable
  to contain
context/contextual
  to contextualize
continuity/continuous
  to continue
contract/contraction/contractile/contractibility
  to contract
contrast/contrastive
  to contrast
contribution/contributive/contributing
  to contribute
convergence/convergent
  to converge
converse/conversion
  to convert
convex
cooperation/cooperative
  to cooperate
coordinate/coordination
  to coordinate
core
corollary
correlate/correlation/correlative
  to correlate
correspond/corresponding/correspondence
  to correspond

corroborate/corroborative
  to corroborate
criterion/criteria
critic/critical
  to criticize/to critique
cube/cubical
  to cube
cumbersome
current/currently
curve/curvature
cycle/cyclic/cyclical
cylinder/cylindrical
damage
  to damage
data
decrease
  to decrease
deductive/deductively/deduction
  to deduce
definition/definitive/definite
  to define
demonstration/demonstrator/demonstrative
  to demonstrate
density/denseness/dense
depth/deep
  to deepen
derivation/derivative
  to derive
design
  to design
detail
  to detail
determination/determinant/determinate/indeterminate
  to determine
development/developmental
  to develop
diagonal/diagonally
diameter/diametrical/diametrically
difference/different
  to differ
dilution
  to dilute
dimension/dimensional
direction/direct/indirect/directly/indirectly
  to direct
distinguishable/distinguished
  to distinguish
distribution/distributable/distributive
  to distribute
divergent
  to diverge
diversion
  to divert
divide/division
dynamics/dynamo/dynamic
earth

ecology/ecological/ecologically
economy/economics/economist/economical
   to economize
edge
education
   to educate
effect
electricity/electric/electrical/electrification
   to electrify
element/elementary/elemental
elevation/elevator
   to elevate
elimination
   to eliminate
ellipse/ellipsis/elliptical
emphasis/emphatic
   to emphasize
empty
   to empty
energy/energetic
   to energize
entropy
equal/equality/inequality/equation
equilibrium/equilibration
   to equilibrate
equivalence
   to equal/to be equal to
estimate/estimation
   to estimate
even/evenness
   to even out/to even up
examination/examinable
   to examine
exception/exceptional
   to except
excess/excessive
   to exceed
exertion/exertive
   to exert
expansion/expansibility/expandable/expansible
   to expand
experiment/experimentation/experimental
   to experiment
explanation/explanatory
   to explain
exponent/exponential/exponentially
expression/expressiveness/expressivity/expressive/
    expressively
   to express
extensibility/extensive/extendable
   to extend
facility
   to facilitate
factor/factorial
   to factor
fall/falling
   to fall

figure
   to figure out
finite/infinite
fluid/fluidity
foot/feet
form/formative/formation
   to form
formula/formulaic
foundation/foundational
   to found
fraction/fractional
frequency/frequently
frozen
   to freeze
function/functional
   to function
fundamental/fundamentally
generation
   to generate
geography/geographical
geometry/geometrical
globe/global
government/governmental
   to govern
graph/graphic
   to graph
gravity/gravitation/gravitational
   to gravitate
hard/hardness
   to harden
heat/hot
   to heat
height/high
horizontal/horizontally
humidity/humid
hyperbola/hyperbolic
hypothesis/hypothetical
   to hypothesize
ideal/idealism/ideal/idea
   to idealize
identity/identification/identical
   to identify
illustration/illustrative
   to illustrate
imitation/imitative
   to imitate
immediacy/immediate/immediately
implication
   to imply
importance/important
incline/inclination
   to incline
inclusion/inclusive
   to include
increase
   to increase

individual
  to individuate
inductive/inductively
  to induce
industry/industrial
  to industrialize
inertia/inert
influence/influential
  to influence
initial/intially
  to initiate
insert/insertion
  to insert
instrument/instrumental
integer
integral/integration
  to integrate
interpretation
  to interpret
intersect/intersection
  to intersect
interval
introduction
  to introduce
intuition/intuitive
  to intuit
knowledge
  to know
laboratory/lab
largeness/large
  to enlarge
lateral/equilateral/laterally
less
  to be less than
life/alive
  to live/to be alive
limit/limiting/limitation
  to limit
line/linear/non-linear
load/loaded
  to load
locus/location/locatable
  to locate
logic/logical/logically
long/length
machine/machinery
macro
magnitude/magnitudinous
maintenance
  to maintain
major/majority
manipulation/manipulative
  to manipulate
mass
material/materialistic
  to materialize

math/mathematics/mathematical/mathematician
maximum/maximal
  to maximize
measure/measurement
  to measure
mechanics/mechanical/mechanistic
  to mechanize
mega
meter/metric/metrical/metrically
method/methodology/methodologist
    methodical/methodological
micro
minimum/minimal
  to minimize
minor/minority
minus
mixture
  to mix
mobile/mobility
  to be mobile
mode/modality/modular
  to modulate
model
  to model
molecule/molecular/molecularity
momentum
more
  to be more than
motion/motionless
  to motion/to put in motion
multiple/multiplicity/multiplication
  to multiply
nature/natural
negation/negative
  to negate
negligence/negligent/negligible/negligibly
negotiation/negotiable/negotiability
  to negotiate
norm/normal/normally/normative
number/numerical/numerous/numerically
  to number/to enumerate
object
  to object/to objectify
obvious/obviously
  to obviate
occasion/occasional/occasionally
occurrence
  to occur
odd/oddness
operation/operative
  to operate
opposite/opposition
  to oppose
orbit/orbital
  to orbit

order/ordinal
 to order
ordinary/extraordinary/ordinarily
origin/original/originally
 to originate
parabola/parabolic/parabolical
parallel/parallelogram/parallelism
part/partial
peculiar/peculiarity
per capita
per/percent/percentage
permit/permission/permissible
 to permit
perpendicular
pervasive
 to pervade
phase
 to phase out/to phase in
phenomenon/phenomena
photograph/photography/photographer/photographic
 to photograph
physics/physical
plan
 to plan
point
 to point
policy/politics/politician/political
poly
positive
 to posit
potential/potentially
pound
 to pound
power/horsepower
 to power
precision/preciseness/precise
preliminary
principal/principally
principle
problem/problematic
procedure/process
 to proceed
product/production
 to produce
progress/progression
 to progress
project/projection/projectile/projective
 to project
property
proposal/proposition
 to propose
pull
 to pull
pursue
 to pursue

push
 to push
quality/qualitative/qualifiable/qualifiably
 to qualify
quantity/quantitative/quantifiable/quantifiably
 to quantify
radius/radii
random/randomly
 to be random
rate/ratable
 to rate
ratio/rational/irrational
rationale
real/reality/unreal
 to realize
reason/reasonable
 to reason
reciprocal/reciprocally
 to reciprocate
recognize/recognizable
recommendation
 to recommend
record
 to record
rectangle/rectangular
reduction
 to reduce
reflection
 to reflect
regulation/regular/regulative
 to regulate
relationship/relative
 to relate
release
 to release
remainder
 to remain
repetition/repetitive
 to repeat
report
 to report
representation/representative/representable
 to represent
resemblance
 to resemble
resistance
 to resist
resource/resourceful/resourceless
respective/respectively/with respect to
restriction/restrictive
 to restrict
result/resultant
 to result
resumption/resumptive
 to resume

reverse/reversal
   to reverse
revolution
   to revolve/to revolt
rotation/rotational
   to rotate
rough/roughness
   to roughen
row
satisfaction/satisfactory
   to satisfy
saturation
   to saturate
scale/scalar
scheme/schematic
scope
score
   to score
second/secondly/secondarily
   to second
separation/separate/separable
   to separate
sequence/sequential
   to be in sequence
set/setup
   to set up
significant/significantly
   to signify
similar/similarity
simplification/simplicity/simple
   to simplify
simultaneous/simultaneity
situation/situational
   to situate
slope
   to slope
smooth/smoothness/smoothly
   to smooth
soft/softness
   to soften
solution/solvable/unsolvable
   to solve
specificity/specific
   to specify
speed
   to speed up
sphere/spherical
spiral
   to spiral
square
   to square
stability/instability/stable/unstable
   to stabilize
standard
   to standardize
state/static/statics

statistics/statistical/statistically
step
   to take a step
straightness/straight/straightforward
strength/strong
   to strengthen
string
   to string
structure/structural
   to structure
submission/submittal/submittable
   to submit
substitution
   to substitute
subtraction
   to subtract
summary/summation
   to summarize
supplement/supplementary
   to supplement
survey
   to survey
symbol/symbolic
   to symbolize
symmetry/symmetrical
system/systematic
   to systematize
table/tabular
   to tabulate
technique/technology/technical
temperature/temperate
theory/theorem/theoretical
   to theorize
thermometer/thermal
thickness/thick
   to thicken
thinness/thin
   to thin out
topography/topographic/topographical
topology/topologic/topological
trace
   to trace
trait
transfer/transferable
   to transfer
transition/transit/transitory
transportation/transportable
   to transport
trapezoid/trapezoidal
treatise/treatable
   to treat
triangle/triangular
   to triangulate
type/typical
   to type
ultimate/ultimately

unit/unity
    to unite/to unify
usually/unusually/usual/unusual
value/valuable
    to value
variation/variant/variable
    to vary
velocity
verification/verifiable
    to verify
vertical/vertically
view/viewpoint
    to view
visual/visually/visualization
    to visualize

volume
waste/wasted
wave
weakness/weak
weight
    to weigh
wheel
    to wheel
work/worker/workable
    to work
year/yearly
zero

Acknowledgments

Unit 2: Pronunciation—"Specific pronunciation compensation strategies": Eric Nelson; Exercise 6 to practice compensation strategies: Susan Gillette

Unit 4: Functional Language—excerpts from a speech by Elaine Tarone entitled "Cross Cultural Differences in Nonverbal Communication" in Exercises 3 and 5.
Grammar—examples of definitions: Eric Nelson

Unit 5: Focus 2—"Timing in waiting for answers" and "Practice responding to student answers" adapted from materials developed by Karin Smith
Pronunciation—structure of examples for practicing rhythm in Exercise 13: Clifford Prator and Betty Wallace Robinett; transcript for lab presentation on Hooke's Law in Exercise 14: Jerry Thiessen

Unit 6: Grammar—materials and exercises on negative questions adapted from materials developed by Karin Smith
Needs Assessment—questions for use in interviews: Susan Gillette

Unit 8: Functional Language—list of functions: Linda Mealey
Functional Language—material on rhetorical questions based on materials developed by Karin Smith
Assignment Presentation—layout of assignment: Caren Hohenstein Abdelaal

Unit 9: Pronunciation—Exercise 3 on -s/es suffixes based on materials developed by Eric Nelson

Unit 10: Needs Assessment—the issue of re-entry and suggested peer observation: Deniz Gokcora

APPENDICES

ITA Test concept and some teaching skill categories: based on the TEACH Test by Roberta Abraham and Barbara Plakans, Iowa State University. Also adapted from SPEAK® materials with permission of Educational Testing Service.

ITA Test language categories and descriptors: Educational Testing Service

ITA Test procedure, scoring scale, and some teaching skill descriptors: Karin Smith and other members of the staff of the University of Minnesota TA English Program

Some field-specific questions: Linda Mealey, Anthony Winklemann

Some field-specific topics for general interest: Linda Mealey, Cheng Chih Sung

Sociology problem: Jim Keefe

BIBLIOGRAPHY

Teaching Assistant training: Linda Kruger
Teaching Assistant training: ITAs: Gayle Nelson

REPRINTED BY PERMISSION OF PRENTICE HALL, ENGLEWOOD CLIFFS, NEW JERSEY:

Allen R. Angel, *Intermediate Algebra for College Students* 2/e (1988), pp. vii–x, 41, 58, 59, 92, 105, 307, 390, 539–44.

Betty Schrampfer Azar, *Understanding and Using English Grammar* (1989), pp. 11, 29, 120, 144, i1–i7.

James M. Barrett, Peter Abramoff, Krishna A. Kumaran, and William F. Millington, *Biology* (1986), pp. vii–xx, 34, 117, 137, 601, 603, 1080, 1083, 1084, and 1135–68.

Mark L. Berenson and David M. Levine, *Basic Business Statistics* (1989), pp. xi–xviii, 895–904.

Jay Bolemon, *Physics: An Introduction* 2/e (1989), pp. 93, 169, 586–93.

Theodore L. Brown and H. Eugene LeMay, *Chemistry: The Central Science* (1988), pp. viii–xviii, 4–5, 87, 207, 371, 589, 1003–28.

Karl E. Case and Ray C. Fair, *Principles of Economics* (1989), pp. v–xxviii, 4, 54, 180, 192.

Vincent Del Toro, *Electrical Engineering Fundamentals* (1986), pp. v–xii, 21, 34, 50, 73, 911—21.

Douglas C. Giancoli, *Physics* 2/e (1985), pp. 2, 3, 97, 341, 393, 394, 472, 721.

Robert T. Grauer, *Structured Cobol Programming* (1985), pp. vii–xiv, 199.

Robert L. Kruse, *Programming with Data Structures: Pascal Version* (1989), pp. v–x, 52, 275, 350, 351—52, 407.

Richard I. Levin, *Statistics for Management* (1987), pp. 131—32, 311, 498.

Richard I. Levin and David S. Rubin, *A Short Course in Business Statistics* (1983), pp. 8, 9, 51, 100, 169.

Deena R. Levine and Mara B. Adelman, *Beyond Language: Intercultural Communication for English as a Second Language* (1982), p. 47.

Warren J. Luzadder and Jon M. Duff, *Fundamentals of Engineering Drawing* (1989), pp. v–ix, 73, 118, 149, 197, 203, 663–72.

John J. Macionis, *Sociology* (1989), pp. v–xi, 6, 33, 55–57, 183, 553, name index, subject index.

James G. MacGregor, *Reinforced Concrete* (1988), pp. 27, 47, 77, 96, 128, 166, 168, 337, 502, 785–99.

James L. Newman and Gordon E. Matzke, *Population: Patterns, Dynamics, and Prospects* (1984), p. 65.

James A. F. Stoner and R. Edward Freeman, *Management* 4/e (1989), pp. AIE-73, AIE-81, AIE-97, AIE-102, AIE-113, AIE-125; v–xx, 26, 84, 104, 121, 265.

G. J. Thuesen and W. J. Fabrycky, *Engineering Economy* 7/e (1989), pp. vii–xiv, 4–5, 14–15, 32, 38, 57, 70, 71, 398, 705–17.

Stephen Worchel and Wayne Shebilske, *Psychology* (1989), pp. 17, 191, 225, 265, 267, 490.

Also:

R. Edward Freeman, case study: "The Use and Abuse of Joyce Roberts," in Stoner and Freeman, *Management* 4/e, p. 325. Reprinted by permission of R. Edward Freeman.

J. L. Horn and G. Donaldson, graph from "Cognitive Development II: Adulthood Development of Human Abilities," modified and reprinted with permission of the publishers from *Constancy and Change in Human Development: A Volume of Review Essays* by Orville Brim and Jerome Kagan, eds., Cambridge, MA: Harvard University Press. Copyright © 1980 by the President and Fellows of Harvard College.

Saundra Hybels and Richard L. Weaver, II, *Speech Communication* (Litton Educational Publishing Co., 1974), pp. 69–77. Reprinted by permission of Wadsworth, Inc.

James G. MacGregor, *Reinforced Concrete* (1988), pp. 96, 166, 502. Figures reprinted by permission of James G. MacGregor, 9239 1118th St., Edmonton, Alberta, Canada T6G 178.

Bibliography

Culture

Althen, G. 1988. *American ways: A guide for foreigners in the United States*. Yarmouth, Maine: Intercultural Press.

Barnes, G. A. 1984. *The American university: A world guide*. Philadelphia: ISI Press.

Cui, S., and Messerschmitt, D. 1985. *American university encounters*. Hayward, Calif.: Alemany Press.

Jorstad, H. 1981. Inservice teacher education: Content and process. In *Proceedings of the National Conference on Professional Priorities*. Hastings-on-Hudson, N.Y: ACTFL.

Kohls, R. 1984. *The values Americans live by*. Washington, D.C.: Meridian House International.

Levine, D. A., and Adelman, M. B. 1982. *Beyond language: Intercultural communication for English as a second language*. Englewood Cliffs: Prentice Hall Regents.

Solheim, M. 1986. Confronting the familiar. *International Student 2*, 3: 20–23.

Stewart, E. 1972. *American cultural patterns: A cross-cultural perspective*. Yarmouth, Maine: Intercultural Press.

Wendt, J. R. 1984. DIE: A way to improve communication. *Communication Education 33* (October): 397–400.

Field-Specific Textbooks

Angel, A. R. 1988. *Intermediate algebra for college students*. Englewood Cliffs, N.J.: Prentice Hall.

Azar, B. S. 1989. *Understanding and using English grammar*. 2/e. Englewood Cliffs: Prentice Hall Regents.

Barrett, J. M.; Abramoff, P.; Kumaran, A. K.; and Millington, W. F. 1986. *Biology*. Englewood Cliffs: Prentice Hall.

Berenson, Mark L., and Levine, David M. 1989. *Basic business statistics: Concepts and applications*. Englewood Cliffs: Prentice Hall.

Bolemon, J. 1989. *Physics: An introduction*. Englewood Cliffs: Prentice Hall.

Brown, T. L., and LeMay, H. Eugene. 1988. *Chemistry: The central science*. Englewood Cliffs: Prentice Hall.

Case, K. E., and Fair, R. C. 1989. *Principles of economics*. Englewood Cliffs: Prentice Hall.

Del Toro, V. 1986. *Electrical engineering fundamentals*. Englewood Cliffs: Prentice Hall.

Giancoli, D. C. 1985. *Physics*. Englewood Cliffs: Prentice Hall.

Grauer, R. T. 1985. *Structured COBOL programming*. Englewood Cliffs: Prentice Hall.

Kruse, R. L. 1989. *Programming with data structures: Pascal version*. Englewood Cliffs: Prentice Hall.

Levin, R. I. 1987. *Statistics for management*. Englewood Cliffs: Prentice Hall.

Levin, R. I., and Rubin, D. S. 1983. *A short course in business statistics*. Englewood Cliffs: Prentice Hall.

Luzadder, W. J., and Duff, J. M. 1989. *Fundamentals of engineering drawing*. Englewood Cliffs: Prentice Hall.

MacGregor, J. G. 1988. *Reinforced concrete*. Englewood Cliffs: Prentice Hall.

Macionis, J. J. 1989. *Sociology*. Englewood Cliffs: Prentice Hall.

Stoner, J. A. F., and Freeman, R.E. 1989. *Management*. Englewood Cliffs: Prentice Hall.

Thuesen, G. J., and Fabrycky, W. J. 1989. *Engineering economy*. Englewood Cliffs: Prentice Hall.

Worchel, S., and Shebilske, W. 1989. *Psychology: Principles and applications*. Englewood Cliffs: Prentice Hall.

Language

Alexander, L. G.; Kingsbury, R.; and Chapman, R. 1978. *Take a stand*. New York: Longman.

Azar, B. S. 1989. *Understanding and using English grammar*, 2/e. Englewood Cliffs: Prentice Hall Regents.

Barnes, G. A. 1982. *Communication skills for the foreign-born professional*. Philadelphia: ISI Press.

Chan, M. 1987. *Phrase by phrase: Pronunciation and listening in American English*. Englewood Cliffs: Prentice Hall Regents.

Cook, A. 1991. *American accent training*. Hauppauge, New York: Barron's Educational Series, Inc.

Dickerson, W. B. 1989. *Stress in the speech stream: The rhythm of spoken English*. Urbana: The University of Illinois Press.

English Language Services, Inc. 1967. *Drills and exercises in English pronunciation: Stress and intonation, part 2*. New York: Collier Macmillan International.

English, S. 1988. *Say it clearly: Exercises and activities for pronunciation and oral communication*. New York: Collier Macmillan.

Gilbert, J. 1978. Gadgets: Nonverbal tools for teaching pronunciation. CATESOL Occasional Papers 4.

———. 1984. *Clear speech: Pronunciation and listening comprehension in American English*. Cambridge: Cambridge University Press.

Graham, C. 1978. *Jazz chants: Rhythms of American English for students of English as a second language*. New York: Oxford University Press.

Grate, H. G. 1974. *English pronunciation exercises for Japanese students*. Englewood Cliffs: Prentice Hall Regents.

Hagen, S. A. 1988. *Sound advice*. Englewood Cliffs: Prentice Hall Regents.

Hughes, G. S. 1981. *A handbook of classroom English*. London: Oxford University Press.

Lackstrom, J.E.; Selinker, L.; and Trimble, L.P. 1972. Grammar and technical English. *English Teaching Forum 10*.

McLaughlin, M.L. 1984. *Conversation: How talk is organized*. Beverly Hills, Calif.: Sage Publications.

Morley, J. 1979. *Improving spoken English*. Ann Arbor: University of Michigan Press.

———. ed. 1987. *Current perspectives on pronunciation: Practices anchored in theory*. Washington, D. C.: Teachers of English to Speakers of Other Languages.

Nilsen, D. L., and Nilsen, A. P. 1973. *Pronunciation contrasts in English*. Englewood Cliffs: Prentice Hall Regents.

Pifer, G., and Mutoh, N. 1977. *Points of view*. Rowley, Mass.: Newbury House .

Prator, C., and Robinett, B. W. 1985. *Manual of American English pronunciation*, 4/e. New York: Holt, Rinehart, & Winston.

Raimes, A. 1990. *How English works: A grammar handbook with readings*. New York: St. Martin's Press.

Rooks, G. 1988. *The non-stop discussion workbook: Problems for intermediate and advanced students of English*, 2/e. Rowley, Mass.: Newbury House.

Ruetten, M. 1986. *Comprehending academic lectures*. New York: Macmillan Co.

Selinker, L.; Tarone, E.; and Hanzeli, V., eds. 1981. *English for academic and technical purposes*. Rowley, Mass.: Newbury House.

Sheeler, W. D., and Markley, R. W. 1991. *Sounds and rhythm: A pronunciation course*. Englewood Cliffs: Prentice Hall Regents.

Sims, J., and Peterson, P. 1981. *Better listening skills*. Englewood Cliffs: Prentice-Hall.

Stern, D. A. 1987. *The sound and style of American English: A course in foreign accent reduction*. Los Angeles: Dialect Accent Specialists, Inc.

Trimble, L.T. 1985. *English for science and technology: A discourse approach*. Cambridge: Cambridge University Press.

Weinstein, N. 1982. *Whaddaya say? Guided practice in relaxed spoken English*. Englewood Cliffs: Prentice Hall Regents.

Wong, R. 1987. *Teaching pronunciation: Focus on English rhythm and intonation*. Englewood Cliffs: Prentice Hall.

Young, L., and Fitzgerald, B. 1982, 1983. *Listening and learning: Lectures, modules I—VII*. Rowley, Mass.: Newbury House.

Language: Listening and Speaking Diagnostic Tests

Educational Testing Service. 1985. *The speaking proficiency English language assessment kit (SPEAK)*. Princeton: Educational Testing Service.

Gilbert, J. 1984. "Clear listening test." In *Clear Speech: Pronunciation and Listening Comprehension in American English*, 3–6. Cambridge: Cambridge University Press.

Prator, C., and Robinett, B. W. 1985. "Accent inventory." In *Manual of American English Pronunciation*, 4/e, ix–xiv. New York: Holt, Rinehart, & Winston.

Teaching

Adler, M. J. 1984. *The Paideia Program: An educational syllabus*. New York: Macmillan Co.

Brown, G. 1978. *Lecturing and explaining*. London: Methuen.

Centra, J.; Frosh, R. C.; Gray, P. J.; and Lambert, L. M. 1987. *A guide to evaluating teaching for promotion and tenure*. Littleton, Mass.: Copley Publishing Group.

Felder, R.M.; Leonard, R.; and Porter, R. L. 1987. *Teaching effectiveness for engineering professors*. North Carolina State University School of Engineering.

Goodwin, S. S.; Sharp, G. W.; Cloutier, E. F.; Diamond, N. A.; and Dalgaard, K. S. N. *Effective classroom questioning*. Champaign-Urbana: University of Illinois Office of Instructional and Management Services.

Gullette, M. M., ed. 1984. *The art and craft of teaching*. Cambridge: Harvard University Press.

Hill, W. F. 1977. *Learning through discussion: Guide for leaders and members of discussion groups*. Beverly Hills, Calif.: Sage Publications.

Hurt, H. T.; Scott, M. D.; and McMroskey, J. C. 1978. *Communication in the classroom*. Reading, Mass: Addison-Wesley.

Kayfetz, J., and Stice, R. 1987. *Academically speaking*. Belmont, Calif.: Wadsworth Publishing Co.

Kolb, D. A. 1981. "Learning styles and disciplinary differences." In *The Modern American College*, eds. A. W. Chickering and Associates. San Francisco: Jossey-Bass.

Leeds, D. 1988. *PowerSpeak: The complete guide to persuasive public speaking and persuading*. New York: Prentice Hall Press.

McKeachie, W. J. 1986. *Teaching tips: A guide book for the beginning college teacher*, 8/e. Lexington, Mass.: D.C. Heath & Co.

Marincovich, M., and Rusk, L. 1987. *Excellence in teaching electrical engineering: A handbook for faculty and teaching assistants*. Palo Alto, Calif.: Stanford Center for Teaching and Learning.

Teaching Assistant Training

Abbott, R. D.; Wulff, D. H.; and Szego, C. K. 1989. Review of research on TA training. *New Directions for Teaching and Learning 39* (Fall): 113–16.

Allen, R. R., and Reuter, T. 1989. *Teaching assistant strategies: An introduction to college teaching*. Dubuque, Iowa: Kendall/Hunt Publishing Company.

Boehrer, J. 1989. "Suggestions for watching tapes with TAs." *Employment and Education of Teaching Assistants: Readings from a National Conference*, 134–35. Columbus: Ohio State University.

Boehrer, J., and Sarkisian, E. 1985. The teaching assistant's point of view. *New Directions for Teaching and Learning 22* (June): 7–20.

Carroll, J. G. 1977. Assessing the effectiveness of a training program for the university teaching assistants. *Teaching of Psychology 4*, 3: 135–37.

———. 1980. Effects of training programs for university teaching assistants: A review of empirical research. *Journal of Higher Education 51*, 2: 167–80.

Chism, N. V. N., and Warner, S. B., eds. 1989. *Institutional responses and responsibilities in the employment and education of teaching assistants: Readings from a national conference.* Columbus: Ohio State University.

Chism, N. V. N.; Cano, J.; and Pruitt, A. S. Teaching in a diverse environment: Knowledge and skills needed by TAs. *New Directions for Teaching and Learning 39* (Fall): 23–35.

Davey, K. B., and Marion, C. 1989. Evaluating TA development programs: Problems, issues, strategies. *Employment and Education of Teaching Assistants: Readings from a National Conference*, 118–25. Columbus: Ohio State University.

Ervin, G., and Muyskens, J. A. On training TAs: Do we know what they want and need? *Foreign Language Annals 15*, 5: 335–44.

Grasha, A. F. 1978. The teaching of teaching: A seminar on college teaching. *Teaching of Psychology 5*, 1: 21–23.

Menges, R. R., and Rando, W. C. 1989. Graduate teaching assistants' implicit theories of teaching. *Employment and Education of Teaching Assistants: Readings from a National Conference*, 83–-90. Columbus: Ohio State University.

Nyquist, J.; Abbott, R. D.; Wulff, D. H.; and Sprague, J., eds. 1991. *Preparing the professoriate of tomorrow to teach: Selected readings in TA training.* Dubuque, Iowa: Kendall/Hunt Publishing Company.

Parrett, J. L. 1989. A ten-year review of TA training programs: Trends, patterns, and common practices. *Employment and Education of Teaching Assistants: Readings from a national conference*, 67–79. Columbus: Ohio State University.

Sprague, J., and Nyquist, J. D. 1989. TA supervision. *New Directions for Teaching and Learning 39* (Fall): 43–45.

Weimer, M.; Svinicki, M. D.; and Bauer, G. 1989. Designing programs to prepare TAs to teach. *New Directions for Teaching and Learning 39* (Fall): 61–64.

Wright, D. L. 1989. TA training resources. *New Directions for Teaching and Learning 39* (Fall): 128–30.

Teaching Assistant Training: ITAs

Abraham, R. G., and Plakans, B. S. 1988. Evaluating a screening/training program for NNS teaching assistants. *TESOL Quarterly 22*: 505–8.

Anderson-Hsieh, J. 1990. Teaching suprasegmentals to international teaching assistants using field-specific materials. *English for Specific Purposes 9*: 195–214.

Ard, J. 1987. The foreign TA problem from an acquisition-theoretic point of view. *English for Specific Purposes 6*: 133–44.

———. 1989. Grounding an ITA curriculum: Theoretical and practical concerns. *English for Specific Purposes 8*: 125–38.

Bailey, K. M. 1982. Teaching in a second language: The communicative competence of non-native speaking teaching assistants. Ph.D. diss., University of California, Los Angeles.

Bailey, K. M.; Pialorsi, F.; and Zukowski/Faust, J., eds. 1984. *Foreign teaching assistants in U. S. universities.* Washington, D. C.: National Association for Foreign Student Affairs.

Bernhardt, E. 1987. Training foreign teaching assistants: Cultural differences. *College Teaching 35*: 67–69.

Boyd, F. A. 1989. Developing presentation skills: A perspective derived from professional education. *English for Specific Purposes 8*: 195–203.

Briggs, S.; Hyun, S.; Aldridge, P.; and Swales, J. 1990. The international teaching assistant: An annotated critical bibliography. Ann Arbor: The English Language Institute, University of Michigan.

Brown, K. 1988. Effects of perceived country of origin, educational status, and native speakerness on American college student attitudes toward non-native instructors. Ph.D. diss., University of Minnesota, Minneapolis. (DAI, 49, 1710A–1711A).

Byrd, P., and Constantinides, J. C. 1988. FTA training programs: Searching for appropriate teaching styles. *English for Specific Purposes* 7: 123–29.

Constantinides, J. C. 1989. "ITA training programs." In *Teaching Assistant Training in the 1990s*, 79–86, eds. R. D. Abbott and D. H. Wulff. San Francisco: Jossey-Bass.

Davies, C. E.; Tyler, A.; and Koran, J. J., Jr. 1989. Face-to-face with English speakers: An advanced training class for international teaching assistants. *English for Specific Purposes 8*: 139–53.

Davis, B. K. 1984. A study of the effectiveness of training for foreign teaching assistants. Ph.D. diss., Ohio State University, Columbus.

Dege, D. B. 1981. "Format and evaluation of the cross-cultural component of a foreign teaching assistant training program" (Report No. CS 503 583). Minneapolis: University of Minnesota. (ERIC Doc. Reproduction Service No. ED 207 100).

———. 1983. Verbal and nonverbal communication behaviors in multicultural groups: An exploratory analysis. Ph.D. diss., University of Minnesota, Minneapolis.

Douglas, D., and Myers, C. 1989. TAs on TV: Demonstrating communication strategies for international teaching assistants. *English for Specific Purposes 8*: 169–79.

Franck, M. R., and DeSousa, M. A. 1982. Foreign TAs: A course in communication skills. *Improving College and University Teaching 30*: 111–14.

Gillespie, J. K. 1988. Foreign and U. S. teaching assistants: An analysis of verbal and nonverbal classroom interaction. Ph.D. diss., University of Illinois.

Gillette, S. 1982. "Lecture discourse of a foreign TA: A preliminary needs assessment." Minneapolis: University of Minnesota (ERIC Doc. Reproduction Service No. ED 250 907).

Hinofotis, F. B., and Bailey, K. M. 1980. "American undergraduates' reactions to the communication skills of foreign teaching assistants." In *On TESOL '80*, 120–33, eds. J. C. Fisher, M. A. Clarke, and J. Schachter. Washington, D.C.: TESOL.

Inglis, M. A. 1988. Variables that affect undergraduates' evaluations of non-native speaking teaching assistants' instruction. Ph.D. diss., Memphis State University.

Kaplan, R. G. 1989. The life and times of ITA programs. *English for Specific Purposes 8:* 109–24.

Keye, F. Z. A. 1981. An exploratory study of students' written responses to foreign teaching assistant presentations. Ph.D. diss., University of Minnesota, Minneapolis.

Landa, M. 1988. "Training international students as teaching assistants." In *Culture, Learning, and the Disciplines: Theory and Practice in Cross-Cultural Orientation* (pp. 50–57), eds. J. A. Mestenhauser, G. Marty, and I. Steglitz. Washington, D.C.: National Association for Foreign Student Affairs.

Landa, M., and Perry, W. 1984. "An evaluation of a training course for foreign teaching assistants." In *Foreign Teaching Assistants in U. S. Universities*, eds. K. M. Bailey, F. Pialorsi, and J. Zukowski/Faust. Washington, D. C.: National Association of Foreign Student Affairs.

McMillen, L. 1986. Teaching assistants get increased training. *The Chronicle of Higher Education*, October 29.

Matross, R.; Paige, M. R.; and Hendricks, G. 1982. American students' attitudes toward foreign students before and during an international crisis. *Journal of College Student Personnel*: 58–65.

Nelson, G. 1989. The relationship between the use of personal examples in foreign teaching assistants' lectures and uncertainty reduction, student attitude, student recall, and ethnocentrism. Ph.D. diss., University of Minnesota, Minneapolis.

———. 1992. The relationship between the use of personal cultural examples in international teaching assistant lectures and uncertainty reduction, student recall, student attitude, and ethnocentrism. *The International Journal of Intercultural Relations, 16*.

Orth, J. L. 1982. University undergraduates' evaluational reactions to the speech of foreign teaching assistants. Ph.D. diss., University of Texas, Austin.

Pialorsi, F. 1984. "Toward an anthropology of the classroom: An essay on foreign teaching assistants and U. S. students." In *Foreign Teaching Assistants in U. S. Universities*, 16–21, eds. K. M. Bailey, F. Pialorsi, and J. Zukowski/Faust. Washington, D. C.: National Association for Foreign Student Affairs.

Rentz, M. D. 1987. Diplomats in our own back yard: How we treat foreign students on our campuses can have lasting consequences for our country. *Newsweek*, February 16, 1987, p. 10.

Rice, D. S. 1984. "A one-semester program for orienting the new foreign teaching assistant." In *Foreign Teaching Assistants in U. S. Universities*, 69–75, eds. K. M. Bailey, F. Pialorsi, and J. Zukowski/ Faust. Washington, D. C.: National Association for Foreign Student Affairs.

Rounds, P. L. 1987. Characterizing successful classroom discourse for NNS teaching assistant training. *TESOL Quarterly 21*: 643–70.

Sadow, S. A., and Maxwell, M. A. 1982. "The foreign teaching assistant and the culture of the American university class." In *On TESOL '82*, 253–58, eds. M. A. Clarke and U. J. Handscombe. Washington, D. C.: TESOL.

Sarkisian, E. 1984. "Training foreign teaching assistants: Using videotape to observe and practice communicating and interacting with students." In *On TESOL, '84*, 325–31. eds. P. Larson, E. L. Judd, and D. S. Messerschmitt. Washington, D. C.

Sequeira, D. L., and Costantino, M. 1989. "Issues in ITA training programs." In *Teaching assistant training in the 1990s*, 79–86, eds. J. D. Nyquist, R. D. Abbott, and D. H. Wulff. San Francisco: Jossey-Bass.

Shaw, P. A.,and Garate, E. M. 1984. "Linguistic competence, communicative needs, and university pedagogy: Toward a framework for TA training." In *Foreign Teaching Assistants in U. S. Universities*, 22–42, eds. K. M. Bailey, F. Pialorsi, and J. Zukowski/Faust. Washington, D. C.: National Association for Foreign Student Affairs.

Smith, J. 1989. Topic and variation in ITA oral proficiency: SPEAK and field-specific oral tests. *English for Specific Purposes 8*: 155–67.

Stevens, S. G. 1989. A "dramatic" approach to improving the intelligibility of ITAs. *English for Specific Purposes 8*: 181–94.

Turitz, N. J. 1984. "A survey of training programs for foreign teaching assistants in American universities." In *Foreign Teaching Assistants in U. S. Universities*, 43–50, eds. K. M. Bailey, F. Pialorsi, and J. Zukowski/Faust. Washington, D. C.: National Association for Foreign Student Affairs.

Turner, J. F. 1988. TA perception of problem and TA perception of role in teaching Spanish, Ph.D. diss., Ohio State University.

Young, R., ed. 1989. Special issue: The training of international teaching assistants. *English for Specific Purposes 8*.

Zukowski/Faust, J. 1984. "Problems and strategies: An extended program for foreign teaching assistants." In *Foreign Teaching Assistants in U. S. Universities*, 76–88, eds. K. M. Bailey, F. Pialorsi, and J. Zukowski/Faust. Washington, D. C.: National Association for Foreign Student Affairs.

Teaching Assistant Training: "The ITA Problem"

Bailey, K. M. 1983. Foreign teaching assistants at U. S. universities: Problems in interaction and communication. *TESOL Quarterly*: 308–11.

———. 1984. "The 'foreign TA problem.'" In *Foreign Teaching Assistants in U. S. Universities*, 3–15, eds. K.M. Bailey, F. Pialorsi, and J. Zukowski/Faust. Washington, D. C.: National Association for Foreign Student Affairs.

Berdie, D. R.; Anderson, J. F.; Wenberg, M.; and Price, C. S. 1976. Improving the effectiveness of teaching assistants–Undergraduates speak out. *Improving College and University Teaching 24*: 169–71.

Constantinides, J. C. 1987. The 'foreign TA problem'–An update. *NAFSA Newsletter 38*: 3, 5.

Constantinides, J. C., and Byrd, P. 1986. Foreign TAs: What's the big problem? *Journal of International Student Personnel 3*: 27–32.

Fisher, M. 1985. Rethinking the "foreign TA problem." *New Directions for Teaching and Learning 22*: 63–73.

Fiske, E. B. 1985. When teachers can't speak clear English. *New York Times*, June 4.

Heller, S. 1986. Problems arise in foreign-student programs. *The Chronicle of Higher Education*, October 29.

Schwartz, J.; Gibbs, L.; Dietz, K.; Kelley, T.; Himmelsbach, E.; and Bock, P. 1985. Let's talk it over: Foreign TA's, U.S. students fight culture shock. *Newsweek on Campus*, December.

Teaching Assistant Training: ITA Materials

Althen, G. 1988. *Manual for foreign teaching assistants*. Iowa City: University of Iowa Press.

Byrd, P.; Constantinides, J. C.; and Pennington, M. 1989. *The Foreign Teaching Assistant's Manual*. New York: Collier Macmillan.

Douglas, D., and Myers, C. 1990. *Teaching Assistant Communication Strategies* [Videotape and instructor's manual]. Ames: Iowa State University Media Production Unit.

Pica, T.; Barnes, G.A.; and Finger, Alexis G. 1989/90. *Teaching matters*. Rowley, Mass.: Newbury House.

Wennerstrom, A. 1991. *Techniques for teachers: A guide for nonnative speakers of English*. [Workbook and videotape]. Ann Arbor: The University of Michigan Press.

Index

Body movement, 3, 12, 14, 135
Boredom, 12, 90
Breathing:
    to counteract nervousness, 148
    diaphragmatic, 56–57
Broad questions, 72–73
Business administration field-specific materials, 182–185
Case study, 35, 117–119
Cause and effect, 35, 149
Characteristics:
    of good teacher, 8–9, 49–51
    of U. S. undergraduate students, 85–86
Cheating, 85, 144
Check, comprehension, 3, 4, 15, 21, 43, 91, 93–94, 97–98, 109–110, 136, 149, 166, 177
Chemistry field-specific materials, 186–189
Choice questions, 3, 93, 100, 102
Chronology, 35
Civil engineering field-specific materials, 190–192
Clapping:
    for practice of the three-second rule, 71
    for pronunciation practice, 65, 83
Clarity:
    of presentation, 3, 29, 110–111, 123, 160, 168, 173, 175
    of response to questions, 3, 94–95, 97–98, 136, 160, 169, 173, 177
Classroom:
    behavior, 11–13, 86
    culture, U. S., 154
    expressions, 17–19
    management, 90
    situations, 27–28
    terms, 16–17
    use of questions, 105–106
Clause, relative, 7, 66, 112
Cleanliness, 13
Closing, 3–4, 5, 20, 57–59, 109
College preparation, 86
Collocation, 23
Commanding, 48–49
Comment tag, 101
Communication:
    cross-cultural, vii, x, 157
    nonverbal, 3, 11–13, 57–58, 135, 144, 150, 160, 162, 169, 173, 176
Communication strategies, 36
Comparison and/or contrast, 35, 54, 150
Compensation strategies:
    grammar, 25–26, 152–153
    pronunciation, 21–25
    use of visuals, 30
Completeness, 110
Complex grammatical constructions, 26
Complex sentences, 25, 26
Compounds:
    adjective and noun, 45–46
    nouns, 45–46
    three-noun, 45–46
    verbs, 45–46
Comprehensibility, 2, 5, 151–153, 160, 174
Comprehension:
    aural, 3, 69–71, 90, 136, 157, 160, 169, 173, 177
    check, 3, 4, 15, 21, 43, 91, 93–94, 97–98, 109–110, 136, 149, 166, 177

monitoring student, 94
    of reduced function words, 81
Computer science field-specific materials, 193–196
Concern:
    about correctness, 148–149
    for students, 15, 84, 176
Conciseness, 2, 3, 7, 91, 94–95, 110, 123, 136, 149, 166, 175, 177
Concluding expressions, 4
Conclusions, 3–4, 5, 20, 57–59, 109
Confidence, 3, 11, 14–15, 136, 148, 176
Confusion, 12
Conjunctions, 62, 80–81
Connectors:
    double, 26
    logical, 117–119
Consonants:
    clusters, 80
    identical, 80
    linking, 80
    phonetic symbols, 22
    reduction of, 80–81
    voiced, 139–141
    voiceless, 139–141
    word-final, 78
Contact, eye, 3, 12, 14, 59–60, 108–109, 135, 176
Content:
    appropriateness, 3, 135, 176
    choices, 108
    relevance, 3
Context, 70
    familiar, 3, 123, 175
    for learning new information, 134
Continuing a two-part presentation, 134–135, 137–138
    feedback form, 169
Contractions, 78
Contrasting:
    ideas, 6
    information, 115
    words, 6
Contrast:
    comparison and, 35, 54, 150
    with opposite, 24, 54, 150
Control, 123–124, 135–136, 152, 168, 169
Core sections, x
Correctness, concern about, 148–149
Course:
    duplicating materials for, 132
    information, 19, 20
    requirements, 19, 20
    topics, 19, 20
Cross-cultural communication skills, vii, x, 157
Cross-cultural differences, 8–9, 11–13, 15, 33, 49–51, 57–58
Cultural awareness, x, 15
Cultural differences, implication of, 153–154
Cultural patterns, steps in analyzing, 77
Culture, U. S.:
    academic, 143–145
    classroom, 154
Defining a term, 52–53, 60, 61, 66
    feedback form, 164
Definitions, 16–17, 150
    formal, 53, 60–61, 66
Deletion of sounds, 6, 78–82, 139
Demonstrations, 24, 31, 88, 109